THE
YELLOW
PERIL

THE
YELLOW
PERIL

Chinese Americans
in American Fiction
1850–1940

William F. Wu

ARCHON BOOKS
1982

First published 1982 as an Archon Book,
an imprint of The Shoe String Press, Inc.,
Hamden, Connecticut 06514

Printed in the United States of America

Library of Congress Cataloging in Publication Data

Wu, William F., 1951-
  The yellow peril.

  Bibliography: p.
  Includes index.
  1. American fiction—History and criticism
2. Chinese Americans in literature   3. Yellow peril
in literature.   I. Title
PS 374.C46WI   813'.009'35203951   81-12701
ISBN 0-208-01915-4   AACR2

This is dedicated to my parents
William Quokan Wu
and
Cecile Franking Wu

and also
to the memory of Marvin Felheim

CONTENTS

Acknowledgments

Prof. Marvin Felheim was Director of the Program in American Culture at the University of Michigan during the first four of my five and a half years in graduate school. I worked primarily with him, spiritually and scholastically, during that time. He was chairman of my dissertation committee throughout most of the preparation of this dissertation. Unfortunately, he passed away as the project entered its final stages. However, this volume reflects his influence and direction in great proportion and should be listed among those in the preparation of which he had a significant role.

Thanks are due to Alan Wald, who assumed the chair of my dissertation committee in the project's late stages, and therefore the greatest responsibilities of analysis and criticism, on short notice. I also wish to thank Larry Goldstein, who filled the vacant spot in my committee on equally short notice. These were important contributions.

Dr. John B. Foster and Robert E. Briney, publisher of *The Rohmer Review*, provided helpful correspondence. B. Tyger of the San Francisco Academy of Comic Art located and filled a misplaced order of mine without which the chapter on pulp magazines would have been difficult and perhaps impossible to write. I also thank Michael D. Toman, erstwhile unemployed rogue reference librarian, for research suggestions. Special thanks and appreciation are due to Susan G. Cohen, but I managed to finish this anyway.

Introduction

My purpose in writing this work has been to explore the depiction of Chinese immigrants and their descendants in American fiction, from the mid-nineteenth century entry of the first Chinese immigrants in significant numbers, to the eve of World War II. I consider both the immigrant Chinese and the American-born generations that followed them to be Chinese Americans, but will sometimes identify the groups separately in recognition of the fact that the historical experience and treatment of the immigrants in fiction has been different from that of their descendants. The fiction treated in this study includes short stories and novels both by white Americans and Asian Americans.

I am defining the term *Yellow Peril* as the threat to the United States that some white American authors believed was posed by the people of East Asia. As a literary theme, the fear of this threat focuses on specific issues, including possible military invasion from Asia, perceived competition to the white labor force from Asian workers, the alleged moral degeneracy of Asian people, and the potential genetic mixing of Anglo-Saxons with Asians, who were considered a biologically inferior race by some intellectuals of the nineteenth century. The Chinese immigrants were the first target of this attention, since they were the first Asian immigrants to reach the United States in large numbers. This study will focus on American fiction about Chinese Americans in an attempt to analyze the growth and development of attitudes about them.

My thesis is that the Yellow Peril is the overwhelmingly dominant theme in American fiction about Chinese Americans in the years with which this study is concerned. It is expressed through the variety of images of the Chinese Americans that appear, especially in their relation to, and their role as part of, the United States. The historical causes and literary subject matter change, but the theme neither disappears nor abates.

Each work of fiction has been studied individually for the images it contains. Prior to the turn of the century, the Yellow Peril is perceived only as stemming from the Chinese. In the twentieth century, especially in the pulps, the Japanese joined the Chinese as a perceived menace to Europe and North America. The overall process of evaluation relies primarily on detailed analyses of the characters under consideration. This has been done with an awareness that the American public as a whole sometimes did not distinguish carefully among Asian ethnic groups, so that events involving one Asian ethnic group often affected the image of another. Some works are obscure and these have been quoted at greater length than more available ones.

Relatively few critical sources have been cited; this is due to a dearth of relevant studies. The less important works of fiction have naturally received little critical attention and, often, when such attention was concerned with pertinent stories, the authors had little or nothing to say about the depiction of Chinese Americans. This observation is intended only as an explanation, and not as a value judgement of earlier scholarship with different goals.

The scope of this study stretches from the first Chinese immigrants' arrival in the United States in the 1850s to the eve of World War II and the alliance of the United States with one Asian nation, China, against another, Japan. The early part of the period under consideration saw the entrance of Chinese immigrants into the American labor pool on the West Coast, the development of Chinatowns, and the institutionalization of legal discrimination against Chinese Americans in laws that included, or were later expanded to include, other East Asian ethnic groups as well.

The early immigration of the Chinese was brought about by a number of factors, including a major civil war in China in the 1850s and 1860s, an increase in the number of Chinese trading ports, and the California Gold Rush. This new face-to-face contact between the Chinese and white Californians produced new images of the former in American fiction. The earliest fiction reflects their activities throughout the West Coast states with historical accuracy as miners, merchants, migrant workers, domestic servants, launderers, and other kinds of laborers. These images change in the 1880s after the beginning of Chinese exclusion. The Chinese Exclusion Act of 1882 stopped the legal immigration of all Chinese except teachers, students, merchants, diplomats, and tourists. A period of riots and violence against the Chinese immigrants already in the United States drove them out of rural areas and smaller communities into the larger Chinatowns such as those in San Francisco, Sacramento, and Seattle. American authors followed them to Chinatown and produced fiction that focuses on these communities as exotic, filthy, and crime-ridden ghettoes. The images of the Chinese change for the worse, as they now appear as a more violent and dangerous people. Drugs, prostitution, and murder are depicted as accepted elements of Chinatown society. At the same time, a few authors write about missionaries' efforts to convert the Chinese Americans, usually with an attitude of condescension. A very few works exhibit no concern over the Yellow Peril.

The fear of the Yellow Peril is closely tied to national and international events. In the late nineteenth century, the phenomena most discussed in American fiction that related to this fear were the immigration of the Chinese to the United States and the social and legal developments that concerned them. At the end of the century, Japanese immigrants reached the continental United States in significant numbers and the Boxer Rebellion in China nearly destroyed the Manchu dynasty and the treaty system that European powers, the United States, and Japan enjoyed with that government. With the annexation of the Philippines by the United States, Pilipino immigration began also. Japan announced itself as a world power with its victory in the Russo-Japanese War of 1905–6. Internal strife continued in China until 1949, always threatening to upset the establishment of foreign powers in that country. The relation of historical events and their significance to fiction about Chinese Americans has been drawn whenever relevant.

In the twentieth century, some writers examine seriously the cultural differences and contacts between Chinese Americans and white Californians, but most still exploit the Chinatowns for what they consider quaintness, mystery, and exotic flavor. Lurid tales of vice, gambling, and tong wars stand alongside sympathetic portrayals of the victims of subsistence-level wages, persecution by law enforcement officials, and cultural friction. No authors describe the actual social structure of Chinatown based on the Six Companies pyramid and the Bachelor Society. When fiction by Chinese Americans first appears, it is set in these communities, which represent the home of Chinese American culture. The 1930s were also, of course, the heyday of pulp magazines and of the Yellow Peril depicted in them.

The word *stereotype* is used often in discussions of mass media without being defined, but a clear definition of a Chinese American stereotype is important to this discussion. The use of the word *stereotype* to describe literary devices and characters was originally a metaphor drawn from the printing industry, though now the literary meaning is the major definition. A block of moveable type, of course, is

set with individual letters and symbols and can be changed slightly or
greatly at will. A stereotype is made in one piece from a mold of the entire block of moveable type. It is an exact copy of the original and can
only be used to reproduce that page of type. Since it is a solid block, it
cannot be modified; alterations must be made by setting a new block of
moveable type, after which another stereotype can be cast from a fresh
mold. A literary stereotype, then, is a reproduction of an earlier image
without significant creative changes.

New literary stereotypes of Chinese Americans accumulate over
the years, but even concurrent ones are often contradictory. Many
stereotypes circulated between 1850 and 1940. The Chinese Americans
were viewed as inscrutable, wildly excitable, of low intelligence, and
of high and complex intelligence. They are described as extremely able
workers yet low on the evolutionary scale. Occupational stereotypes include tong killers, heartless husbands, female slaves, and torturers, as
well as loyal domestic servants and successful merchants. The key to
defining these contradictory images as racial and ethnic stereotypes is
their unchanging nature. When an author makes Chinese immigrants
launderers and characterizes them as violent and emotional only
because they are Chinese by ancestry, these qualities are stereotypes. If
an author creates a well-motivated, individually characterized Chinese
immigrant who launders clothes because of legal and economic restraints
which bar him from other occupations, that character is an artistic creation of the author placed in an accurate historical context, not just a
stereotype taken from the imprint of earlier expressions in society or
literature. In this study, the word *stereotype* refers to descriptions of
Chinese Americans that I judge are based on race and ethnicity rather
than on serious attempts by the author at characterization.

The depiction of Chinese Americans in relation to the
Yellow Peril can be divided into four categories. They are:

1. Fiction by white authors in which the author depicts Chinese
   Americans as a threat to the well-being of the United States or
   other Americans.
2. Fiction by white authors in which the author depicts Chinese
   Americans specifically as nonthreatening to the rest of the
   United States and as innocent victims of ethnic and racial prejudice.
3. Fiction by white authors in which the author depicts Chinese
   Americans without regard to the question of whether or not
   they threaten the well-being of the United States or other
   Americans.

4. Fiction by Chinese Americans, from the viewpoint of Chinese
American characters, in which the author depicts Chinese
Americans as a group dealing with the perception held by
white American characters of them as a threat to the well-
being of the United States and other Americans.

The discussions of each work of fiction considered in this study
make clear into which category each work falls. Each chapter contains, in either the text or the notes, what I believe is the complete list
of fictional works belonging under each chapter title, excepting the
chapter on pulp magazines, which contains a representative sampling
of pulp fiction about the Chinese Americans.[1] Also, some uncollected
short stories must certainly have escaped notice. When Chinese is
anglicized from the Mandarin dialect, the Pinyin system is given first,
followed by the Wade-Giles system in parentheses. Anglicized terms
from other dialects are used as given by the original author or source.

The individual depictions of Chinese American characters have
been described in the analyses of each story, but here I offer the outline
of a theoretical model of a Chinese American character which, if
created in fiction, I would consider nonracist. My purpose in presenting this model is to provide a basis for comparison with the many
characters described throughout this study. The parameters of this
model are few and simple:

1. The character does not possess any particular personality traits
solely as a result of race or genetic heritage, but has a normal
range of human emotions and motives which are realistically
shaped by the cultural environment of the character.
2. The character is clearly an individual who has personal concerns that are realistic and convincing within the context of the
story and recognizable as normal human affairs.
3. All descriptions and values of Chinese culture and history and
of American culture and history are accurate and used ap-
propriately in regard to the character.

These guidelines are so basic that setting them down may seem
superfluous. However, most of the Chinese American characters
reviewed here fail to measure up to them in one way or another. I
believe that this failure is directly related to the concept of the Yellow
Peril, and that a realistic character portrayal of a Chinese American in
an accurate historical context could not sustain the vision of a Yellow
Peril.

For many years, the accepted interpretation of the growth of

American hostility toward the Chinese immigrants was that expressed by Mary Coolidge in *Chinese Immigration*. Coolidge isolates the dominant role of Irish immigrants in the agitation against the Chinese over labor issues in the 1870s as the activating circumstance behind this hostility, which supposedly followed a favorable atmosphere when the Chinese first arrived.

> The clamor of an alien class in a single state—taken up by politicians for their own ends—was sufficient to change the policy of a nation and to commit the United States to a race discrimination at variance with our own professed theories of government, and so irrevocably that it has become an established tradition.[2]

Stuart Creighton Miller refers to this interpretation as the California thesis, and argues persuasively against it in *The Unwelcome Immigrant: The American Image of the Chinese, 1785–1882*.[3] He points out that hostility toward the Chinese had both an older historical context and a nationwide geographical one. Central to both contexts is the myth of the American melting pot of peoples.

> Cultural anxiety over the admission of such an unfamiliar and dissimilar migrant as the Chinese was not confined to any one section of the country either. Eastern editors articulated such fears at least as early as they were expressed in California. Americans have generally assumed that the theory of the melting pot involved a two-way process whereby immigrants contributed to the cultural matrix in the process of becoming "Americanized." Until the coming of the Chinese, however, no immigrant group had differed sufficiently from the Anglo-American root stock to compromise basic social institutions such as Christian religion and ethics, monogamy, or natural rights theory, not to mention the doctrine of material progress for the individual. Faced with the concrete possibility that it might become necessary to sacrifice substantial elements of these axiomatic beliefs in the name of a melting-pot hybrid "Americanization," many editors and legislators frankly shifted their ground. Social foundations were not negotiable. The immigrant had to become a convert and shed his foreign, heathen ways. The alternative was total exclusion of culturally distant groups, and a melting pot that was limited rather than infinite in scope.[4]

Miller adds that racist theory in the nineteenth century linked the genes of the Chinese to their thoughts and habits. This was fuel for the argument that they were unassimilable; supposedly, their behavior was as unchangeable as their physical racial characteristics. These concepts were not confined to the West Coast, either. The historical background of this hostility is even older, and Miller terms it the most crucial factor in the success of the movement for Chinese exclusion.

> Californians did not have to expend much effort in convincing their compatriots that the Chinese would make undesirable citizens. The existing image of the Chinese in America had already done it for them. For decades American traders, diplomats, and Protestant missionaries had developed and spread conceptions of Chinese deceit, cunning, idolatry, despotism, xenophobia, cruelty, infanticide, and intellectual and sexual perversity. This negative image was already reflected in American magazines and geography textbooks before 1840, a fact that is at variance with the assumption made by many diplomatic historians that Americans respected the Chinese and sympathized with them during the Anglo-Chinese wars. These wars—in conjunction with the Taiping Rebellion, the Burlingame Mission, Tientsin Massacre, and emigration of Chinese "coolies" to the western hemisphere—coincided with the development of the first recognizably modern mass media in the United States. The immediate result was a notable jump in American awareness of China, if the greatly increased coverage given to that nation in the mass media after 1840 is any index. It was the unfavorable, previously developed, trader-diplomat-missionary view of the Chinese that was available to the editors for popularization during this period in which occurred a chain of sensational events in China.[5]

Historical events and literature written prior to 1850 are beyond the scope of this study, but here at the outset I will make clear that I accept Miller's contention that the image of the Chinese in the United States before their arrival was negative in character. Specific controversies developed after their immigration began, but the groundwork had already been laid for the racism they faced.

Gunther Barth presents a thesis in *Bitter Strength: A History of the Chinese in the United States 1850-1870* that must also be mentioned. He distinguishes between Chinese sojourners, who intended to remain in the United States only long enough to earn and save money before returning to China, and Chinese immigrants, who intended to remain in the United States permanently. He says that the early arrivals from China were nearly all sojourners, and he places much of the burden of anti-Chinese hostility on their shoulders.

> The sojourners intended to make and save money quickly, and to return to China to a life of ease with the family which their drudgery had maintained. In the clutches of debt bondage or under contract to labor companies, they became docile subjects of bosses and headmen, still directed in the United States by the dictates of the Chinese world, sustained by a control system based on family loyalty and fear. The sojourners shouldered the burden of daily toil in an alien environment in defense of their own system of values. They rejected new standards, and clung to their culture to give meaning to the ordeal.
>
> The sojourners' goal influenced the American reaction. Their world raised up specters that challenged American values. The work camps which regimented anonymous hordes of laborers resembled gangs of Negro slaves. The control system extended debt bondage and despotism to the United States. Chinatown, which harbored indentured migrants in dilapidated structures, suggested filth and immorality as the sojourners' second nature. These images impressed themselves firmly on Americans and determined the reaction towards the Chinese even after the sojourners had abandoned their traditional goal for the promise of a life defined no longer in terms of mere survival, but of liberty.[6]

This thesis perhaps should be modified in degrees for two reasons that Barth does not confront. I do not mean to say that many Chinese arrivals were not sojourners, but that evaluating their status and historical impact may be more involved than Barth indicates. The first reason is that a solid background of anti-Chinese hostility existed in the United States before the Chinese reached this country, as Miller describes. The sojourners were coming into an atmosphere that was neither favorable nor even neutral. In addition, the distinction between a sojourner and an immigrant lies solely in the migrant's personal goals, which are hard for a scholar to measure. One who arrives as a sojourner intending to return to China becomes an immigrant upon deciding to stay or upon realizing that for financial reasons returning is impossible. Likewise, one who has few personal bonds in

China and is at first willing to stay in the United States becomes a sojourner if the harshness of life and prejudice against the Chinese in the United States bring about a discouraged change of heart. Historical evidence of such personal decisions is usually ambiguous and this is the second reason for accepting Barth's thesis with reservations.

Barth mentions that hardly any Chinese in the United States tried to get citizenship during the 1850s and 1860s, and he also notes that the outcome of such attempts was predetermined against them anyway. This latter point would seem to nullify the importance of the scarcity of applicants; one has no idea how many people might have applied if they had felt they had any chance of success. Barth also says that the sojourners strengthened the animosity against them by keeping together and not reaching out to form bonds with white American society, thereby inviting hostility through alienation. Yet all immigrant groups to the United States have shown this tendency in degrees, in order to maintain a familiar cultural and social atmosphere while they adjust to new surroundings. The degree to which these groups have become and remained ingrown varies, but generally, those who have been the targets of the greatest prejudice have huddled together the most resolutely. Certainly Barth is correct in saying that this formation of a tight immigrant society was used against the Chinese as evidence of their unassimilability, but it is only one arc in a vicious circle. Since the hostility toward the new arrivals from China began almost upon their landing, at the very least one might surmise that the cause-and-effect relationship of animosity toward, and self-imposed isolation of, the Chinese migrants developed simultaneously. Second, Barth measures the development of sojourners into immigrants partly by their acculturation into white American society. This is logical enough in the framework of the melting pot concept Miller describes, where immigrants are welcomed only if they drop their foreign, or non-Western European, ways. However, in passing, one might also observe that in the multicultural context of nineteenth century California, a group of Chinese arrivals conceivably could have wished to live in the expansive, gold-bearing new land permanently away from the tight social obligations and economic limitations in China, and yet maintain their traditional values and customs just as the original English immigrants did when they chose to live in colonies isolated from the Native Americans and chose to continue speaking English and wearing their native European clothing. Barth's system would categorize such people as sojourners.

No discussion of the Yellow Peril in American fiction is complete without at least the barest mention of seemingly unrelated events that occurred in Eastern Europe six centuries before Chinese immigrants first reached North America. In the thirteenth century, Mongol armies under the rule of Genghis Khan and his descendants twice swept across Asia into Eastern Europe, conquering all they faced. Though they defeated the individual and allied European armies sent against them, they halted their second European invasion when the successor of Genghis Khan died in East Asia. The Mongols returned to Mongolia to take part in the selection of a successor, and when they came again into Eastern Europe they settled in Russia as rulers of defeated territory but did not press their military designs farther into Europe. The other Europeans did not know what had saved them. However, the surprise and power of the initial Mongol onslaught had made a deep impression on the European chroniclers of the day.

The Mongol invasions of Europe and their later settlement in Russia represent the first time that detailed historical records were kept of major confrontations and subsequent long-term political accommodations between East Asians and Europeans in large numbers.[7] Large numbers of East Asians and Europeans did not meet again to reside permanently in the same land until they both entered the Pacific Coast of the United States from opposite directions. A detailed examination of the relationship between these two events would require another full study, but one particular result of the Mongol invasions should be mentioned here.

The European chroniclers, monks who recorded the coming of the Mongols, expressed their fear mainly through three issues. One was that the Mongols could not be defeated in direct action. Militarily, this was true at the time; Europe was saved by the timely death of Genghis Khan's successor, not by any military might of the Europeans. Another issue is that the Mongols were believed to be coming in huge numbers. This was not true, but seems to have been a belief caused by the lightning mobility of the Mongols, all of whom were mounted and wore very light armor compared to the Europeans. Their speed caused the Europeans to think they saw many Mongol units when they were actually confronted by a few units appearing quickly in widely separated places. Finally, the European monks were concerned about the non-Christian, "heathen" nature of the Mongols. Some chroniclers called the Mongols the punishment of God out of Tartarus, from which the Mongols also came to be called Tartars; this was facilitated by the coincidentally similar Persian word for them, *Tatars*, that reached Europeans.

In California, the three arguments levelled first against the immigration of the Chinese are surprisingly similar. White Californians claimed that the Chinese laborers could not be beaten in direct competition, allegedly because they worked too hard and survived on less wages. Second, anti-Chinese agitators claimed that the Chinese would swarm over the Pacific and inundate white America, though in California, for instance, in the 1850s, the rate of Chinese immigration was second to that of Irish immigrants and was closely followed by that of German immigrants. It did not even approach the combined immigration from all European countries. Finally, the "heathen" state of the Chinese immigrants was assailed in the fear that they would morally corrupt the Christian values of the United States.

The European monks' reactions to the Mongol invasions have an apparent relation to the American anti-Chinese forces' claims against Chinese immigration. The depth of this relation depends upon the literature and events of the six centuries between them. However, the white American fear of the Yellow Peril has its roots among Europeans who survived a Mongol whirlwind from the Gobi Desert seven centuries ago.

I

The Chinese Immigrant on the Frontier

The first Asian immigrants to the United States were Chinese who landed in California. They took part in the Gold Rush, in the boom years of the mining camps, and in the development of cities such as San Francisco and Sacramento. Several factors brought this about. The Opium War in 1839–40 caused an increase in trade between China and the West, opening new port cities and altering the economics of those cities; in addition, word of the new frontier country, with its unmined gold and its urgent need for labor, spread through the ports of China. Perhaps the most lasting factor in immigration, though, was the Taiping Rebellion. This was a civil war in China that raged for fourteen years and contributed to widespread suffering not only by the direct effects of war, but also by causing the neglect of dikes and farmland which resulted in flood and famine. This long-term social and political upheaval encouraged many Chinese to risk their fortunes outside the country, and California was a prime destination.

These immigrants from Asia were the first free nonwhites to arrive in the United States in significant numbers. The Africans had been brought by force, and the territories of the Native Americans and Mexicans had been conquered and occupied militarily. By contrast, the Chinese came by choice. They sometimes voluntarily indentured themselves in exchange for passage, and in nearly all cases they endured harsh conditions during the journey. The resulting immigration profoundly affected the formation of institutionalized racism in the United States at both state and federal levels.

The early hostility toward the Chinese in California was first manifested legally in the Foreign Miners' Tax in the early 1850s. This was a California levy officially directed toward any non-U.S. citizens working in the mines, but in reality it was primarily enforced against the Chinese. By the time the law was declared unconstitutional, the Chinese were estimated to have paid 85 percent of the five million dollars collected in revenue.[1]

The sources of conflict between the Chinese and white Californians are complex. In addition to racial differences, the religious, cultural, and linguistic differences were much greater than those among Europeans of different backgrounds. The focal point of conflict, however, was labor. After the transcontinental railroad was completed in 1869, jobs were scarce. During the recession of the 1870s, Irish American demagogue Dennis Kearney aroused white workers into a frenzy of assault, riots, and lynchings against the Chinese, who were accused of taking jobs from white workers. The anti-Chinese movement grew quickly, and legal discrimination followed proportionally.

Many legal developments against the Chinese occurred. One of the most important was an 1854 decision by the California Supreme Court stating that, as non-whites, the Chinese were untrustworthy, and that their testimony was unacceptable in a court of law.[2] In 1879, a U.S. Supreme Court decision denied them the right to become naturalized citizens.[3] These and similar measures culminated in 1882 in the first Chinese Exclusion Act. This was the first restriction that the United States had ever placed on immigration; the right to immigrate was denied to all Chinese except a few in the merchant, tourist, diplomat, teacher, and student categories.[4] Many Chinese remained in the U.S., however, often the victims of continuing atrocities. The two sides in the conflict, Chinese and white, continued to live together in rough, suspicious proximity.

The earliest American fiction about the Chinese immigrants was written during the 1860s and 1870s and set in the California frontier. Bret Harte, Joaquin Miller, and Ambrose Bierce are well-known authors who wrote about Chinese immigrants in some of their stories about the American frontier. Margaret Hosmer, a writer who lived in California from about 1855 to 1875, wrote a novelette that will be considered. All four authors lived in a social atmosphere hostile to the Chinese immigrants. Interestingly, however, none of them depicted the Chinese immigrants as a threat, instead taking more tolerant or even sympathetic positions.

The prevailing stereotype of the Chinese immigrants at this time was that of a "coolie," or unskilled laborer. Coolies were considered physically small, dirty, and diseased. In manner, they were allegedly humble and passive, but also sneaky and treacherous. They supposedly all looked alike and were depraved morally, given to theft, violence, gambling, opium, and prostitution. The most durable of their alleged traits was inscrutability, a quality that remains part of the Chinese American stereotype to the present. The fiction considered in this chapter was written with an awareness of this stereotype, but these four authors are not writing about the Yellow Peril itself.

Bret Harte, the foremost writer of frontier fiction from the early days of the mining camps and wagon trains, was an Easterner who lived in California from 1854 to 1871. He produced fiction both during this period and after leaving to return East, where he lived until 1878. In that year he moved to England, where he spent the rest of his life.

Harte was one of the first local colorists, popularizing this school with his picturesque stories of western frontier life. He emphasized details such as clothing, manners, and dialect among the divergent groups in California such as Native Americans, Chicanos, Chinese immigrants, Irish Americans, and WASPs. Chinese immigrants appear in his fiction, therefore, as part of the California scenes he portrays throughout his work; they are seldom major characters. They are prominently featured in four of Harte's short stories, which will be discussed first in chronological order.[5]

"Wan Lee, the Pagan" (1874) tells the story of a Chinese boy from babyhood to his death as a child from a mob. One of the important characters is Hop Sing, a merchant who first arranges for the care of the baby. Harte's presentation of this character not only illustrates a clear break from the general coolie stereotype, but also suggests in more detail what kind of stereotype of the Chinese he was encountering.

> Before I describe him I want the average reader to discharge from his mind any idea of a Chinaman that he may have gathered from the pantomime. He did not wear beautifully scalloped drawers fringed with little bells—I never met a Chinaman who did; he did not habitually carry his forefinger extended before him at right angles with his body, nor did I ever hear him utter the mysterious sentence, "Ching a ring a ring chaw," nor dance under any provocation. He was, on the whole, a rather grave, decorous, handsome gentleman. . . . His manner was urbane, although quite serious. He spoke French and English fluently. In brief, I doubt if you could have found the equal of this Pagan shopkeeper among the Christian traders of San Francisco.[6]

The other Chinese supporting characters are launderers, domestics, coolies, and a juggler. They are all presented as loyal and skillful, yet sometimes uncooperative. Wan Lee himself exhibits these traits in abundance, beginning with his first job delivering newspapers. Every paper is delivered on time at the proper place, but how? In the form of hard-pressed cannonballs, delivered by a single shot and a mere *tour de force* through the glass of bedroom windows. They had received them full in the face, like a baseball . . . in quarter sheets, tucked in at separate windows . . . in the chimney, pinned against the door, shot through attic windows, delivered in long slips through convenient keyholes, stuffed into ventilators, and occupying the same can with the morning's milk.[7]

Wan Lee is promptly removed to the typesetting end of the newspaper business, where he soon gains a passable ability to read English. His mischievousness reaches its high point when he substitutes a line of Chinese type for an intended quote from a prominent politician. The politician subsequently complains angrily to the paper. The Chinese throughout the community enjoy the joke, however, as the line of Chinese had portrayed Wan Lee's immediate superior in the typesetting room saying that Wan Lee has made a fool of him. The quote ran, "'China boy makee me belly much foolee. China boy makee heap sick,' as Wan Lee translated it."[8]

Harte finishes his account of Wan Lee with a sideswipe at California's white Christians. Wan Lee befriends a white girl and carries her books and makes toys for her; in exchange, she sings and reads to him, and takes him to Sunday school. Wan Lee's end comes quickly and senselessly, during two days of riots when "a mob of half-grown boys and Christian school-children"[9] attack "unarmed, defenseless foreigners, because they were foreigners and of another race, religion, and color, and worked for what wages they could get."[10] Wan Lee's death is stark and sudden, and is shown to have no relation whatever to his individual identity, but only to his Chinese and pagan identity.

In "The Queen of Pirate Isle" (1887), written after Harte had permanently left the West, a page named Wan Lee does odd jobs in a mine-owner's house, but plays with the household children in his free time. Harte utilizes the children's play and elements of humor to show a softer side of racial interaction, frequently putting Wan Lee in the role of hero and leader. On the way to visit the mine, one of Wan Lee's playmates falls part of the way down a cliff, and Wan Lee rescues her by flipping his long queue over the side. This prompts a miner down below to say, "Darned ef I ever want to cut off a Chinaman's pigtail again, boys."[11] The amused miners later disguise themselves as pirates and pretend to abduct the children, but the masquerade fails when Wan Lee recognizes the self-proclaimed pirate chieftain as a miner who owes forty dollars to his father, a launderer. Finally, when the "pirates" suggest throwing Wan Lee into a dungeon, his friends insist that he be allowed to return home with them. By presenting this group identity among the children, Harte suggests rather idealistically that the coming generation of Californians may not suffer the same divisions as his.

The protagonist of "See Yup" (1898) is named for one of the dialects spoken by immigrants from Guangdung (Kwangtung) Province. He represents the kind of witty, fast-moving character that Wan Lee, "the Pagan," might have been as an adult. Harte essentially gives that Wan Lee his revenge, as See Yup dupes the white Californians repeatedly to make his fortune. The humor and mischievousness of this character are similar to those in the earlier story; the primary difference is that See Yup does not die.

See Yup represents all of his fellow immigrants, in both his appearance and tribulations. He is a launderer who

> looked like any other Chinaman, wore the ordinary blue
> cotton blouse and white drawers of the Sampan coolie, and,
> in spite of the apparent cleanliness and freshness of these
> garments, always exhaled that singular medicated odor—
> half opium, half ginger—which we recognized as the com-
> mon "Chinese smell."[12]

See Yup is routinely harassed by local schoolboys and cannot collect on all his bills, one customer being "an Irishman, whose finer religious feelings revolted against paying money to a heathen."[13] Yet See Yup's victories more than even the score. He evades the Foreign Miners' Tax, "an oppressive measure aimed principally at the Chinese, who humbly worked the worn-out 'tailings' of their fellow Christian miners," by capitalizing on the inability of white Californians to identify the individual Chinese.[14] See Yup pays his own tax, then passes the receipt to twelve of his compatriots, who successfully avoid paying any tax by showing it to the tax collector whenever he visits. See Yup next draws the miners, all plagued by indigestion, into buying his Chinese medicines. His business is good until a Western doctor takes the miners aside and tells them the contents of their Chinese medicines. Harte is not specific here, but relates that the miners do not patronize See Yup any further.

See Yup's final gambit nets him twenty thousand dollars and is followed by his permanent departure from the community. The money is in payment for rights to mine the tailings, or refuse ore, which he has been working throughout the story. He draws the miners into making their offer by publicly consigning one five-hundred-dollar shipment of gold repeatedly through Wells, Fargo. The shipment is received at San Francisco and secretly returned to See Yup, who then publicly sends it out again. The miners believe each shipment to San Francisco is a new load of gold dust mined from the tailings. He salts the tailings with this dust just before leaving, and by the time the tailings are played out, a few weeks later, he is nowhere to be found.

Harte is careful to excuse See Yup from moral culpability, however. The story ends with the observation that See Yup was probably not liable for legal action. No legal evidence pointed to his having salted the tailings, and he had never actually claimed that his weekly shipment to San Francisco came from them. This inference was drawn by the community as a result of spying and hearsay. Furthermore, See Yup had never offered to sell the tailings. He had simply received an offer, coupled with threats. The miners themselves had been more active in the fraud than he. One of Harte's reasons for giving this conclusion is certainly to indicate the thoroughness of See Yup's plan, but of course his getaway has already succeeded anyway. Another function of this conclusion is to assure the reader that the protagonist of the story is, indeed, See Yup, and that he is morally blameless, having merely taken advantage of the miners' greed and aggression.

In "Three Vagabonds of Trinidad" (1901), Li Tee is a waif whose Chinese guardians were driven from their washhouse by angered miners, leaving him alone. Because of his race, the mining town barred him from public school and Sabbath school, for

> although as a heathen he might have reasonably claimed attention from the Sabbath-school the parents who cheerfully gave their contributions to the heathen *abroad*, objected to him as a companion of their children in the church at home.[15]

The prevailing sentiment which drives Li Tee into the forest, where he takes up with an Indian and a dog, is expressed by a prominent citizen:

> "The nigger of every description—yeller, brown, or black, call him 'Chinese,' 'Injun,' or 'Kanaka,' or what you like— hez to clar off of God's footstool when the Anglo-Saxon gets started. . . . It's our manifest destiny to clar them out—that's what we was put here for—and it's just the work we've got to do!"[16]

Eventually, the townspeople hunt down the outcasts. All three suffer from want in the wilderness, but Li Tee dies first, of starvation, because he is the one most closely tied to civilization. The Indian and the dog are killed the same day by hunters from the town.

These four stories present Harte with a certain dilemma. Because his sympathies are with the persecuted Chinese immigrants, he often writes of them in a favorable manner. As a local colorist, however, he must also portray anti-Chinese attitudes more representative of Californian sentiment. In these stories he resolves the dilemma by using plots that deal specifically with the attitudes of white characters toward the Chinese immigrants.

In the following stories, Harte uses Chinese immigrants in significant supporting roles. Here the Chinese immigrants do not appear as positively as in the four stories discussed above, partly because they receive less attention. Harte resolves his dilemma in these stories less effectively since anti-Chinese statements by white characters are sometimes left unanswered. A close look at the presentation of the Chinese immigrants in these stories, however, indicates that Harte still treats them favorably.

In "A Belle of Canada City" (1900), Harte strikes a delicate balance. A stage driver here speaks for the bulk of white California:

> I reckon they're everwhar in Californy whar you want 'em and whar you don't; you take my word for it, afore long Californy will hev to reckon that she generally *don't* want 'em, ef a white man has to live here. With a race tied up together in a language ye can't understand, ways that no feller knows,—from their prayin' to devils, swappin' their wives, and havin' their bones sent back to Chiny—whot are ye goin' to do, and where are ye? Wot are ye goin' to make outer men that look so much alike and act alike, and never in ways that ye kin catch on to! Fellers knotted together in some underhand secret way o' communicatin' with each other, so that ef ye kick a Chinaman up here on the Summit, another Chinaman will squeal in the valley![17]

These opinions are not contradicted directly, but Harte allows the behavior of the Chinese people in the story to speak for itself. The servant Ah Fe and his colleagues maintain their loyalty to their master and play a crucial part in transmitting his messages and sheltering his daughter under bad conditions. The balance in this story is even; however, taken with the rest of Harte's work, one can see that this story stands with those considered above in presenting the Chinese as positive characters.[18]

Other works where the Chinese appear in lesser roles include the novel *Gabriel Conroy*, three novelettes, and seventeen short stories. These will be discussed briefly in chronological order. In one short story written in California, "The Christmas Gift That Came to Rupert: A Story for Little Soldiers" (1864), a children's story, Harte once again uses children as a device to unite the white and Chinese Californians.[19] Fung Tang is a page, unconverted to Christianity, who is nevertheless allowed to join his master's household in celebrating Christmas. As a listener, he is part of the frame around the story, not in the story itself. By giving the story an integrated audience, Harte subtly suggests that the children of California have certain interests in common. However, another work from California, the novelette "N.N.: Being a Novel in the French Paragraphic Style" (1865), presents a Chinese launderer as one of an undifferentiated mass: "These Chinese are docile, but not intelligent. They are ingenious, but not creative. They are cunning in expedients, but deficient in tact. In love they are simply barbarous."[20]

Harte's years in the Eastern United States produced only three works that include Chinese Americans. One was "Wan Lee, the Pagan," discussed above; the others are "An Episode of Fiddletown" (1873), and *Gabriel Conroy* (1875–76). Both of the latter stories include household servants named Ah Fe, but there is no evidence to indicate whether or not they are the same character, or related to the Ah Fe in "A Belle of Canada City."

In "An Episode of Fiddletown," Ah Fe searches at one point for his mistress, who has deserted the household. The subplot detailing Ah Fe's efforts adds nothing to the central plot, but deepens the background of frontier California by developing the Chinese as a part of its society, with their own experiences and subculture. It also allows Harte to illuminate the persecution which Ah Fe encounters, and to express his own opinions of that persecution with dry humor.

> On the road to Sacramento he was twice playfully thrown from the top of the stage-coach by an intelligent but deeply intoxicated Caucasian whose moral nature was shocked at riding with one addicted to opium smoking. At Hangtown he was beaten by a passing stranger, purely an act of Christian supererogation. At Dutch Flat he was robbed by well-known hands from unknown motives. At Sacramento he was arrested on suspicion of being something or other, and discharged with a severe reprimand—possibly for not being it, and so delaying the course of justice. At San Francisco he was freely stoned by children of the public schools; but by carefully avoiding these monuments of enlightened progress, he at last reached in comparative safety the Chinese quarter, where his abuse was confined to the police and limited by the strong arm of the law.[21]

Harte carefully notes that Ah Fe, for all his trouble, still responds to abuse with small offenses of his own. His loyalty is selective and he is not oblivious to ill treatment. After arriving in San Francisco, he returns an apron belonging to his former mistress's daughter, along with a forty-dollar gift for her living expenses. Concurrently, he steals a scarf from an Irish handmaid who has treated him rudely.

In *Gabriel Conroy*, the servant Ah Fe has a similar task. The protagonist of the story has left home, and Ah Fe is sent to find him. He enlists the aid of a Chinese labor gang, who immediately drop their work and scatter in all directions. Gabriel Conroy is located within a half hour, and the Chinese are all back at work in another half hour. Ah Fe has one more tribulation, however. A murder was committed during that hour on the road which he himself had taken. When Ah Fe is questioned by authorities, Harte has him play the standard inscrutable role: "He returned his questioner's glance with ineffable calmness and vacancy, patiently drew the long sleeves of his blouse still further over his varnished fingers, crossed them submissively and Orientally before him. . . ."[22]

This use of an image which was a stereotype even in Harte's time is rare in his work. If there is a positive value in presenting it here, that value would derive from the fact that Ah Fe is, and has been, acting consistently on the side of good to support the protagonist. However, this usage goes against the bulk of Harte's efforts in depicting the Chinese, which run counter to the prevailing image of the day.

The remainder of Harte's writing, produced in England late in his career, include Chinese characters only in roles so minor that they are more a part of the setting than characters. In most of these works, the Chinese appear as servants in homes, mining camps, hotels, and rooming houses; the most striking settings are a millionaire's mansion and a bandit's den. The large picture Harte presents indicates primarily that Chinese servants could be found anywhere in the West where employers could afford them. In the rest of the stories, Harte depicts the Chinese as a pervasive work force throughout the range of laboring-class jobs. They appear several times as farm laborers, representing the little-known fact that the Chinese were California's first migrant workers. They also work as carriers, using baskets balanced on long shoulder-poles, and they appear again in mining and laundry work, for which they are better known historically.[23] Individually, these roles are too small to make a significant contribution to the image of the Chinese in the West.

Although this study focuses on fiction, one exception must be made. Of all Harte's many pieces dealing with the Chinese, the most popular and well known is the narrative poem, "Plain Language from

Truthful James" (1870), or "The Heathen Chinee."[24] Without discussing it, this work would be incomplete.

The poem presents a contradiction. Fundamentally, it tells how Truthful James and Bill Nye try to cheat Ah Sin at cards, and find that instead Ah Sin cheats them. To this extent, the story is similar to the final trick of See Yup, who uses the white miners' own greed against them. Here Harte ends with the ironic complaint of the loser: "That for ways that are dark / And for tricks that are vain / The heathen Chinee is peculiar. . . ."[24] When the poem first appeared, Harte's irony was probably lost on many readers caught up in the anti-Chinese movement, which mushroomed in the 1870s. The white characters in the poem clearly exhibit racist attitudes, and their expression of these probably contributed to the poem's early acceptance. One assumes that the vernacular style, the irony, and the story itself account, deservedly, for its continued popularity since then. John Burt Foster states that the growing anti-Chinese attitudes were an element "Harte seems to have taken advantage of when he substituted the phrase 'We are ruined by cheap Chinese labor' for the original line 'Henceforth I'm opposed to cheap labor,' which even became 'Or is civilization a failure?' in the page proof." Foster also says, "Harte was deeply ashamed of the poem, and indeed it does seem to repudiate the forthright stand he took on race relations. . . ."[25]

With Harte's other work in mind, one can see that this poem stands outside the general pattern. In regard to the depiction of the Chinese, the most similar work of Harte is "A Belle of Canada City," where the responsibility of portraying Western characters accurately required the anti-Chinese tirade of a stagecoach driver, quoted earlier. In that instance, of course, the balancing factor in favor of the Chinese was Ah Fe's loyal behavior. Ah Sin's winning at cards does not have inherent moral value, though, so it does not serve a positive purpose in the same way. Harte's implied criticism of his white opponents' hypocrisy is therefore perhaps too subtle, at least for its time, when many readers were disinclined to perceive it.

By contrast, Ambrose Bierce rarely left any doubt about where he stood on any issue, usually being against it no matter what it was. On the question of the Yellow Peril, he was against the hostility directed at the Chinese immigrants. His fiction set on the frontier can be classified as local color, though much of his fiction cannot.

Bierce lived in California from the end of the Civil War to the turn of the century, except for three years in England in the early 1870s. The work of Bierce that involves the Chinese, like that of Harte, constitutes only a small fraction of his total output. Nevertheless, as a Western writer, this awareness of the Chinese in California as a social and politically significant element is natural and to be expected in some of his fiction.

Bierce's first published short story, "The Haunted Valley" (1871), deals with anti-Chinese sentiment without including a Chinese character. The primary trait of the main character, Jo Dunfer, is a violent hatred of the Chinese, vividly expressed. The tension in the story line involves the fate of Ah Wee, a supposed Chinese worker at Dunfer's remote cabin who was killed by him. The climax arrives with the discovery that Ah Wee was not a Chinese man, but a girl, presumably Chinese, Dunfer had won in a poker game in San Francisco, and had accidentally killed in a fit of jealousy. Dunfer had buried her out by the cabin and then identified her in town as a coolie he had hired. Dunfer claims to have killed Ah Wee for not learning to cut down trees like a white man. This saves him from legal retribution, as the jury finds that Ah Wee "came to 'is death by a wholesome sentiment workin' in the Caucasian breast."[26] Ever since, Dunfer has kept his cover intact by expressing his antipathy toward the Chinese at every chance.

Until the end of the story, the reader assumes that Ah Wee really is a Chinese man. Dunfer's antagonism toward Ah Wee and the Chinese in general is frequently expressed, providing the reader with a firm picture of the anti-Chinese mood of the day. The alleged reason for Ah Wee's death, that "he" would not cut down trees in the correct manner, is obviously silly. In presenting it, and Dunfer's prior knowledge that the jury will accept it, Bierce illustrates the extremity which anti-Chinese prejudice had reached.

His "Mortality in the Foothills" (1872) is a single ironic paragraph, stating that Chinese and Indians should no longer be thrown down a certain mine shaft. In a twist, Bierce refers the reader to an old well which is just as good for the purpose and more accessible, besides.[27]

The short story called "The Night-Doings at 'Dead Man's'" is the strangest of Bierce's work dealing with the Chinese. The main character is another white recluse in a remote cabin, named Hiram Beeson. A former Chinese domestic of Beeson lies buried beneath the cabin; however, for no reason given, Beeson had cut off his queue and nailed it to the cabin wall before the burial. Claiming that the Chinese believe they cannot enter heaven without their queues, Beeson has stood guard over the queue for over two years, foiling the attempts of the dead Chinese domestic to rise from his grave under the floor to get it. The story itself involves the appearance of a mysterious stranger, the death of Beeson, and the disappearance of the queue.

The salient and peculiar fact regarding the Chinese in this story is that detailed explanations are not considered necessary. Beeson does not give the cause of his domestic's death, the reason he removed the domestic's queue, or his motive for guarding it from its owner for over two years. The assumption that the reader will accept these developments as given again suggests that common white attitudes toward the Chinese immigrants were so hostile that harsh treatment of the domestic, no matter how mysterious, is acceptable without further elaboration. At the same time, Bierce's description of the Chinese domestic is less than flattering. The servant gives off the scent of opium, is covered with mold from the grave, and takes the queue in his "horrible yellow teeth."[28]

Two of Bierce's *Fantastic Fables* (1911) concern the Chinese in the United States, and a third has an apparent connection.[29] Bierce's tone is again ironic in "A Radical Parallel," where white Californians are driving the Chinese out of a town. Upon hearing that some Chinese in China seek to drive foreigners from that country, they "were so greatly incensed that they carried out their original design."[30] In "A Treaty of Peace," Bierce mentions four wars by 1894 between China and the United States, all of which had resulted from atrocities against each other's emigrant citizens. The treaty establishes a tally of scalps to be kept by each government. The country with the most is awarded a thousand dollars per scalp, with a payoff every ten years in Mexican dollars. The title character in "The Returned Californian" is a hanged man who goes to St. Peter in 1893. St. Peter allows him to enter heaven, taking the fact that he was hanged in California as evidence that California has been settled by Christians. This ironic comment seems to refer to the widespread lynchings that went unpunished at that time. It does not mention the Chinese by name or specific implication, but they were frequently the victims of such actions during this period. John Burt Foster includes this fable as one which concerns the Chinese in California.[31]

Unlike Harte, Bierce never presented the Chinese positively as individuals. His efforts on their behalf were all negative in tone, criticizing their persecutors with the irony typical of much of his work. While Bierce certainly never sounds very favorable toward the Chinese himself, this lack of positive depiction alone is not necessarily an indication of special antipathy toward the Chinese on his part, since he frequently wrote pieces where none of the characters were very likeable.

Joaquin Miller's *First Fam'lies of the Sierras* (1876) is largely the result of time he spent in the California mines and mountains in the 1850s. Miller was another local colorist of the West. The one Chinese character in this novel is Washee-Washee, who of course launders clothes in the isolated mining camp called "The Forks." He is not exactly a villain, but neither is he the persecuted figure presented by Harte and Bierce. His character is that of a playful rascal, annoying but less than an object of real hatred.

After the Widow arrives in camp, the first respectable woman to reside there, the miners take their clothes to her to be washed. She soon takes in Washee-Washee as an assistant, and shortly after that clothes begin to disappear. The miners confront Washee-Washee, but when the Widow asks about the commotion, they are too shy in her presence to speak.

> But who ever saw an embarrassed Chinaman? The innocent little fellow, turning his soft brown almond eyes up to the Widow, told her, as poor Sandy stared straight down the hill, that this dreadful "Amelikan" wanted him to leave her, and to go home with him, to be his wife.[32]

When the miners trap Washee-Washee with a trove of stolen goods and present him and the evidence to the Widow, she begs for his release. She tells Washee-Washee to stop stealing, and that it is "not right."[33]

> The Chinaman understood the first proposition perfectly, but not the last at all. To him all this was simply a bad investment. To him it was only a little shipwreck; and having been taught by the philosophers of his country to prepare for adversity in the hour of prosperity, he was not at all lacking in resignation now. He rose up, smiled that patient and peaceful smile of his, and wended his way to his home.[34]

Washee-Washee's response is that of an amoral individual, equally devoid of conscience and malice. He is not the devilish Wan Lee of Bret Harte who delivered papers destructively, but a semi-innocent heathen without knowledge of sin. Although Harte's launderers were usually cheated by their customers, and Miller's Washee-Washee is caught cheating them instead, he is still more of a mascot than a villain. The miners' intent of lynching him seems to be a reflex; when the Widow intercedes for his life, they readily agree. They also will not run him out of town, since he would die in the wilderness, so they decide to reform him. To this end, the Judge lectures him and the "Parson," named because he is the most profane man in camp, curses him. This non-religious attempt to imbue Washee-Washee with a sense of guilt is deemed "a little missionary business."[35] The only result, however, is that Washee-Washee falls asleep.

The Widow, whose moral presence is felt throughout the camp, soon brings about a true change in Washee-Washee. His behavior as her assistant is excellent, and he begins carrying a Bible. When the Widow marries, however, he must leave her house.

Miller's most evocative description of Washee-Washee involves his decline after this point. He cannot go into business again, but he remains in camp. Finally, he begins smoking opium, which Miller presents as a crutch for failure and loneliness, not a casual vice of the Chinese. He dies unnoticed, and Miller provides for the first time a vision of the Chinese which is neither condescending nor criminal.

> Every five years there is a curious sort of mule caravan seen meandering up and down the mining streams of California, where Chinamen are to be found. . . . In this train or caravan the drivers do not shout or scream. The mules, it always seemed to me, do not even bray. This caravan travels almost always by night, and it is driven and managed almost altogether by Chinamen. These Chinamen are civil, very respectful, very quiet, very mournful both in their dress and manner.[36]

This is the caravan that collects coffins bearing the remains of the Chinese. They are returned to China. Washee-Washee finally leaves The Forks aboard the Caravan of Death.[37]

Margaret Hosmer wrote a novelette called *You-Sing: The Chinaman in California: A True Story of the Sacramento Flood* (1868). Hosmer's stated purpose in writing this is to present a picture to white Americans in order to further missionary efforts to convert Chinese Americans. The story describes the relationship between You-Sing, a worker first in the mines and now a domestic, and his former employer and friend, Mr. Murdoch. The Murdoch family is new to Sacramento, having just joined Mr. Murdoch from the East, and the three children quickly learn anti-Chinese prejudice from the local children. The family's black maid is particularly hostile toward You-Sing and teaches the Murdoch boy to throw sand on him and call him names. You-Sing's experience with white children keeps him away from them whenever possible, and he is neither meek nor forgiving. When he comes across one of the daughters, Mary, stuck in the mud with a friend, he stops to jeer.

> The Chinaman stood still and laughed heartily at her perturbation; he had been teased and insulted so much by the American boys and girls that it gave him pleasure to see anything disagreeable happen to them.[38]

This merely completes the vicious circle of hostility. Mary cannot understand why her parents object to the anti-Chinese sentiment in the West. After this early run-in with You-Sing, Mary says to her friend, "I think they are the worst people in the world . . . I don't know what papa means by saying they are just what we make them. I'm sure nobody makes You-Sing wicked; it is his own bad nature."[39]

Mr. Murdoch had removed You-Sing from the mine and found him the position as a domestic because of the persecution he had received from the boss, Sidney Duck. When Mary suggests that You-Sing should forgive Duck for his nasty treatment, You-Sing again shows no sign of forgiveness or passivity. His awareness of Duck's criminal activities reflects the inadmissibility in court of Chinese testimony.

> No, no; me ought to get him welly hard lickee. He too muchee bad. Ah, me know—Mellickan lawman no believe poor John Chinaman, and so wicked Sidney Duck no hide all bad things from me. Ah, me know all about him, and by'me-by [sic] people catchee, and killee. Me welly glad then.[40]

The flood develops while Mr. Murdoch is away at the mine, and You-Sing takes the responsibility of saving his wife and children. He does this by helping them to the roof of their house and waving down boats to take them away. When the family members are separated, he reunites them and they relocate in San Francisco. Mary and the other children are now convinced of You-Sing's good character, though the maid remains untrusting. Mr. Murdoch has been murdered by drowning during the flood, and You-Sing, who feels indebted to his late employer for taking him out of the mine, remains with the family. Throughout this period, Hosmer shows You-Sing to be a loyal servant with courage, initiative, and a personal sense of honor, deserving of Mr. Murdoch's early praise. One is reminded of tales from the South, in which appreciated loyal ex-slaves remained with their masters during the trials of Reconstruction.

Eventually, You-Sing takes the Murdochs back to Sacramento. There he runs a laundry with a Chinese friend and refers sewing jobs to Mrs. Murdoch, who earns an income that way. Finally You-Sing witnesses an altercation in a Chinese gambling establishment, which brings about a just end to the story.

In this gambling house, other Chinese, also habitually harassed by whites, are gambling with an unfriendly white man. These Chinese are no more tolerant than You-Sing: "at last one of the Chinese, goaded to anger by the insults of the drunken man, sprang up and caught him by the throat. . . ."[41] On this occasion, You-Sing fulfills his debt to his late employer by learning the identity of Mr. Murdoch's murderer. This is the villain Sidney Duck, who also stole the Murdoch family's assets. Their income is restored, and You-Sing receives a job, a bank account, and private tutoring in English, since he is not welcome in the schools on account of race. Surprisingly, even though the book was published by the Presbyterian Publication Committee, Hosmer does not tie the last loose end with his conversion to Christianity.

> Mary grieved to find that You-Sing, with all his devotion to his friends, was yet a stranger to the true spirit of the Christian. . . .
> Thus we will leave them, trusting, as they did, that the Lord, who had chosen so humble a worker for his will, never meant to despise or reject him.[42]

This ending does not indicate a respect for You-Sing's lack of interest in Christianity, however. Perhaps Hosmer was just being realistic. Her view of the Chinese is sympathetic, but distinctly missionary. Writing of herself in the third person as author, she says in the preface:

> These intelligent, apt, industrious, but heathen people, awakened her warm sympathy, and she earnestly desires that others should think and feel and work for them. Unless we bless them with our Christianity, they will curse us with the vices and wickedness of heathenism. To interest the people of the United States in them is the aim of this story, the events of which are entirely true, though not occurring in the exact order in which they are here narrated.[43]

Hosmer's religious purpose distinguishes her from the local colorists, who were more interested in telling entertaining tales of the locale for their own sake.

In sum, the earliest and most significant works of American fiction dealing with the Chinese immigrants on the frontier share three basic elements. First, each one views the Chinese as individuals with specific characterization, participating in California society as history has recorded, as laborers and domestics, sometimes in integrated communities, more often in segregated ones. Second, none of these works holds a particularly important place in American letters. Hosmer's work is an obscure didacticism, while scholars interested in western local colorists mention the Chinese immigrant characters of Harte, Bierce, and Miller briefly if at all; the stories discussed above are usually examined for their other features. Finally, all of these authors write with an awareness of the widespread hostility with which the frontier Chinese lived.

Harte and Hosmer are particularly conscious of this. Harte does the best job of presenting the Chinese with individual human characteristics, both good and bad, though as a non-Chinese he occasionally falls prey to the stereotypes of the day himself. On the other side, he at least does not idealize the Chinese to a large degree, as even his sympathetic characters cheat and annoy their white harassers. His presentation of the Chinese as individuals with a normal range of emotions is the most realistic of these works. By contrast, Hosmer, working in a missionary tradition, takes a more saccharine approach.

To assure her readers that the Chinese deserve their sympathy, Hosmer indicates that their trials and their anger are the fault of white people in the West, and that in reality the Chinese are good people whose only flaw is their heathenism. So far, given her purpose, this is not damaging. In making the character of You-Sing appealing to her readers, however, she idealizes his virtues as a servant. As a missionary writer, she may see his slavish loyalty and unselfish efforts as positive Christian values. Certainly the character works well within the story, since she has given him ample motivation for appreciating Mr. Murdoch. Still, if the character is not exactly contrived, it is nevertheless carefully selected for her purpose, showing her readers that the Chinese are not threatening or to be feared. This message prevails even though her Chinese characters on rare occasions do sometimes get angry and jeer and fight; these unpleasant reactions are blamed solely on their Christian tormentors and, with unintentional irony, on their heathen state. Hosmer specifically intended that You-Sing would charm her readers back in the parlors of Philadelphia. On the whole, her sympathy is the patronizing and condescending affection common to those wishing to "enlighten" people of another culture.

Bierce's Chinese immigrants are almost incidental to his work; the tenor of these stories and fables is the exposure of hypocrisy, deceit, and cruelty on the frontier. While he seems to present the Chinese immigrants as individuals, he actually manages to avoid this, as one sees when Ah Wee's identity remains uncertain, and the story of the dead Chinese domestic ends without a clear explanation. In these stories, and in his fables, Bierce appears to have included the Chinese not because he was especially sympathetic toward them, or even because he was particularly interested, but simply because they comprised a part of the West about which he wrote. Even so, his approach is significant in that he, too, writes of them with more sympathy than hostility.

Miller comes the closest of these writers to presenting his Chinese character in a stereotyped pattern. Washee-Washee is a mascot, whose attempts at theft are humorous in their transparency. He is a cheater who remains unreformed by the rough miners but whose eventual conversion to Christianity by the Widow marks a success of Christianity over heathenism. This connection between Christianity and morality is precisely what Hosmer suggests in her preface, and here it reflects the same kind of condescension on Miller's part toward the Chinese. However, if his depiction of Washee-Washee as a thief is more negative than any presentation by Hosmer, his lyrical account of the Caravan of Death is more representative of the frontier Chinese in history than Hosmer's happy ending, where You-Sing has a job, a bank account, and white friends.

Despite their presentation of the Chinese as individuals, these writers made little attempt to understand the Chinese culture or viewpoints. Empathy is beyond consideration. At the authors' best, Harte sympathizes on many occasions with the plight of the Chinese, though he still fails to see the situation through the eyes of his Chinese characters. Even when he considers them desirable and admirable people, their culture and habits remain quaint and curious. Perhaps at the authors' worst, Miller envisions the Chinese as subhuman pets incapable of morality until they are converted to the Christianity of the West. Certainly most disappointing is Hosmer's attempt at a liberal depiction of the Chinese, at the price of an unrealistic ending and the showcasing of her main character's servile qualities. Overall, their works probably did not alter the image of the Chinese immigrants in readers' minds. Though their handling of the Chinese in these stories ran against the contemporary climate of opinion, that handling still accentuated the differences between the Chinese immigrants and their neighbors, and minimized the similarities.

This period between 1850 and 1882 saw Asians and whites mingling in their everyday lives for the first time in North America. On one hand, the immigration of Asians to the Pacific Coast was just as likely to occur in this age of growing trade and industry as the immigration of Europeans had been to the Atlantic Coast. On the other hand, their coming as free immigrants ran directly against the doctrine of Manifest Destiny which granted the West to the traditional American population of that time, from the stock of Western and Northern Europe. The tolerant stance of these authors toward the newcomers from Asia is remembered now because of the recognition accorded to Harte, Bierce, and Miller. Unfortunately, this stance is less representative of white sentiment at this time in California than the novels of Chinese invasion to be considered next.

II
Early Novels of Chinese Invasion

The harsh attitudes toward the Chinese immigrants in the later decades of the nineteenth century were grounded in the stiff competition for jobs on the West Coast and the turbulent growing pains of the labor movement. Numbers became important: the number of dollars in a wage, the number of jobs available, and the number of workers competing for those jobs. The Chinese Exclusion Act of 1882 resulted in part from this concern over numbers. Yet in stopping the immigration of Chinese laborers only, the United States took a racial stand as well as an economic one. This stand revealed a genuine fear of immigration specifically from China, and this fear was based on culture and race, not just on politics and economics. The Scott Act of 1888 proved this by redefining the term *Chinese* to mean anyone of Chinese descent, regardless of citizenship, nation of birth, and nation of residence.[1] No matter how many generations one's family had been in the Western Hemisphere, in Europe, or in another part of the world, proof of original Chinese ancestry was sufficient to keep one out of the United States under these laws. No other nationality was defined in this manner by U.S. immigration laws.

The fear of massive Chinese immigration created its own particular type of fiction and is revealed in the novels by Atwell Whitney, Robert Woltor, Pierton W. Dooner, and Oto Mundo discussed below. These authors are in the naturalist school, seeing the world in terms of inevitably clashing forces. These xenophobic novels were written during roughly the same time as the works about the Chinese immigrants on the frontier, but their focus is on the future. The Mongol invasions of Europe in the thirteenth century are reverberating here; with these works, the term *Yellow Peril* comes into its own, as the United States is shown to be seriously threatened, clearly doomed, or destroyed in all of them.

The novel *Almond-Eyed: The Great Agitator; a Story of the Day* (1878), by Atwell Whitney, marks a transition from the local color written about the immigration of the Chinese to fantastic images of open war. This apologue is set in imaginary Yarbtown, California, a microcosm in which missionary-minded Christians, Chinese and white workers, and factory owners interact. The nature of Yarbtown, despite its nominal placement in California, is that of a small New England town. The people constitute a single community based around one Presbyterian church and several small factories. Deacon Spud runs the church and owns the factories. His name, referring to a potato, would seem to suggest Irish descent. However, unlike real Irish Americans, the Spud family favors the coming of the Chinese. Whitney's introduction of the Chinese into this homogeneous community symbolizes their entry into the United States as a whole.

The Chinese are presented entirely as a group, with no individual characterization, though individual figures occasionally take the spotlight as representatives of the group. Analysis of their traits simply involves an examination of their group activity, which proves to have no redeeming qualities. However, upon their first arrival to work in the factories, Deacon Spud charitably rises in church to offer a resolution: "'Resolved, that we will do all in our power to urge upon them the teachings of Christ and bring them to a knowledge of their darkness.'"[2]

The hero, Job Stearns, is a well-travelled laborer. His first name reflects the tribulations he experiences in the novel. Prophetically, he immediately sets the tone for the novel: "'The conversion of one Chinaman in five hundred will not counterbalance the evil which the presence of the other four hundred and ninety-nine have done.'"[3] The tension in the plot comes from the events which gradually prove his attitude right.

The characteristics of the Chinese are revealed in three stages. Their first trait is a solid heathenism which even special religious classes cannot affect. The failure of these classes to make any progress is best illustrated when Stearns, venturing into Chinatown to keep an eye on its inhabitants, immediately comes across an altercation among three of its people. "The two Chinamen had the woman pressed to the floor, and one of them was engaged in the elevating, Christianizing operation of decapitating her with a pick handle. . . ."[4]

The Chinese are also enthusiastic gamblers. Their money has come from driving long-time white residents out of businesses such as vegetable peddling and laundering. In regard to competition, Whitney explains in the third-person omniscient narrative that the Chinese "can do anything. They follow our hard-working people close on their heels, steal their trades, cheapen labor, and then sit down to a dinner of rice and potato sprouts, such as a hearty white would starve on."[5]

The concept of the Chinese contaminating Yarbtown is more than symbolic. The Yarbtown Chinatown grows into a noxious hilltop slum, with a stream of refuse rolling down toward Aristocracy Street. The filth produces smallpox and, ironically, Deacon Spud is the only fatality mentioned. He pays with his life for having tried to convert the Chinese, with Job Stearns attending him in his illness when everyone else avoids him.

The Chinese mount their greatest economic threat at the same time that the most serious moral charge against them is presented. The high tide of Chinese involvement in Yarbtown in economic terms comes with Simon Spud's wholesale hiring of Chinese workers at the factories he inherited from his father, and in moral terms with the regular attendance of school children at the Chinese opium den. Whitney charges that Chinese immorality is beneath white sinning:

> Our immorality is out of reach of the young; theirs is of a different stamp, cheap—easily indulged in and unhedged by any remains of horror and conscientious scruples. Ours is hidden in gilded temples at whose doors one must knock and pay to enter; theirs is an open pool of filth in whose putrid waters the child may dabble his feet.[6]

Eventually, the unemployed white workers riot, burning both the Chinatown and the factories during the celebration of the Chinese New Year, when the noisy festivities at first camouflage the conflagration. However, the ultimate outcome of the novel is ambiguous: owner Simon Spud leaves town, while laborer Job Stearns stays on to manage the new factories being built. They will employ only white workers. Yet the Chinatown is also rebuilt and the racial conflict in Yarbtown reaches a point of stasis. Whitney concludes:

> The stream of heathen men and women still comes pouring in, filling the places which should be occupied by the Caucasian race, poisoning the moral atmosphere, tainting society, undermining the free institutions of the country, degrading labor, and resisting quietly, but wisely and successfully, all efforts to remove them, or prevent their coming. Good people, what shall be done?[7]

An answer to this question—nothing—is given in Robert Woltor's *A Short and Truthful History of the Taking of Oregon and California by the Chinese in the Year A.D. 1899* (1882). Published in the same year as the first Chinese Exclusion Act, this novel purports to be a history written at the turn of the century. If possible, Woltor's Chinese are even less individual than Whitney's. Only a few actual characters appear in the story, since the structure of the work is closer to that of a history than that of a novel. Of the characters who do appear, even fewer are Chinese. The one significant Chinese character is Prince Tsa Fungyan, leader of the invasion, which he opens with a direct naval attack on San Francisco. Religion is also an issue here: "When, in conclusion, he stated his object and purpose, Prince Tsa bore less resemblance to a human being than he did to Milton's Satan."[8]

Woltor offers a summary of Chinese immigration and settlement prior to 1880, and of relevant Chinese history. A number of his historical "facts," however, are false, and without them his version of the future would be impossible. Among others, he claims or suggests that the Chinese are deliberately concentrated in urban ghettoes for their strategic military value, that they are culturally unassimilable, that their immigration is encouraged by the numerous poor whites because lower Chinese wages mean lower prices, and that the Chinese are acting as one large organism with conquest their only motive.

Woltor ignores the pervasive presence of the Chinese in rural areas as miners, migrant agricultural workers, and servants throughout the West Coast states. His claim of cultural unassimilability had resulted largely in his own time from the great differences between Chinese culture and the culture of the frontier; the passage of time, of course, has disproven the charge beyond argument. His suggestion that lower wages paid to the Chinese made them welcome among the poor was based on the idea that the rich could buy more expensive goods made by white labor, but the poor wanted the lower prices on goods made by Chinese labor. This also directly opposes the truth of his own time, when the working class violently protested the hiring of the Chinese. Finally, of course, the Chinese in reality simply responded to the economics of the frontier in moving from one area to another. Woltor's indication that they act in automatic concert without visible leaders or organization is one of the earliest presentations of a particularly long-lived and fabricated character trait, a quality of mindlessness and puppetlike mass obedience. It reaches its greatest vogue in fiction with these stories of invasion, but persists as part of the Yellow Peril concept even to the present.

Woltor's next historical distortion is the assertion that beginning in 1880 the government of China decided to become a maritime power and needed nothing more than this decision in order to succeed. He

ignores the numerous defeats China had suffered from European
powers ever since the Opium War, and the spheres of influence and
extraterritoriality which those governments had carved away from the
Chinese government. The decaying and increasingly ineffective
Manchu government becomes, in Woltor's novel, a world maritime
power by 1899.

At the time of invasion, Chinese Americans rise throughout
California cities as a fifth column. In open warfare, a certain dullness
of mind in the Chinese is an asset, as Woltor explains:

> Our enemy, moreover, possess two great elements becoming
> the most sanguinary warfare, which may well be the envy of
> warmer-blooded races, namely a stoic indifference to pain,
> which makes them fearless to deeds of blood, and a certain
> coolness in moments of excitement and danger, when calm-
> ness is invaluable. The Caucasian shudders at the sight of
> blood—the Mongolian, though his life blood oozes out, at
> sight of the vital fluid becomes stoic. Did they but possess
> the proper dash in action, with able leaders no troops on
> earth could stand on the same parallel, as warriors. For-
> tunately, "dash" is a natural gift of the Caucasian, and the
> Mongolian character cannot acquire it.[9]

The "Asiatic swarm" of Chinese is victorious on the Pacific Coast, and
at the end of the novel threatens the rest of the United States.[10] Woltor
sees a religious quality to this conquest reminiscent of the medieval
monks' vision of the Mongols as tools of their God's vengeance.

> Now, it is somewhat curious that in the Sixteenth verse of
> the first chapter of the Revelation of St. John the angel who
> held the keys of hell and death is thus partially described:
> "And he had in his right hand seven stars: and out of his
> mouth went a sharp two-edged sword: and his countenance
> was as the sun shineth in his strength.". . . We can not be
> blind to the fact that Prince Tsa comes from Oriental
> regions, where the sun shines first on earth and proves its
> powers; that the plume of a peacock surmounts his man-
> darin cap, and that with his right hand he draws from its
> dragon-mouthed scabbard a two-edged sword, whose blade
> is marked symbolic of the Seven Stars.[11]

Just as Whitney's vision of 1878 gave ominous rumblings for a
future such as Woltor's, this vision of partial conquest presages a complete defeat of the United States by China. In effect, Pierton W.

Dooner provides it in *Last Days of the Republic* (1880), a novel that contains many parallels to Woltor's novel.

Appearing two years before the first Chinese Exclusion Act, Dooner's novel begins with a supposedly historical account of Chinese immigration to the U.S. up to 1880. This account is also twisted subtly, granting the Chinese government strength and deliberation it did not have. The account describes Chinese immigration as a conscious maneuver toward eventual conquest of the U.S. and considers the Six Companies to be the arm of the Chinese government charged with conducting this infiltration. In reality, the Chinese government had prohibited emigration and was simply powerless to stop it; the Six Companies had no roots in China, being a new organization which developed in the U.S. as a response to new conditions. Dooner also assumes for his extrapolation unlimited immigration of Chinese laborers for an indefinite period. Their coming actually was stopped in 1882, but he foresees, instead, a modification of the Naturalization Laws, allowing Asians or "Mongolians" to become citizens. With his vision of a strong, conquest-minded government and of unlimited immigration, he weaves a double helix of Chinese character traits and labor relations into the next twenty years.

Dooner's Chinese characters are no more individualized than Whitney's. However, his group characterization does not involve outright depravity, but a cunning and devious desire for power. Viewed as a monolithic mass with a single, common ambition, the Chinese workers suddenly appear very efficient, "for it is their enterprise, their thrift, their industry—in short, their virtues, that have made them invincible and insupportable, and not the exercise of any degrading or vicious habit."[12]

The apparent contradiction with Whitney's reasoning is, of course, partly a difference in point of view. For the white workers and merchants, the Chinese ability to save money and cut prices and wages is threatening and pernicious. For the Chinese, it is sound business practice in a competitive market. However, the sympathy of the narration allows no mistaking of interpretation—the efficiency of the Chinese is consistently viewed through the suffering of the white laboring class.

One crucial character trait allows the Chinese immigrants to reduce the United States to a province of China. This is absolute, unquestioning, immediate obedience to the government of China, such as Woltor also ascribes to his Chinese. Dooner's image of the Chinese as a mindless mass is required in order to make plausible the slow process of infiltration and the subsequent arming and training of the Chinese in the United States.

The Chinese conduct their infiltration with quiet, deliberate success. The capitalist class, seeing the thrift of the Chinese, has lowered wages and decides to encourage immigration by granting the rights of naturalization to them. Opposing them are members of the white working class, who are being driven out of their jobs wherever the Chinese appear. Once naturalized, the Chinese take part in the electoral process and carry the state governments of California, Nevada, and Oregon. Massive riots by white laborers follow, but have no result.

The Deep South is deemed vulnerable to the influx of Chinese labor in its effort to construct a viable economic system without chattel slavery. The aristocracy of the South welcomes the Chinese on account of the perceived racial and national characteristics they possess, failing to understand that this image is partly a front for conquest.

> Compared with the Pacific Coast States, the progress of the Coolie throughout the whole territory known as the Slave States, might be said to have been without any obstacle worthy of the name. The inhabitants were delighted with them as a substitute for the negroes . . . they could not have provided themselves with a model more suitable . . . than . . . the Coolie. He was so eminently stupid in great things, and so quick and keen in small; so devoted to toil, and so averse to sentiment; so obedient, so cunning, so ignorant, so unassuming, and so servile, that the Southern land-owners once more imagined themselves the masters of a race of slaves,—but this time willing slaves—and a prospect of permanence to the institution.[13]

For these reasons, the Chinese are also welcomed in New England to work in the great manufacturing centers of the nation. In time, they become citizens and vote in these areas, too. Once the Chinese come into power in the Deep South and New England, they begin their military preparations.

The obedient, uncurious characterization of the Chinese is crucial for the arming and military training that they receive. It is done on an individual basis in the United States, organized by the government in China.

> The citizen only knew that he was called upon to reform the habits of every-day life to which he had been accustomed, by devoting a considerable portion of his time to the performance of military evolutions and the manipulation of arms. He had no information as to how many besides himself

might be so employed. . . .[14]

This process is careful and unhurried. The training and possession of weapons is decreed a secret, and the secret is kept. Time offers no danger to an enterprise carried out to the letter with blind conviction.

The Chinese strike when they are ready, and the "War of the Races" spreads quickly. The patience and efficiency of the Chinese has produced its desired military strength; though American forces win substantial early victories in the Midwest and Middle Atlantic states, they falter from the force of numbers and the lack of resources held in New England, the Deep South, and the Far West. The novel ends with the organized forces of the United States confined to a defensive posture around Washington, D.C., assaulted on all sides, clearly doomed.

After the passage of the first Chinese Exclusion Act in 1882, the number of Chinese immigrants in the United States naturally levelled off. Throughout the 1880s, continuing atrocities against the Chinese by whites drove the Chinese out of many smaller communities and most rural areas. For protection, they gravitated to the larger Chinatowns, such as those of San Francisco and Sacramento. Through normal attrition, the number of Chinese in the United States dwindled in the 1890s and any realistic expectation of Chinese conquest was long dead. Surprisingly, another novel of Chinese invasion was published near the turn of the century, placing the date of invasion further into the future, and no longer relying on existing Chinese immigration as a potential fifth column.

Oto Mundo's *The Recovered Continent: A Tale of the Chinese Invasion* (1898) appeared the year before the Boxer Rebellion, which signaled to the world that a new internal force in China might topple the old Manchu Dynasty. Mundo imagines such an occurrence in 1933, when a Chinese revolution immediately revitalizes China into a major power. The novel itself reads slightly less like a straight history than the three works just considered; unlike the others, it is not really a philippic. Essentially, it is the story of Toto Topheavy, a white man who initially was an idiot. Experimental surgery has converted him to a genius and, spurned in the Western world in the first half of the novel, he disappears for a time. After the Chinese revolution of 1933, China begins wars of expansion into Southeast Asia, against the holdings of England and France, and into Russia. As the wars gradually involve more and more of the world, Toto Topheavy proves to be the leader and moving force of the new China.

Mundo not only does not characterize the Chinese as individuals, but in fact presents no actual Chinese characters. Nor does he bother with the labor issue, where infiltration is a nonmilitary form of invasion. Instead, he moves directly to the issue of military conquest. Toto Topheavy is the only character who appears on the Chinese side, as his armies conquer all of Asia and move westward into Europe. Mundo's characterization of the Chinese as a group is unoriginal, merely repeating the stereotypes of his predecessors. His Chinese are "raging savages" who do the bidding of their leader without thought or question.[15] The critical stage of the war occurs in Eastern Europe and the eastern Mediterranean, which is lost to the Europeans with the news that "'FOUR HUNDRED MILLION CHINESE ARE POURING LIKE A FLOOD OVER EUROPE!'"[16] This region was also the site of the actual victories of the Mongols over allied European forces, though Mundo does not indicate an awareness of this. Eventually, Toto Topheavy and his Chinese hordes conquer the Western world, finishing with the United States.

These four novels agree that the Chinese are at least a threat to the United States, and possibly to the world. They raise questions of moral character and economics and sheer numbers to explain this threat. However, while they share the conclusion that China is a threat, their arguments do not all mesh with one another.

As reflections of popular sentiment, the Whitney and Dooner novels indicate the ambiguity toward Chinese moral traits which might be expected in any racial controversy. The significance does not lie in Whitney's extreme condemnation or in Dooner's ironic respect, but in the fact that they both consider the Chinese to be undesirable in spite of their contradictory biases. Whitney wants Chinese immigration stopped because Chinese immigrants are diseased and depraved; Dooner wants it stopped because they are straightlaced and efficient. One is tempted to look further, in the interests of logic, for a reason that they share.

Economic competition is prominent in *Almond-Eyed: The Great Agitator; A Story of the Day* and fundamental to *Last Days of the Republic.* Neither book suggests that Chinese labor is of poor quality, but simply that it costs less in wages. The numerical facts of Chinese immigration become a concern after enough Chinese laborers are seeking jobs in the United States to bring focus to the issue. On the grounds that the Chinese accept lower wages than whites, white labor unions refuse them membership and the means for them to demand higher ones. Writing before any limit to immigration had ever been placed on anyone wishing to enter the United States, Whitney and Dooner were alarmed at their vision of white labor's future on the Pacific Coast. The significance, once again, lies in the number of Chinese immigrants arriving in this region.

Certain character traits become staples of Yellow Peril characterization at this point, leading to an abundance of water imagery. Dooner provides the crucial element by developing further Whitney's one-dimensional characterization of the Chinese immigrants as a mass of identical people. Dooner takes the implicit suggestion that they have no individuality another step with explicit descriptions of the Chinese acting with rigid, unfaltering obedience. This view of the Chinese as a solid unit eliminates the need for true characterization and yet offers at the same time a threat which is sufficiently dangerous and threatening to satisfy the reader. The water imagery appears in all four of these novels, where the solid entity of Chinese stream out of China, pour into the United States, and wash away all opposition in a cresting flood tide. In its simplicity, this literary device is similar to the tactics of demagoguery that were also rampant in this age.

Woltor develops these staples even further. Dooner states that the Chinese in the United States obey the government of China without knowledge of each other's activities and without any curiosity. Woltor does not even raise the question of the individual Chinese laborer's response to orders, but simply relates their activities as though they are in a sort of mental lockstep without need of communication among themselves. They are nearly perfect soldiers, possessing no mental, and little physical, sensitivity. As they become increasingly zombielike, of course, they also become increasingly subhuman. The more clearly the Chinese appear less than human, the more frightening, and dramatically effective, these novels are.

Mundo writes after Chinese exclusion had become well established, when the labor question is not so immediately pressing. He approaches the subject of invasion without using the Chinese in the United States as infiltrators, instead including the United States among other areas of the world threatened by Chinese military invasion. In terms of character, he distills the fears of Whitney and Dooner and arrives at a single cause for the perceived threat: numbers. The morality issue relies upon numbers for its significance; similarly, the question of jobs does not reach regional or national importance without the involvement of large numbers of people. Mundo concentrates strictly upon the advantages of a modern nation whose only unique attribute is a massive population. The argument that such a nation would be invincible needs no support from discussions of morals or economics.

This is not to suggest that the issues of morality and economics were insignificant or completely fraudulent. In addition, a perceived threat provokes a reaction regardless of its foundation, just as a real one will. However, the contrasting evaluations of those issues by Whitney and Dooner—which nevertheless lead to the same conclusions—suggest that a fear of the number of Chinese people in the world underlay the many specific suspicions, fears, and hostilities of white Americans at this time toward the Chinese which were expressed through more tangible issues.[17]

The enduring element in this type of fiction is the development by Woltor and Dooner of the Chinese as masses of mindless automata. This typing of the Chinese echoes the medieval monks' belief that in the Mongol invasions of Europe, the armies of Genghis Khan vastly outnumbered the European forces they defeated. Typing the Chinese as automata also results from the failure of these writers to seek any understanding of Chinese cultural behavior or interests. Instead of characterizing the individual Chinese, these authors claim simply that the Chinese have no individual character. The race wars they depict climax the inherent conflicts that Social Darwinists believed existed between old and new societies. Part of the reason these naturalist authors treat Chinese characterization lightly is because they believe that the behavior of the Chinese is due to their race and not to free will. In the context of the novels, therefore, the Chinese cannot be dealt with on a rational basis as humans, but can only be confronted and opposed as an irrational force. These nineteenth century fantasies of Chinese invasion faded with the Exclusion Acts, but the naturalist interpretation of issues regarding the Chinese immigrants continues to dominate fiction about them for the next several decades.

These novels have a minor place in American literature and have been deservedly forgotten during the century since their publication. I do not mean to emphasize their importance out of perspective by treating them in such detail. However, they do reflect a sentiment toward the Chinese in the United States that was not at all minor, and we shall see in subsequent chapters that many of the traits first ascribed to the Chinese Americans in these novels recur as fundamental character traits in many works by important American authors who followed.

III
Short Fiction of the *Overland Monthly* and the *Californian*

Two magazines consistently presented short fiction with important Chinese characters in the late nineteenth and early twentieth centuries. They were the *Overland Monthly* (1868–75, 1883–1935) and the *Californian* (1880–82), an interim journal from the same publishers during the hiatus in publishing the *Overland Monthly*. Both were published in San Francisco. Of their eighty-one pieces of short fiction, sixty-nine involve Chinese immigrants to the United States. Taken as a group, these stories represent a fairly narrow category, being short fiction published in San Francisco and subject to the commercial pressures and length restrictions of monthly magazines, as well as to editorial taste. Stories by important authors such as Frank Norris and Ambrose Bierce are present; the first editor of the *Overland* was Bret Harte, though none of his fiction about the Chinese immigrants appeared in these magazines. This cache of short fiction represents many authors and indicates their wide range of attitudes and subject matter regarding Chinese immigrants.

Limin Chu, in *The Images of China and the Chinese in the "Overland Monthly," 1868–1875, 1883–1935*, divides these stories into the following nine categories: Chinese invasion, opium, vengeance, "Dark Ways and Vain Tricks," love stories, miscegenation, domestic servants, comedies, and "Angels, Yellow and White."[1] Since Chu's groupings are logical and obviously reflect the major aspect of each story in regard to the Chinese characters involved, I have chosen to use his categories rather than invent less relevant and less useful ones simply for the sake of a greater claim to originality. "Dark Ways and Vain Tricks" includes miscellaneous crimes and mysterious activities; "Angels, Yellow and White," contains stories of sacrifice and good deeds. Unlike Chu's study, this one will consider only representative stories in some of the categories, though citations for the rest can be found in the notes. Also, this examination will take the stories within each category in chronological order to facilitate a look at developing trends.

Four stories appeared dealing with Chinese invasions of the United States. These are "The Battle of Wabash" (1880) by an author named only Lorelle, "The Sacking of Grubbville" (1892) by Adah F. Batelle, "The Year 1899" (1893) by William W. Crane, and "The Revelation" (1911) by R. P. Pearsall. The years of these stories correspond roughly to the period of novels on the same subject, and the stories themselves bear a strong resemblance to those novels.

"The Battle of Wabash"[2] moves into the future from 1880 to 2078. In antecedent action, Chinese immigration and intermarriage with whites have produced by this time an American population with a ratio of about three Chinese Americans to one white American. In a paroxysm of vengeance, the Chinese Americans beheaded all the descendants of Dennis Kearney because of the anti-Chinese agitation he led; Chinese influence has even gone so far as to place a mandarin on the bench in the City Hall of San Francisco, where the decapitation of a chicken has replaced a hand on the Bible in the administration of an oath. The Chinese have moved from the Pacific Coast into the Deep South, where they have not only taken over but have built up a manufacturing center to rival the Northeast. Concerted efforts have succeeded in securing the rights of naturalized citizenship for the Chinese immigrants. Significantly, Lorelle indicates that citizenship is sought only as a prelude to eventual conquest, and not because Chinese immigrants have any interest in attaining equal legal status or democratic rights.

By 1940, a Chinese American had become governor of California and along the way, increasing the sense of threat to white American readers, he married a white woman. Finally, in 2080, a Chinese American billionaire runs for the presidency. Awakening with great suddenness, the white population prepares for war and attempts to strike quickly and destroy the Chinese Americans.

A Chinese American army is created, however, that uses Fabian tactics at the cost of half a million lives until reinforcements arrive from China. The Chinese Americans are depicted as uncaring about their casualties, expressing the idea that Asians simply do not value human life. The first army rendezvouses with its reinforcements in southern Illinois and they surround the white Americans' forces. The Battle of Wabash ends with five million Chinese casualties, but they have completely destroyed their opposition. Lorelle presents the victors exercising particular cruelty in slaughtering white troops who are willing to surrender.

Robert Woltor's *A Short and Truthful History of the Taking of California and Oregon by the Chinese in the Year A.D. 1899* appeared in 1882, two years after this story. The *Californian* suggested Woltor stole the idea from a story presented in the *Californian*, apparently referring to "The Battle of Wabash."[3] Limin Chu points out that Pierton W. Dooner's *Last Days of the Republic* (1880), which appeared the same year as "The Battle of Wabash," actually has more similarities, such as the naturalization of the Chinese immigrants, their early entrance into the South, and the tactics of military conquest.[4] All three of these works project the reader into the future, and while they clearly tie the social issues regarding Chinese immigration in the 1880s to distant disaster, the threat they describe is perhaps blunted somewhat by its distance in time.

This is not a problem in "The Sacking of Grubbville."[5] Grubbville is a small town a hundred miles from San Francisco. Rumors begin to reach Grubbville of trouble in the larger city's Chinatown, and the residents of Grubbville are frightened because they had voted for the most strident of the anti-Chinese politicians. Even so, the townsfolk continue to patronize their own Chinese laundry and some of them express the thought that Irish whiskey may be a greater evil than the Chinese presence. The climax of the story comes when word is shouted to the watch along the river levees from a passing boat, that the Chinese have risen up against agitation by the Irish in San Francisco.

The people of Grubbville hear that the Chinese have seized San Francisco by force and have imprisoned all the police, the Irish mob leader, and the mayor as well. They prepare to defend themselves for impending attack. At the end of the story, however, these developments all prove to be rumors gone rampant; San Francisco is in fact peaceful with business as usual. Batelle's story illustrates a possible violent takeover by the Chinese in a manner plausible at the time of the story, and in this way may have presented a sharper threat than the fantasies did. The readiness of Grubbville's inhabitants to believe that the Chinese immigrants have risen up against their oppression also indicates an awareness that the treatment of the Chinese was unjust. A latent sense of guilt might therefore be inferred on the part of the white Californians who were taken in by the rumors.

William W. Crane's "The Year 1899"[6] returns to the Yellow Peril on a lavish scale. Not only are all the Asian nations except Japan joined in a confederacy under the Chinese, but the assault on the United States involves alliances with Native and Black Americans as well. In Asia, the name of Genghis Khan is invoked to inspire enthusiasm. The Asian confederacy attacks Europe and the United States simultaneously with the destruction of all Christian countries as their goal. The United States is especially blind to the conspiracy, with the State Department repeatedly ignoring warnings of the coming attack.

Heavy infiltration into the Deep South from the Atlantic and Gulf Coasts precedes the Chinese attack. The Chinese infiltrators settle in empty or swampy lands and proceed to improve them, at the same time befriending and secretly organizing the Black population. The United States government has continued to ignore warnings, most recently of Black invasions from the Caribbean. Washington officials finally realize the danger when the great chief of the Cherokees reports that two Chinese people approached him about a plot against whites, and that most of the inhabitants of American reservations have already joined. News soon arrives that Americans and Europeans in China have been massacred; Black rebels have killed all the whites in Cuba and Puerto Rico; all of continental Europe has fallen to the Asian invasion.

The United States Navy fails to stop the huge invasion fleet coming across the Pacific. Despite heavy losses, this fleet is so massive that it continues to advance in a huge body and lands successfully. The Chinese and Blacks in the South, however, are defeated. They attack out of the swamplands; Crane has the Blacks easily routed while the Chinese, led by hatchet killers from the Chinatowns, fight until they are killed. Finally, the United States is saved by a deus ex machina; the Hindus and Moslems in the Asian army that invaded Europe have begun to fight each other and so China abandons the confederacy and recalls all its troops for defense, including the large force in the United States. The United States, Great Britain, and Japan join in the attack on China proper. All over the world, conquered nations rise up and the danger from China ends.

Crane's work is unusual in that he has gone into a consideration of other American minority groups, Native Americans and Blacks. This seems ironic in view of current concerns over American minority rights. Though Crane obviously thought little of nonwhites, he recognized that they had shared suffering at the hands of whites and might be induced to join a conspiracy. The worldwide scope of the story removes its sense of immediacy to the reader, but the conclusion still conveys a message to the reader of the story's time: the United States is intact but still vulnerable to Asian invasion. Since it was not saved by its defensive efforts, but by the collapse of the Asian confederacy, Crane has repeated the actual events of the Mongol invasions of Europe, which were halted by concerns of the Mongols in Asia and not by any European maneuvers or victories in the field.

"The Revelation," by R. J. Pearsall,[7] uses a science-fiction device.

The story begins with three white characters with differing opinions of the Chinese. Cruikshank says the Chinese are simply beneath consideration. Morgan feels that whites are no better, though an apparent lack of patriotism on the part of the Chinese causes him to doubt they will mount a threat to the West. Brent, who had been a naval surgeon in Peking, tells an anecdote to contradict their attitudes. His information constitutes the revelation referred to in the title.

The science-fiction part of the story is the use of hypnosis by a German scientist named Von Haltung who was also in Peking. He was experimenting with a means to have thoughts in the mind of one person occur also in the mind of another. Brent volunteered to be the second subject and Von Haltung's Chinese servant, Wang, was paid to be the first.

At the end of only a few minutes of the experiment, Brent feels great revulsion every time he looks at Wang. The reason is that Wang's mind is filled completely with cruelty, lust, and all the baser impulses. However, Brent and Von Haltung next visit Tsai Ching, an able official in the Chinese government. He is persuaded to participate in their endeavors immediately and Brent goes into a simultaneous trance. The result is a series of startling visions which owe a great deal to the Boxer Rebellion, that had occurred twelve years before this story appeared.

The first vision is that of an argument between Tsai Ching and another Chinese official. This is followed by a vision indicating Tsai Ching's high position in the secret Society of Myriad Swords, which represents the Boxers. In the third vision, Brent sees a Chinese servant murder Von Haltung in his bedroom and take a tray from his safe to Tsai Ching. This is followed by a sweep of shorter visions, including the execution of a criminal, the sacking of a foreign settlement in China, and many unrecognizable faces.

The next clear scene shows a conference of Chinese leaders with Tsai Ching presiding. The Chinese official exhorts his colleagues against the foreigners in China, again following the main thrust of the Boxer Rebellion. Brent watches an uprising occur overnight, as Tsai Ching suddenly replaces the Manchu Emperor and orders the extermination of all foreigners in China. This is accomplished in six hours. Then a large, modern, well-equipped army proceeds to take over all of Asia.

Brent's final vision is broad, showing him the victorious procession of the Chinese army, three million strong, into Europe. East Europeans flock to its banners and, as it moves toward the Atlantic, more Chinese follow out of Asia and settle in the conquered territory of

Europe. In the fall of 1928, a European and Asian armada invades the United States with an army of four million. The American military fights valiantly but falls under the weight of numbers, leaving all the earth to the Chinese.

These visions take only five minutes, and Tsai Ching does not realize after the trances are over that his future plans have been revealed. As soon as possible, Brent gets Von Halsung away and gives him the details. They foil Tsai Ching's plan by allowing Von Halsung's servant, Wang, to steal a tray of jewels from his master's safe and take them to Tsai Ching. There they have the Chinese police arrest Tsai Ching for arranging the theft, and by executing him a few weeks later they end the conspiracy.

Limin Chu points out that in addition to the Society of Myriad Swords and their antiforeign stance, several other details indicate that Pearsall was deliberately writing an analogue of the Boxer Rebellion. Chu cites references in the story to the murder of foreign missionaries and their Chinese converts, the looting of a foreign settlement, the planned assassination of Von Halsung, and the character of Tsai Ching. Historically, the Boxers did kill foreign missionaries and Chinese Christians, destroyed churches and besieged the Legation Quarter in Peking, and murdered the German minister to China. Chu suggests that Tsai Ching represents Prince Tuan, who was in supreme command of the Boxers.[8] Apparently Pearsall wished to illustrate two ideas: first, that the Boxer Rebellion, if it had succeeded, might have unified China and gone on to conquer the world; second, that eliminating the leader of the group early would have ended the movement. Neither suggestion seems likely, but the first results from taking the Boxers' antiforeign stand to the extreme, and the second seems to come from the old idea that the Chinese people are a mindless mass, easily molded by an occasional leader and without initiative of their own. Like the novelists of Chinese invasion, these authors are naturalists writing about fundamentally inimical forces.

The tales of opium offer little that is new in their characterization of the Chinese as a threat to white Americans. As a group, their significance lies in their presentation of the Chinese as dealers and users of the drug; that the Chinese do this is more an underlying assumption than any kind of accusation. A brief summary of these stories, therefore, seems sufficient here.

"The Dramatic in My Destiny" (1880), by Emma F. Dawson, contrasts a decent boardinghouse where the white protagonist, York Rhys, lives and a very sordid vision of San Francisco's Chinatown.[9] Hoping to do business in China, Rhys is studying Chinese with a sophisticated

Chinese immigrant, Tong-ko-lin-sing, whose name appears to be Manchurian.[10] Tong is urbane and cultured, fluent in four languages, but also greedy and arrogant. His tutoring of Rhys results in the latter's addiction to opium, which is the point of the story. A sidelight on the author's attitude toward the Chinese appears at Rhys's boardinghouse, where a Chinese cook named Si-ki works. He is depicted as a sickly, sneaky creature who at one point caresses the hand of a white woman. For this he is beaten with a cane until it breaks. By the end of the story, he has contracted leprosy. One assumes that Dawson does not mean to imply that he caught it from the woman's hand. Chu suggests that Dawson's turning Si-ki into a leper may reveal "a pathological hatred of miscegenation."[11]

"Chung's Baby" (1898), by Phil More, is set in a run-down mining town in the Sierras called Washout, where a man named Chung lives in a cabin with his baby.[12] The protagonist of the story is a broken-down white man named Opium Billy who survives on odd jobs, chores, and baby-sitting for Chung. The last is especially important, because Chung smokes opium and when he is out Opium Billy helps himself to Chung's supply. One day Opium Billy awakes from his opium sleep to find the cabin on fire and filled with smoke. He first staggers to the door, then returns to save the baby, who was overcome while playing dominoes. He carries the child outside, but too late; they both die from smoke inhalation. Nevertheless, the addict is recognized for a heroic death. Chung's only contribution to the story is to provide the opium and the baby.

The sense of threat in the opium tales grows out of the assumption that the Chinese customarily smuggle and supply the drug as well as smoke it. These stories claim that white Americans who befriend the Chinese will have their bodies and lives contaminated by opium as a result. Overall, however, these stories maintain this stereotyped assumption without developing it or weakening it.

Revenge is a common theme in fiction and ordinarily would not have special significance. However, in the five stories in this category, the lust for vengeance is deliberately tied to assumed values in traditional Chinese culture, suggesting that revenge is more important to the Chinese than to others. These stories are set in the United States and the insistence of the Chinese immigrants upon violent revenge is the threat they represent. Again, two particular stories will characterize the group.

"The Revenge of a Heathen" (1890), by Charles R. Harker, actually shows a change of heart on the part of the main character.[13] Ah Lee is a cook on a ranch where he is hated by all the white cowboys as well as by the foreman, Murphy. Only Murphy's small son Tommie will be his friend, but when Murphy discovers this he strikes Ah Lee's face with a whip. Ah Lee spends a sleepless night in pain and anger during which he plans to repay Murphy by hurting Tommie. Shortly after, however, Tommie falls into a pond and nearly drowns; Ah Lee immediately jumps in and saves him. All thoughts of revenge are forgotten. Oddly, this first tale of planned revenge in 1890, published at a time when the social atmosphere on the West Cost is still thought to be quite strongly against the Chinese, is the only one in which the Chinese seeker of vengeance is presented as a good enough individual to change his mind.

A more typical story in this category is "The Revenge of Ching Chow" (1924), by L. Warren Wigmore, where vengeance becomes an obsession.[14] Ching Chow has plans to kidnap a slave girl named Purple Dawn, who is owned by a Chinatown merchant, and Ching Chow has put many months of effort into this plot. However, a white missionary named Miss Patterson unknowingly foils the plot by having the police free Purple Dawn from the merchant. Ignoring the police, Ching Chow blames Miss Patterson, who never does realize what happened. Ching Chow devises another long-range plot to kill her for her interference.

The plot involves the construction of a brick reservoir. During the months it is being built, Ching Chow attends Miss Patterson's Bible class in order to gain her confidence. Throughout this period, he gradually forgets about Purple Dawn and concentrates solely on the murder of Miss Patterson. When the reservoir is almost finished, he drugs her and carries her to it; however, in removing the heavy manhole cover, he lets it strike his leg. He stumbles over her body into the hole and dies, leaving her to recover safely. In this story, Ching Chow presents a particularly dangerous threat because his choice of Miss Patterson as a target for revenge is irrational.

Changes do occur over time in the stories of vengeance. In 1890, Ah Lee has a change of heart and saves his intended victim; in the next several stories, individual Chinese figures, including a jade god, seek their revenge by killing or trying to kill white victims. Few have any more justification than Ching Chow. Finally, in 1926, the reader is presented with an entire Chinatown full of violent crime with no end in sight.

The category titled "Dark Ways and Vain Tricks" holds fourteen stories about the mysterious activities of the Chinese in California. Most are about crimes. The particular crimes in these stories vary, but all contribute to the image of the Chinese not only as criminals, but as especially devious and secretive ones. Three of them deal with how the

Chinese immigrants are victimized by this image. Chu's selection of the title, derived from Harte's poem "Plain Language from Truthful James," is singularly appropriate. Four of these stories deserve discussion.

Frank Norris, in "Thoroughbred" (1895), begins to develop characters and conflicts that appear prominently in his later *Moran of the Lady Letty: A Story of Adventures off the California Coast* (1898).[15] One of the main characters is Jack Brunt, who has left his working-class roots behind and made a fortune in real estate. He is interested in marrying Barry Vance, whose wealthy father approves of Brunt more than she does. Barry is undecided because she is also receiving attention from Wesley Shotover, the wealthy but indolent descendant of privateers and naval officers. Shotover has a special liking for Barry's Great Dane, but Brunt says that good dogs can be purchased for much less than what she spent for him. Barry replies that her dog is a thoroughbred, though Brunt obviously cannot appreciate this distinction.

Norris uses the Chinese immigrants to separate Brunt, the driving, self-made man, from Shotover, the lackadaisical blueblood. The Vance estate borders Chinatown, and one afternoon the three young people are on a tennis court near the street. Earlier, Barry thinks to herself, "After all, no one is ever afraid of a Chinaman."[16] This incident proves her wrong.

An injured, frantic Chinese immigrant suddenly leaps the hedge bordering the Vance estate, bleeding and talking excitedly. Brunt becomes agitated; Barry is interested. Shotover establishes that the fugitive is being pursued by the members of a rival tong. As his many pursuers charge the fence yelling, Brunt escapes to the safety of the house. Barry remains where she is, watching Shotover face the crowd with a dog whip in his hand.

> Shotover faced them, calm and watchful, drawing the lash of the whip slowly through his fingers, and the Hop Sing Tong, recognizing with a coward's intuition, a born leader and master of men, felt themselves slipping back into the cowed washmen and opium-drugged half-castes of the previous week, and backed off out of reach . . . the great Dane came up to his side. There they stood and kept the crowd in check, thoroughbreds both.[17]

Twenty police officers quickly arrive and forcibly disperse the crowd. After this incident Brunt, having revealed himself as an inferior to Shotover, no longer competes for Barry's affection.

Norris's purpose is to show that the lazy Shotover's aristocratic breeding will manifest its value in a crisis while Brunt's everyday aggressive ambition folds in the face of true danger. Ross Wilbur, protagonist of Norris's novel *Moran of the Lady Letty*, is a more fully realized character of the same type, a pampered club man whose being shanghaied stimulates the release of untapped courage and physical ability.[18]

Norris's emphasis on ancestry over environment results from his naturalist beliefs. Though he clearly considers Brunt a lower form of human than Shotover, he does imply that Brunt should be able to stand off a mob of Chinese tong members alone. This expectation is based on the assumption that the Chinese mob is even lower on the scale of human worth than Brunt. Barry's earlier comment that no one, meaning no white person, fears a "Chinaman" undercuts Brunt even further but also diminishes Shotover's accomplishment. That Norris considers the Chinese a lower form of human than whites, however, remains clear. This is reinforced by the details used to describe them; they are all cowardly bullies, opium smokers, and hatchet killers. Their cowardice is a contribution of Norris's to their image; previously, and to some extent later, tong members are depicted as truly dangerous and capable killers. Norris's ignorance and imagination play a part in their depiction as he not only assumes the above to be common, but also suggests that killers have come from Peking as well as South China and that poison darts are a customary part of their arsenal.

"Baxter's Beat" (1910), by G. Emmerson Sears, is about an unscrupulous reporter in the Chinatown of San Francisco.[19] Baxter wants to scoop his competition on coverage of the Boxer Rebellion, and so approaches Wing Ho Chang, an elderly artist with a small shop. He pays Chang to illustrate Peking, Christian missions in China, and a scene depicting Chinese torture. For the last, when Chang hesitates for lack of information, Baxter gives him something he remembers from a book about Persia. He also has Chang paint the image of a Manchu prince ordering that all white foreigners in China be killed. Then, unknown to Chang, Baxter writes a phony interview in which Chang appears as the speaker for Chinatown's attitudes concerning the Boxers. When the story appears, Baxter's newspaper sells wildly, but Chinatown is furious at Chang for his contribution, believing that this article will bring angry whites down on them. As a mob of Chinatown folk gather near his shop, a white gang does come by also, yelling threats at the whole of Chinatown for the antiwhite stand of the Boxers. Chang and his wife flee for their lives to Baxter's office but are rebuffed by an underling. They leave town, while the reporter continues to exploit the turmoil in Chinatown for another sensational story. Sears suggests here that the image of the Chinese immigrants as a threat is, in some cases at least, explicitly created by whites for reasons not directly related to Chinatown or China.

"Ah Foo, the Fortune Teller" (1915), by Marian Allen, is actually about a domestic servant named Lee Sing.[20] In the opening scene, the reader sees Ah Foo press Lee Sing over a matter not explained; at this point, Ah Foo is little more than a name. The story then turns to Lee Sing's employers, the Osbornes. Elsie Osborne is a spoiled white woman who loves giving parties. Her husband Jerry relies on Lee Sing to keep the books balanced. During one of Jerry's trips out of town as a customs official, however, Elsie gives so many parties that she runs up bills totaling five hundred dollars, above what even Lee Sing can salvage from her husband's salary. Since Elsie does not want Jerry to know about these debts, she accepts Lee Sing's idea of borrowing the money from a Chinatown fortune-teller.

Ah Foo's reputation as a fortune-teller is greatest among the criminal element, and rests largely on what he learns from a police informer who also passes on police information to Ah Foo. The opening scene implies but does not say clearly that Lee Sing may have had ulterior motives for suggesting that his mistress borrow money from the fortune-teller. Also, he could have warned her that money was low before the situation became serious, but instead he simply let her go further into debt. In any case, Elsie Osborn signs over an IOU for five hundred dollars to Ah Foo.

During the trip, Jerry turns up Ah Foo's name on someone else's passport and upon returning calls Ah Foo into his office on suspicion of illegal entry into the country. When Ah Foo arrives, Jerry finds that the doctored passport has disappeared from his safe. He threatens to proceed with Ah Foo's deportation anyway, whereupon Ah Foo produces a photocopy of his IOU from Elsie. Enraged, Jerry lunges at him, but Ah Foo summons Jerry's clerk. Jerry, realizing that Elsie has been upset since his return, calls her on the phone to reassure her and Ah Foo goes free.

Ah Foo, of course, is a shady character with his hand in many suspicious dealings. Lee Sing has been an honest and loyal servant with little power, who may have come under Ah Foo's control in some way not specified in the story. In Allen's depiction of an Asian threat, the honest but subverted servant works in isolation from his people, loyal to his white employers, while the triumphant villain is a part of Chinatown and so symbolically represents his people even to the point of controlling those who appear, and desire to be, decent citizens.

"The provocation of Ah Sing" (1922), by Gordon Grant, is based on several misconceptions.[21] It apparently owes its plot to *The Moonstone*, by Wilkie Collins, as the story is about the theft of a pearl from the forehead of a Buddha in Peking. The first misconception is that such a Buddha might exist in China; jewelled Buddhas originated with Indian tradition and pearls have never been set in the foreheads of Buddhas in China. The second misconception is that tongs in the United States had close ties to the underworld in China. When the pearl disappears, the underworld figures of Peking sling accusations at each other over this sacrilege, and tongs in San Francisco take up the feuds as well. Open warfare is averted by the San Francisco police and the Department of Justice, but all of this activity merely provides the background for the real story.

Ah Sing is a renowned smuggler of opium, guns, and anything else worth smuggling. He works primarily on his ship, the *Nina Maria*, and has never been caught in an illegal act. However, as he sails from Asia toward San Francisco, the legal authorities are certain that he has the pearl and Washington stresses the importance of his capture. In San Francisco, a meticulous search party fails to locate any contraband on Ah Sing's ship. As they give up and prepare to leave, the officer in charge stops to examine an oddly shaped vinegar bottle. A shapeless lump at the bottom proves to be the pearl, destroyed by the vinegar.

The narration does not give Ah Sing's reason for hiding the pearl in the vinegar, though he clearly is unaware of its chemical effect on pearls. However, the officer gives a reason for his placing it there which constitutes the final misconception in the story. He says he took a second look at the vinegar bottle because "the Chinks didn't like vinegar." Supposedly Ah Sing figured no one would look carefully at the bottle.[22] In actuality, vinegar is an integral part of Chinese cooking.

The depiction of the Chinese immigrants in these stories of "Dark Ways" does not appreciably change over time. The three stories sympathetic to them are distributed widely, having appeared in 1894, 1910, and 1921. The stories that dealt with them negatively vary in subject matter, but the degree and kind of hostility they express is fairly constant.

The first of the love stories is also concerned with Chinatown criminals. "A Partly Celestial Tale" (1895), by E. Lincoln Kellogg, is set in a small rural town.[23] Widow Goram runs a boardinghouse full of white miners and cowboys. Tom Quong has been the local launderer for twenty years, but when he imports a Chinese wife without going through the Six Companies in San Francisco, she is kidnapped by Chinatown hatchet killers and taken to a Chinese community nearby.

Widow Goram observes that all the Chinese immigrants are slaves of the Six Companies and that their punishment is usually death. For Tom's sake, she organizes a posse of white men, many of whom are initially reluctant to rouse themselves in his behalf. A gambler says, "We all knows that this here fellow is white—for a Chinaman. . . . But I don't know as I would turn out this time of night just for a Chinaman no matter how white he was. . . ."[24] Eventually, the armed white posse rescues Tom's wife without a confrontation. When Tom hugs her afterward, one of the cowboys who had come hesitantly says, "To see the way they take on each other, a feller might almost think they was humans."[25] This story has more separate elements of the Yellow Peril than most stories in these magazines. The Six Companies and their thugs are clearly threatening, and the white cowboys and miners react to them and to Tom therefore with a mixture of hostility and contempt. However, Kellogg also gives the reader Tom, a sympathetically portrayed Chinese immigrant, and Tom's defender in Widow Goram. Tom is unfortunately not presented here as the rule among Chinese immigrants but as an anomaly.

"The Conversion of Ah Lew Sing" (1897), by M. Austin, is also a love story which takes place in a criminal milieu in Summerfield.[26] The conversion mentioned in the title is actually phony; Lew Sing, who grows vegetables, has been ordered by a tong killer named Foo Chou to take Bible lessons as part of a plot to kidnap Li Choi, a slave girl. She was once owned by the tong member, and has been taking Bible lessons ever since the Mission got hold of her. The tong killer wants her back, but Lew Sing falls in love with her himself. He spirits her away as planned, but instead of heading for the tong killer's hiding place, they go to City Hall for a marriage license. The ending seems unrealistically convenient, however; the tong man, instead of exacting revenge, decides that in his humiliation he will simply leave town.

"A Chinese Ishmael" (1899), by Sui Sin Far, is about a romantic triangle.[27] Leih Tseih is descended from the family of a mandarin but is now poor and has immigrated to the United States on his own. Ku Yum is a slave who wishes to marry Leih Tseih; Lum Choy is a crooked gambler to whom she has been promised by her owners, the Lee Chus. Leih Tseih once slashed him with a knife when he caught the gambler cheating in a game, so they are already enemies. Leih Tseih hides Ku Yum, so Lum Choy seeks redress for her loss and for his knife injury from the Six Companies. He is rebuffed with the explanation that they have no hold over Leih Tseih within Chinatown because he has paid off his debts, and that for the knife attack, Lum Choy should approach the white San Francisco police. He is also reminded that slavery is illegal. Lum Choy leaves angrily and sets his own trap. One night he contacts Leih Tseih about arranging a compromise, but just before this meeting, the gambler fatally wounds himself. When Leih Tseih arrives, the gambler splashes blood on him before dying, leaving Leih Tseih well framed as a murder suspect. Leih Tseih tries to tell Ku Yum to leave him, but she refuses. Since Lum Choy had hoped to separate them by the manner of his death, they decide to foil him by jumping off a cliff together, to be bound together for all time. Their bodies are never found; in Chinatown a legend grows saying that their spirits passed into two sea lions who sometimes wander on the rocky shore together in the moonlight.

Sui Sin Far, whose real name was Edith Eaton, was descended from an English father and a Chinese mother who immigrated from England to the United States when she was young. She may be the earliest writer of American fiction to have Chinese ancestry. This particular story is one of her lesser efforts, but even here her understanding of the Chinese immigrants is clearly that of an insider. This is especially manifested in the dialogue and in the scene with the Six Companies board. In addition, several items in the story are conventions from classical Chinese fiction. One of them is the educated descendant of a mandarin choosing a woman of lower social rank; another is Ku Yum's defiance in favor of love at the end of the story. Finally, their joint suicide is also a common ending to Chinese love stories. The evocative romantic lyricism of the legend about them seems to foreshadow the author's later work, which is much less melodramatic.

The most unpleasant love story is "The Sale of Sooy Yet" (1900), by Marguerite Stabler, where cruelty and selfishness create a marriage.[28] Sooy Yet's father is approached by Man Toy, a tong leader of immense power and wealth who wants a young wife now that he is approaching old age. Sooy Yet has on other occasions been rejected for being ill-tempered and plain, so this time she takes control of matters early. First she arranges to have Man Toy hear her good singing voice without seeing her. She later massages his forehead, which pleases him, at the same time rubbing a poison into his eyes. After Man Toy leaves, his eyes continue to hurt and his head to ache; he thinks constantly of Sooy Yet's voice and hands. He gradually goes blind and is forced to leave his position of power in his tong, after which he wishes even more for Sooy Yet's company. Her father, a poor restaurant owner, requires ten times her original bridal price and receives it; Sooy Yet marries Man Toy, keeps him content with songs and massages, and continues to rub the lotion into his eyes to keep him blind. This is a rare example of cruelty on the part of a Chinese immigrant woman and constitutes the threat in the story, surprisingly making a fairly sympathetic victim of the tong leader.

"Devils, White and Yellow: A Story of San Francisco's Chinatown" (1904), by Andriana Spadoni, is particularly interesting in comparison with the above story.[29] Spadoni is writing from a missionary's point of view about a Chinese slave girl named Ah Quai who is rescued when Ah Fong, who desires to marry her, saves her while allied with missionaries. However, when he asks to marry her, she declines in favor of remaining with the mission. Where Stabler presents Sooy Yet as being so anxious to marry that she blinds and deceives her prospective husband, Spadoni suggests that a Chinese woman under the uplifting influence of missionaries will even turn away a desirable husband.

"The Winning of Josephine Chang" (1920), by James Hanson, is a rarity on two counts.[30] First, it is another of the few stories about Chinese immigrants in these magazines that show no influence or concern with the Yellow Peril. Second, both lovers are Chinese Americans educated and socialized by American society. Josephine's father, Tin Woo Chang, is a rich merchant and important power in the Six Companies whose daughter Josephine is both beautiful and educated in an American university. Her father has her wear an ancestral amulet with some Chinese written characters hidden in it and has proclaimed that no one may marry Josephine unless he can find the hidden words. Many suitors fail with the amulet, but the elder Chang becomes involved when Yee Kwong begins to see his daughter. Yee Kwong is a handsome young diplomat, also educated in the United States. For the first time, Josephine and her father agree on the same suitor. He gives Yee Kwong a crucial clue to help him discover the secret of the amulet without knowing he received help, and the way is free for them to marry. Both Josephine and Yee Kwong take the concern over the amulet lightly as a result of their contemporary American values; her father, as well, is acting more for the sake of the form of a tradition than for its meaning, as is clear when he rigs the contest in Yee Kwong's favor. The result is a story about Chinatown which is culturally accurate and tries to press no particular social or political argument. By contrast, Hanson's next story is a disappointment.

"Behind the Devil Screen" (1921) is an action-packed melodrama with many cultural inaccuracies.[31] The initial paragraph alone holds enough antecedent action for a novel: a beautiful woman is kidnapped from Northern China by a bandit named Fook Chang and taken into the Gobi Desert of Mongolia where she is named Desert Lily. There she is sold to a Tartar priest who then sells her to a travelling Manchu. The first error Hanson makes is in naming this Manchu Ah Fang, which is clearly a name in Cantonese. Ah Fang takes Desert Lily to Mexico and from there into the United States. The actual story begins here.

Wing Fo is the Chinese man to whom Desert Lily was promised and he arrives in San Francisco looking for her. When he locates Ah Fang, the latter demands a huge ransom. Wing Fo first works for low wages on a farm but then wins a lottery; however, the ransom goes up. He happens across Desert Lily's home, however, and the two of them begin to meet in secret. Wing Fo decides to kill the Manchu, but Desert Lily actually does it, by dropping a flowerpot on his head. She thereby inherits his substantial fortune in addition to marrying Wing Fo.

The two protagonists are decent, spirited people and adequately balance the villain of the piece as far as the image of Chinese immigrants is concerned. The wild and melodramatic nature of the story makes it less interesting than Hanson's earlier story, but the real problem is the number of errors Hanson makes. In addition to giving a Manchu a Cantonese name, he ascribes to the Chinese a manner of greeting which is actually Japanese, of inhaling air audibly through tight lips, and he confuses the tongs with the Six Companies. One of his original ideas about Chinatown is his description of tong killers who dress in English tweeds, American silk shirts, Fedoras, striped socks, and oxfords. Such attire is possible but sounds as though the image of Sicilian gangsters has been transplanted to Chinatown from Little Italy.

Some earlier tales of love, like the stories of revenge, depict the Chinese immigrants more favorably than later stories in the same category. In 1895, launderer Tom Quong and his wife are lovers sufficiently liked by whites to receive their grudging aid; later, Ah Lew Sing and Leih Sing take improper steps, such as feigning conversion and plotting murder, but they are sympathetic characters acting out of love. The worst story is from 1900, when Sooy Yet keeps her husband blind deliberately. Two stories are especially interesting, "The Winning of Josephine Chang" and "Devils: White and Yellow: A Story of San Francisco's Chinatown." The first stands alone as the only love story here that is not based on crime and violence, replacing these with a perceptive treatment of young Chinese Americans. The second is an unusual condemnation of Chinatown, expressed through the heroine's decision to remain with white missionaries rather than return to the community. The final story of the seven is no improvement over the earlier ones, as the Chinese husband poisons his unfaithful wife. Variation exists in these depictions, but no clear progress over the span of time involved.

The stories of miscegenation will be considered next as they are also love stories. Nearly as many love stories—six—at least suggesting miscegenation between Chinese immigrants and white Americans appeared in the *Overland Monthly* as love stories about Chinese immigrants alone. The issue was clearly a concern on the West Coast during these years, and generally condemned.

The first story of miscegenation is "The Haunted Valley" (1871), by Ambrose Bierce.[32] It is a complicated story involving one murder committed years before the story opens, another more recent murder, a mysterious message on a tombstone, and a traveler from the East Coast who observes all of this as an outsider. Most of this is irrelevant to the miscegenation, however. The heart of the issue involves Ah Wee, the Chinese cook hired by a man named Jo Dunfer and ostensibly killed for not cutting down trees the way Dunfer wants. This explanation, which is accepted as reasonable by Dunfer's neighbors, is clearly a comment on the depth of anti-Chinese prejudice on the California frontier. Eventually the reader realizes that Ah Wee was a Chinese woman masquerading as a male servant of Dunfer's. He had won her in a poker game and become fond of her; she was killed accidentally in a brawl between Dunfer and one of her earlier admirers. In regard to the interracial couple, Bierce's point seems only to be that a Chinese woman was not likely to be in a position very different from a white woman, except that anti-Chinese hostility required that she masquerade as Dunfer's laborer instead of revealing herself as a woman.

"After Strange Gods" (1894), by Frank Norris, makes an interesting comparison with "The Sale of Sooy Yet," by Marguerite Stabler.[3] Jean Rouveroy is a French sailor working as a guard at the World's Fair in Chicago when he meets Lalo Da, a young woman working at the Chinese Pavilion. This is the name by which Rouveroy calls her; he cannot pronounce her Chinese name, which is not given. She sells chrysanthemums and Jean develops their acquaintance by buying a flower every day. She returns his interest, speaking in broken French learned from her father, who works in Indochina. Five weeks after they have fallen in love, however, Jean is recalled to his ship. Lalo is distraught and leaves for home, pausing in San Francisco to await passage and enjoy the Chinatown. There she runs into Jean, whose ship had been bound for San Francisco, and they spend some time together happily. This period ends when Lalo contracts smallpox. Knowing that she will be disfigured, and afraid of losing Jean again, she tells him to leave her to recover for several months and then kisses his mouth and eyes. As a result, his eyes are infected and in a number of weeks Jean is totally blind and unable to see her scarred face. Together they go live with her father in Tonkin where they weave nets and hammocks for their occupation.

Norris does not dwell on racial differences in this story. Though he says that Lalo is only half-civilized, her behavior is ascribed to her being female. Jean and Lalo do not appear to have cultural conflicts other than the pressures of their geographic origins; neither is actually an immigrant to the United States, so when their work at the fair is finished, they are pulled apart toward their home countries. Lalo's deliberate blinding of Jean is obviously a threat and perhaps a disgusting one, but she is a much more sympathetic character than Stabler's Sooy Yet. Lalo is truly in love and has suffered from parting with Jean once already, while Sooy Yet is a calculating and vicious individual interested only in a wealthy marriage, not in her husband himself.

"The Canton Shawl" (1914), by Hazel H. Havermale, is about a white American named John Sargent who was once captivated emotionally by China when in Canton.[34] Now, after ten years, he has returned as a ship captain. Sargent thoroughly enjoys ambling through Canton and is especially drawn to a certain silk shop where he glimpses an attractive concubine of the owner. He receives, after a while, a secret request to meet her in a deserted garden, where they talk and sing romantically. Finally she bids him farewell, leaving behind her shawl. The next morning the presence of smallpox is confirmed in Canton, requiring that Sargent set sail. He takes the shawl with him, unaware that some of the owner's rouge has been smeared on it. In San Francisco, Sargent falls in love with a Spanish woman named Dolores de Valle, to whom he gives the shawl as a gift from China. When he next returns from a short trip, however, he sees the yellow flag of smallpox flying from Dolores's home. Sargent's miscegenation itself is a small issue in the story until it causes the appearance of smallpox in the United States. At this point the association of disease with interracial mixing symbolizes the racial "contamination" which might result, as well as suggesting the uncleanliness of the Chinese in general.

In most of the stories of miscegenation, the man is white and the woman is of whole or half Chinese descent. One exception is "Ah Choo," (1920), by Esther B. Bock.[35] Ah Choo and a white man work in a packing plant loading heavy cases. The other workers are female immigrants from Italy and Portugal, and Ah Choo with his broken English is often the subject of jokes and ridicule on the job from them and Frank. When Frank negligently hurts Ah Choo's finger, the forewoman, Mabel Martin, binds it with a strip torn from her handkerchief. This and suggestions from her which help him on the job win his devotion so that he spiritually works for her and not only for wages. Meanwhile Frank has been trying to force his attentions on Mabel, who does not want them. Ah Choo murders him undetected, with both personal insults to himself and Frank's behavior toward Mabel in mind. Finally, when he happens to be alone in a remote part of the plant with Mabel one day he throws himself at her feet and proposes. She declines, as sensitively as possible, explaining that she is engaged to the plant foreman. Ah Choo feels humiliated by her and returns to his shack. There he worships his gods, puts on his full Chinese dress, and goes to Mabel's house, cursing her constantly. Swearing to haunt her, her husband, and any children they ever have, he stabs himself to death on her doorstep. In this story Ah Choo is a sympathetic character to some extent, but his hatred at the end makes him also threatening and less likeable. He seems foolish, first for falling for Mabel so easily and completely and then for taking his rejection so badly. His name, suggesting a sneeze, also makes him seem unworthy of respect. He is not an admirable figure but a pitiable one, and the story seems to illustrate that his interest in a white woman is unquestionably improper.

The last two stories of miscegenation show a different kind of dilemma. In "Sweet Burning Incense" (1921), by Jeanette Dailey, Lilian Moore is a young bride whose first visit to Chinatown surprises her when the furniture, screens, paintings, music, and especially the incense seem familiar and pleasant to her.[36] When she eventually has a child, however, she is aghast at her baby's Chinese features. Her husband Maurice is surprised but accepts the child. An aunt finally reveals that Lilian's mother, who died when Lilian was born, was a Chinese immigrant. Lilian has been raised in a society with a distinct prejudice against the Chinese, and she responds by killing herself and her child, both of them suffocating in a room full of smoke from Chinese incense. Dailey strengthens the presence of anti-Chinese feeling by the aunt's concealment of Lilian's racial heritage but does not make a clear statement about miscegenation itself. By writing sympathetically of Lilian, however, who is a product of it, she seems to accept the idea.

In "Shanghai Butterfly: A Short, Short Story" (1933), by Steve Fisher, the protagonist is a young woman named Lexo who has been raised as an orphan in a mission.[37] All she has heard about her parents is that her father is Gordon McDougal and that he deserted her mother, an entertainer known as the Shanghai Butterfly. Lexo has spent all of her young life wanting only to avenge her mother's desertion by killing her father. When she is grown, she sets out on a long search. She finds him finally in the rear of a dusky cabaret in Shanghai, a petty officer standing next to an aging half-white, half-Chinese woman. Lexo identifies herself as his daughter as she pulls out her gun, but as she fires the older woman rushes toward her and is killed. McDougal informs Lexo that she has just killed her mother and he tells the police he shot his wife, explaining to Lexo that he has nothing to live for now. The suggestion is that the missionaries who raised Lexo were ashamed of her having a half-Chinese mother and so lied about McDougal's deserting her. Like Dailey, Fisher seems to accept the miscegenation by virtue of using its offspring as a sympathetic and tragic figure.

None of these stories about miscegenation takes a positive tone. Though Norris's tale seems to have a happy ending, it is reached through an unpleasant and calculated blinding of the husband involved; "The Canton Shawl" and the story of Ah Choo also see disease and death as the result of attempted or actual miscegenation. The last two examine the depth of hostility against the Chinese, again ending in death. Oddly, the one story in which the interracial couple seems to have functioned together the most smoothly and happily is that of Ambrose Bierce, surely an author never accused of overblown sentimentality. This is also the earliest of these stories, but all of Bierce's work is so unusual that one would probably err to conclude much from the fact.

The stories in which Chinese immigrants appear prominently as domestic servants to white employers in the United States have been grouped together because this social role is the most important single image of the Chinese immigrants, including both laundry and cooking duties among the others. Perhaps because the authors may have had actual experiences with Chinese servants, these stories often have a verisimilitude about them that does not exist in most of the stories labeled "Dark Ways and Vain Tricks." The longevity of this image is surprising, having reached into the 1950s and the 1960s on television with the roles of Peter on *Bachelor Father* and of Hop Sing, the cook on *Bonanza*. The earliest presentation of such a role in the *Overland Monthly* appeared almost a century before.

Several of the earliest stories are shallow in their treatment of these characters and warrant only brief explanations. The first story was an attempt to combat the idea that Chinese immigrants made good servants. In "Spilled Milk" (1870), by Mrs. James Neall, Wo Sin constantly makes idiotic and clumsy mistakes.[38] Not all of his failures are due to lack of intelligence, however; he is considered cowardly for refusing to milk a cow that kicks. In "Pete" (1871), by Prentice Mulford, a subplot involving the Chinese servant Ah Sam is attached to the main plot with no real connection.[39] He is simply made to look silly, being found heavily drugged with opium on his wedding night after his bride has been kidnapped. She is found in a hen house by whites he hired to look for her. "Ti Lung" (1884), by Flora De Wolfe, has the same point to make as "Spilled Milk."[40] Ti Lung also makes stupid mistakes and is disrespectful. Finally, when asked to pick currants, he returns with full branches, leaves and all. The last of these stories is "An Episode of the Turnpike" (1884), by C. E. B.[41] In this one, launderer Ah Toy is beaten and run out of the boardinghouse where he works for spitting water on clothes to make steam for ironing. One of the white characters fears Ah Toy applies milk to the biscuits he bakes in the same way.

In the midst of the above stories, one complex and sensitive tale appeared in 1882. This is "Poor Ah Toy" (1882), by Mary T. Mott.[42] Like several other stories in this category about domestic servants, the theme here is miscegenation. These stories are in this category because the subject arises from the contact of domestic servants with their white female employers.

In "Poor Ah Toy," Robert Siddons is a father with three children on a farm outside San Francisco. His wife died in the 1870s and his attractive sister Fanny has come out from Virginia to manage his household. She tries out a succession of Chinese servants and is horrified with most of them. The first seven exhibit all the worst traits that were used to describe Chinese domestics: being dirty, deceitful, stupid, lazy, and superstitious. The first washes his feet in the dish pan; another steals a watch, and the next destroys flannels by boiling them. A lazy one plays stupid in order to avoid having his duties increased; another keeps entertaining his relatives at the house. The sixth refuses to stay because Mrs. Siddons's grave is on the property and the seventh is possibly the worst: he uses the oven to cremate polecats, after which he uses the ashes for Chinese folk medicine. Finally a friend of Fanny's in San Francisco suggests Ah Toy, a young man who is tall, young, clean, and neat. He is an efficient worker and order finally comes to the household.

The news of his mother's death, which comes by a letter, activates a chain of unfortunate circumstances. Ah Toy is bedridden with grief and in addition to a doctor's care, he receives the kind attentions of Fanny, who exercises the same tenderness she used with her favorite slave back in Virginia. Thereafter, Ah Toy is exceedingly grateful. One very hot summer day he happily walks twelve miles into town and back to handle a telegram for Fanny and refuses her generous tip, telling her how much he appreciated her kindness when he was sick. He finishes by saying he is no Tartar, but a gentleman, obviously interested in impressing her beyond his normal duties as an excellent servant.

A suitor named Captain Ward arrives at the farm and stays on past his original expectations. When arrangements are made for him to become a partner in Robert's business, Ah Toy becomes hostile and even openly loses his temper at Captain Ward on one occasion. For this social transgression, Fanny dismisses him angrily. She later finds him in the kitchen, distraught and regretful. As she prepares food, however, he is overcome watching her and impulsively takes her hand and kisses it, as he has seen Captain Ward do. Repelled and disgusted, Fanny exclaims that Robert will kill him for this, but Ah Toy responds by declaring his affection. Later, in her room, Fanny cries and blames herself for the situation. She fires Ah Toy, whose departure puzzles Robert and leaves the children crying. Ah Toy explains that he has decided to go because he is going to die soon.

Ah Toy is replaced on the farm by an incompetent named Gong Wah. However, Fanny neither replaces him nor tries to instruct him, being absentminded and anxious with guilt over Ah Toy, whom she nevertheless finds repulsive in his presumption. Robert chances across Ah Toy one day and reports that he is sick and cried like a child when asking about Fanny and the children. Robert offered to take him back, but he refused. Fanny hears this with apprehension, afraid that if Ah Toy returns, he may declare his transgressions in front of Robert or Captain Ward.

Suddenly Gong Wah's work improves markedly in all his various duties and Fanny suspects Ah Toy is behind this. In addition, one night she believes she hears voices in the kitchen and feels a hand touch her cheek, but when Robert investigates he finds nothing. The next morning, however, she insists on a more thorough search and Ah Toy is found hanged in the stable by his own queue. Gong Wah translates his suicide note, which says that he will always be fond of his mistress and that he hopes to be buried on the farm, to be near her. This is done.

Mott's depiction of Ah Toy is sensitive and sympathetic, but one fact suggests that in one way, at least, she was just as bound by social conventions of the day as the Siddons family and Ah Toy, for whom both miscegenation and servant-mistress romance were grossly improper. Limin Chu notes that neither Ah Toy's affection for Fanny nor Ah Choo's interest in Mabel Martin in "Ah Choo," by Esther B. Bock, are characterized as love.[43] In spite of the fact that they exhibit behavior and feelings usually considered evidence of love in fiction as well as in real life, the word *love* never appears. Mott and Bock in this are perhaps accepting the widespread belief in their time that nonwhites were incapable of experiencing the highest forms of sentiment.

Both Ah Toy and Ah Choo are also victimized, of course, by their working-class status as well as their race, but Ah Toy is a much better specimen of humanity. Ah Choo mounts a threat when Mabel's rejection of him produces hatred and a string of curses against her, her husband, and any children they may have. Even his suicide is aggressive, violating her doorstep. By contrast, after Fanny rejects Ah Toy, his affection continues in his misery. Instead of cursing Fanny, he actually returns to the farm to improve Gong Wah's work and be near her. His visit to her bedroom and subsequent suicide are pathetic and his affection for Fanny, like Ah Choo's for Mabel, develops a little too quickly over a small incident. Still, Ah Toy is a much more sympathetic character in spite of the condescension with which both authors write of their Chinese domestics. To the authors' credit, Chu observes that both stories might have lent themselves easily to comical treatment, but Bock and Mott both chose to examine the issues seriously.[44]

"The Conscience of Quong Wo" (1894), by Horace Annesley Vachell, almost reads as though the character of Ah Choo has been inserted into the plot of "Poor Ah Toy," with the story then converted to a comedy.[45] Sing Lee is a fairly acceptable servant, who is sent by Quong Wo, an employment agent, to a household to work for the corpulent Widow Tracy and her fat and ugly daughter, Cyrulea. One of his two undesirable predecessors has been fired for laughing and saying, when the Widow warns him of hellfire, that she will burn much better than he considering how fat she is. Sing Lee, in contrast to the tall and handsome Ah Toy, smells bad and is generally unpleasant. He attempts to kiss Cyrulea and is severely beaten by a white ranch hand, after which he poisons all the food on the ranch and then kills himself. Quong Wo hears in Chinatown that Sing Lee has bought poison and, guessing its purpose, warns the intended victims just in time. This is the only saving grace in a story otherwise completely given to the worst presentations of the Chinese immigrants as domestic servants.

"Sing Kee's Chinese Lily" (1897), by Mary Bell, is about a household cook whose mistress suggests that he bring his wife from China to join him.[46] His wife, Dew, also works for the Right family when she arrives. During the fruit-picking season when every available hand is working in the fields, Dew disappears. Sing Kee is at first frantic; then suddenly he seems to lose all emotions. Mrs. Right organizes a search party, but Sing Kee declines to go, saying that if Dew has been kidnapped, she will have killed herself. A year later someone finds a disfigured Chinese sandal which is taken as evidence that Dew threw herself into a river and drowned. In his grief, Sing Kee turns to opium and degenerates into a ghostly derelict. Sing Kee's use of opium is an unfortunate stock trait but he is a sympathetic character who at least has ample reason to need such a crutch. The plot is roughly parallel to that of E. Lincoln Kellogg's "A Partly Celestial Tale," except that in this story the abducted wife is never seen again.

Limin Chu raises two more important points in the story. One is that Mrs. Right represents a new figure, that of a white mistress who appreciates the efficiency and loyalty of her Chinese domestic and will do a great deal on his behalf. Such figures probably increase in fiction as the authors come to have greater understanding of these relationships through personal experience. The second point is that the behavior of the Right children is delightfully realistic, as on one hand they like and defend Sing Kee and his wife but on the other hand are not above charging their young friends money for a peek at Dew when this "exotic" wife arrives from China.[47]

The main character of "Ah Gin" (1907), by Eunice Ward, is one of the most positive depictions of a Chinese domestic to appear in these magazines.[48] The story is humorous, with Ah Gin the main source of comedy, but it also has an unmistakably serious side. Ah Gin has been with the Caxton household for many years; when he arrived, the youngest of the four daughters was in the nursery, and now all are grown and married. Ah Gin looks unpleasant, since his face is pock-marked, but he runs the house efficiently and firmly, sometimes ordering about his mistress as well as her daughters. Now that the daughters have their own families and servants, they suggest that their widowed mother dismiss Ah Gin for his occasional improper assumption of authority and replace him with someone more docile. When questioned by their mother, however, about their own servants, they admit to problems such as laziness and bad cooking. One, Leila, has a Japanese immigrant as a domestic who has trouble understanding English. Much of the humor is based on Ah Gin's tyrannical treatment of his employers and his terse and limited English. The Japanese servant is even more a comic figure for his ridiculous efforts at understanding his mistress's orders and the image of the Japanese immigrants suffers to some extent in this comparison with an efficient Chinese domestic.

Ah Gin proves his worth to the Caxton daughters during and after an earthquake and subsequent fires in the neighborhood. When the quake begins, the other servants take flight in a comic flurry of terror, the Japanese immigrant later returning only long enough to snatch up his personal effects. Mrs. Caxton leaves to join her children. Ah Gin remains in the house alone and when his mistress returns two days later, she weeps with relief at finding the household intact and in good order. When Ah Gin learns that the houses of the Caxton daughters have all been damaged, he invites them and their families to dinner with their mother. By this time, all four daughters wish they had a servant such as Ah Gin. The story ends with Ah Gin watching proudly as they dine together in front of him. Within his role as a servant, Ah Gin represents an excellent image of the Chinese immigrants. Despite the humor in his role, he ultimately proves to have courage and compassion in addition to his obvious intelligence and efficiency. Lacking the tendency to quick infatuation of Ah Toy, he poses no threat to the established order and so his depiction to a certain degree goes against the idea of a Yellow Peril.

"Sang" (1917), by Lucy Forman Lindsay, is another story of a faithful and dignified family servant.[49] Sang is an elderly retainer in the Bigby household in a remote mining area of Southern California. When their supplies from the nearest towns are cut off by Mexican revolutionaries under Carranza, Alex Bigby rides out of his mine to get help and food for them and for the Mexican villagers with whom they live. While he is gone, the villagers become angry when his wife, Alice, tells them that even her house has no food left to share. Sang and his mistress take refuge in the home until the hungry villagers set it on fire. As the fire rages, Sang stands defiantly at the door with a knife while his mistress runs for the safety of the mine. When her husband returns with soldiers and food, he finds Sang dead in the smoking ruins of the house and his wife safe in the mine. This depiction of courage and heroic sacrifice is rare among Chinese immigrant characters created by white authors, but of course appears often, as Limin Chu comments, in the traditional literature of China.[50]

The stories about Chinese domestic servants are important as a group for two reasons. One is that many of them depict the Chinese immigrants much more positively than the majority of other stories about them in these magazines. In addition to their racial and cultural origins, of course, they are also working-class individuals. These authors did not attempt a deep understanding of them nor did they actually break away from stereotyped character traits. In some cases, however, they did grant these servants both humanity and the higher attributes of character such as loyalty, courage, and intelligence. The second reason for the importance of these stories is that unlike the stories in some categories considered earlier, these do show a clear change over time. With some exceptions, the worst depictions of the Chinese immigrants as domestics appear the earliest, followed by gradual improvement until one finds in the last several stories a consistent view of these servants as loyal and efficient individuals. One should remember that as servants, however, their value is measured in terms of how well they serve their white employers. Qualities such as independence, outspokenness, and self-assertion are as undesirable as incompetence and laziness, except in Eunice Ward's "Ah Gin." To some extent, the Chinese domestics may parallel the loyal plantation slaves of the Old South in literature, whose praise is also earned by service to whites. So the improvement in their image is genuine but occurs within a narrowly restricted context.

The category of comedies contains nine stories. The images of Chinatown and the Chinese immigrants in these stories do not run to extremes. The worst of the characters panic easily and look silly, with stereotyped references to opium, penny-pinching, gambling, and religious hypocrisy. They are neither as threatening nor as subservient as many of the characters in other categories.

The one distinctive story in this category—"Chinatown: My Land of Dreams" (1919), by the Stevensons— examines the effect of evil Chinese images on a young white couple.[51] Bob and his wife enjoy the spectacle of Chinatown and have befriended an elderly shopkeeper there named Lung Sing and also have become acquainted with a favorite waitress, named Tsien Chu. However, the reputation of Chinatown as a center of violence and depravity has affected Bob's wife, who narrates the story. After returning from a dinner in Chinatown one night, when she has decided to buy a pair of slippers from Lung Sing in the near future, she dreams that she has awakened in a fancy Chinese bed with a canopy and curtains. Lung Sing is no longer a kindly old merchant but an evil presence who has parted the curtains to leer at her. Tsien Chu appears in the dream to rescue her, but an Irish American police officer eyes her suspiciously and then chases after her. Finally she awakens screaming and Bob tells her that she has been thrashing about in her sleep for a long time. Though she gradually recovers from the immediate effects of the dream, a week passes before she is comfortable enough to go buy the slippers she wants from Lung Sing.

Her fears originate from the images of Chinatown that circulated in the early twentieth century, some of which appeared in the *Overland Monthly* itself. More importantly, this is one of the few stories in which a white character exhibits an explicit sexual fear of a Chinese immigrant. In the stories of miscegenation, including those about domestic servants and their employers, miscegenation is usually symbolized by superficial physical contact, mention of marriage, or offspring of such contact. The Chinese immigrants who are involved express sexual interest at most by kissing the white woman's hand. The Stevensons have replaced symbolic references and gestures with an open leer at a woman alone in bed. The story is humorously rendered and perhaps takes as a joke the thought of such an explicit fear on the part of a white woman. This is the only story in this category that took any kind of positive step toward the people of Chinatown. The main character's imaginary terrors seem ludicrous when contrasted with the couple's actual pleasant experiences in the community.

The final category is titled, "Angels, Yellow and White." Each of the three stories in the category features a character of high moral fiber in a close relationship with a member of another race. One will serve to represent the category. This is a frame story, "Poison Jim Chinaman" (1919), by Owen C. Treleaven.[52] In it, an old white man named Old Timer Leagan, who lives in a rural area of California near San Jose, tells the story of Poison Jim to a newcomer. In the story, Jim arrives about forty years earlier and gets his nickname by hiring out his services to farmers to kill ground squirrels with poisoned grain. Later he earns the gratitude of farmers even more by eliminating an entire valley of mustard which threatens to encroach upon their crops. They think Jim is crazy when he requests as payment only the collected seeds. That fall, however, a French dealer in condiments finds that his usual suppliers in South Africa have a failed crop and he buys Poison Jim's mustard for thirty-three thousand dollars. As a result, Poison Jim becomes a rancher and flax grower.

The next several years are unusually dry. One year the crops just barely grow and the livestock are dying off. The Native Americans and poor whites suffer the most and finally an elderly Native man is suspected of theft and is shot to death with his adult daughter, leaving the man's baby granddaughter falling to the ground. Poison Jim takes the baby into his shack and soon leaves the area for a while. Several days later he returns leading twelve wagons laden with supplies from San Jose, worth fifteen thousand dollars altogether. He distributes them by leading the wagon train first to the Native villages and then by the homes of the poor whites. His generosity continues to feed everyone in need in the area until the dry spell ends.

Poison Jim goes about his business quietly, working hard and both making his fortune and displaying his generosity without trying to attract attention. In the same way, Trealeven writes the story in a simple style that lends a sincere tone to the tale. Also, the title is the only important reminder of the Yellow Peril: Poison Jim's name is an ironic contrast to his hardworking and decent character.

The nine categories of fiction that have been used in this chapter indicate that different images of the Chinese immigrants have a different literary history in the *Overland Monthly* and the *Californian*.

Some of the categories show definite qualitative changes over time and some do not.

The four stories of Chinese invasion, for instance, are scattered across thirty-one years. "The Battle of Wabash," "The Year 1899," and "The Revelation" ascribe the same qualities to the Chinese people as the novels about Chinese invasion: they appear easily led, uncaring of human life, and diabolically clever. Militarily, they are uncountably numerous and unstoppably victorious. Actually, throughout all the years during which the stories appeared, China was torn by civil strife and foreign encroachment. These stories of foreign invasion by China seem clearly paranoid in this context. "The Sacking of Grubbville" deals with an uprising in San Francisco's Chinatown, not a direct invasion, and the panicked reaction of Grubbville's population to the rumors of violence might be seen as an expression of white guilt over the treatment of Chinese immigrants in the Western states. The naturalist beliefs in racial hierarchy and confrontation are major elements here, just as in the novels of invasion. These stories do not add much to the images and patterns one sees in the novels of invasion, and they are too few and too widely separated in time to indicate a trend. Yet their existence underscores the importance of this unrealistic idea during these years.

The stories about opium likewise exhibit little that is new. Even aside from comparisons with novels and short stories published elsewhere that clearly try to condemn the Chinese immigrants for using opium, most of the stories in the *Overland Monthly* and the *Californian* assume that the reader shares the authors' association of opium with the Chinese immigrants. The authors probably felt they were realists, simply describing life as they believed it to be. Instead of trying to prove or expose Chinese use of this vice, they tell stories about users and dealers who smuggle it into the United States and introduce it to white Americans. Treatment of the subject changes over time: all but two of the stories appeared between 1880 and 1898 and feature active Chinese immigrants who in some way encourage the drug's use. However, in the early twentieth century, the subject fades from use.

The stories of revenge, on the other hand, grow worse with time. Only one appeared before 1915, "The Revenge of a Heathen" (1890). This is also the most positive story, the only one where the Chinese immigrant has a change of heart and proves not to be a cold-blooded killer after all. The other four stories were published between 1915 and 1926. The Chinese appetite for revenge in these four stories keeps growing; in particular, they tell the reader that the desire for revenge among Chinese immigrants is especially compelling and therefore dangerous. That the category developed as late as it did is odd. Its late appearance and increasingly negative content may result from the authors' attempt to find subject matter regarding the Chinese immigrants that was new and increasingly sensational, after decades of stories about opium and miscellaneous "Dark Ways."

The largest and most consistent category is that of "Dark Ways and Vain Tricks." Relying largely on the idea of Chinese inscrutability, most of them suggest in many different ways that the Chinese are untrustworthy, given to violence, and beyond the understanding of white Americans—ironically, since white Americans wrote all of the stories. Their attitude is that of the muckrakers, exposing evil to a supposedly unsuspecting readership. The three stories that show how the Chinese immigrants are victimized by this reputation appeared at wide intervals, not constituting a trend of their own but emphasizing how influential this general image of mysteriousness and danger was.

The stories of love between Chinese immigrants similarly become neither more positive nor more negative as time passes. "The Winning of Josephine Chang" stands out as the only truly favorable depiction of a romance, being entirely free of violence and betrayal. The other love stories contain too much of the "Dark Ways" image to be very positive. All of the stories of miscegenation make violence, disease, and often death the fate of the main characters. This is another expression of inherent racial differences from the naturalist school. Such ends have two further implications as well. First, these events may be seen as a divine trial or punishment that warns the reader away from such behavior. Second, they may be seen as expressions of how these couples are victimized by society and fate in order to elicit sympathy from the reader. Significantly, none of the authors wrote a completely happy ending for these mixed couples.

The treatment of Chinese immigrants does change over time in the stories about Chinese domestic servants. Within the limits of their roles as servants, their depiction improves markedly from the 1870s to the 1920s. The importance of the limits imposed by this occupational role is hard to measure, but the fact that such characters are socially and economically controlled by white Americans may account for the improvement in their image. Characters in the other categories are not usually under such control through employment and close association with whites, and their relative independence may have been considered a threat in itself.

Humor seems to have taken the edge off the presentation of Chinese immigrants in comic tales where they are not servants. They are all presented in stereotyped ways in this category but without unusually negative images and certainly without any positive reforms. The humor relies on the reader's recognition of these two-dimensional characters, so perhaps the authors were careful not to experiment. They make no real contribution to the overall image of Chinese Americans, but support the status quo.

The final category, of "Angels: Yellow and White," is the product of a narrow time period. The three stories appeared in 1916, 1919, and 1920 and so in both size and duration, this is the most limited category of all. The positive image of the elderly Chinese immigrant in "Poison Jim Chinaman" is an obvious response to the evil images that were so much more common. That these stories appeared no earlier than 1916 probably indicates that they resulted from a slow increase of some white authors' awareness that the Chinese immigrants were a varied people like any other; however, the small number of these stories may result from a lack of readers' enthusiasm. These stories of unqualified kindness and affection between races disappear as abruptly as they appeared, while additional stories depicting the Yellow Peril thrive during the 1920s in *The Overland Monthly*. Certainly the tales of violence, vice, and evil among the Chinese immigrants, or anyone else, are more exciting than these of racial harmony. To this extent, the image of the Chinese immigrants in the *Overland Monthly* and the *Californian* may have suffered largely because of the authors' desire to provide thrills at the expense of balanced, informed, and trustworthy accounts of the Chinese immigrants, their communities, and in some cases their families.

This sampling of stories from the *Overland Monthly* and *Californian* establishes that Chinese Americans were a subject of interest to many authors in the late nineteenth century. The issues are varied and complex, reflecting the social and political tides then current on the West Coast. If the fiction examined in chapter 1 presents the best depictions of Chinese Americans discussed so far, and the novels of Chinese invasion present the worst up to this point, then the fiction considered in this chapter represents a large middle ground in between. Though a qualitatively appraised subject such as the depiction of an ethnic group cannot have a "norm" in a quantitative sense, these stories are as representative of their time and subject as any collection that can be compiled.

IV
Chinatown, 1882–1908: Naturalists, Muckrakers, and Missionaries

American Chinatowns become the primary setting and subject for American fiction about Chinese Americans after 1882. This year, when the first Chinese Exclusion Act was passed, is a somewhat arbitrary choice, as are most specific dates used to mark shifts in literary trends. It is appropriate, however, because exclusion had many important effects on the Chinese immigrants who had entered the United States before 1882. The burgeoning of the Chinatowns was one of the most significant.

Prior to exclusion, nearly 98 percent of the Chinese immigrants lived in communities of twenty-five thousand or less. The fiction of Bret Harte, in particular, reflects their presence throughout the frontier singly and in small communities. Several large Chinatowns existed before 1882 in principal cities such as San Francisco and Seattle; they grew especially in port cities where an immigrant ethnic community could provide a social and cultural haven for the newly arrived. The prejudice and hostility directed at the Chinese immigrants played a large part in the formation of Chinatowns, even before 1882.

The Chinatown of San Francisco is the oldest and largest in the United States. To an extent, its history reflects that of the other Chinatowns, and most of the fiction considered in this chapter is set there. One of the earliest influxes of Chinese immigrants in this community began in 1855 as the unfairly enforced Foreign Miners' Tax drove many of them out of the mountains. One of the largest single influxes probably occurred after the first transcontinental railroad was completed in 1869, and thousands of Chinese immigrant laborers left the Central Pacific to look elsewhere for work. During the decade that followed, demagogue Dennis Kearney ignited a wave of antagonism against the Chinese immigrants, charging that they took jobs away from white workers. Stonings, riots, massacres, and burnings began over these labor questions. The inadmissibility in court of testimony from Chinese victims left them without the protection of law, and from the mid-1870s to the mid-1880s atrocities against them throughout the Western states drove them out of the frontier and many of their smaller communities into the larger Chinatowns where numbers offered greater safety. They were also driven from many of the kinds of work they had been doing in the cities, and were soon left primarily with domestic servant work and the independently-owned ghetto businesses for which they became best known: service work, such as laundries and restaurants, and small shops, catering to the community.

The population was predominantly male. As with most other groups entering the frontier area, the young men came first and ordinarily, in the migrant pattern followed by European immigrants and settlers from the East Coast, the young women would be expected to follow after the men had secured some economic stability. While some Chinese women did enter the country prior to 1882, the first Exclusion Act ended any chance of Chinese immigration following spontaneous patterns. In 1860, the male-female ratio for Chinese immigrants in the United States was 1,858 to 1; by 1890, it was 2,678 to 9.[1] With statistics like these, one easily understands that few families were formed. In addition to the small numbers of Chinese women immigrating, the anti-miscegenation laws of the Western states prevented the Chinese immigrants from marrying women of other races. Despite the existence of some families in the Chinatowns of this period, the Chinatown societies of the time were primarily made up of single men. This situation brought about particular social adjustments on their part.

In the traditional culture of China, the family was the fundamental unit of society. With families nearly an impossibility in the American Chinatowns due to the scarcity of women, a new centralized system was created in response to the new conditions. The first level of the structural pyramid was the *fáng (fong)*. These were comprised of individuals from the same village or small locality in China. Their function was largely social, though the association hall might have lodging facilities for those temporarily in need. The members were often closely related, but blood ties were not the actual basis of membership.

The next level in the pyramid was the family association. These were larger and made up of people with the same surname, under the assumption that all of them were at least distantly related through a common ancestor. Because they had more members, they assumed more functions. Family associations were supported by dues and offered services such as room and board, funeral arrangements, interpreters, and arbitration of disputes between members. They held general meetings, performed ancestral rites, and maintained communication with members' relatives still in China.

Above the family associations were the district associations. In the early decades of immigration, nearly the entire population of Chinese immigrants came from seven districts in Guangdung (Kwangtung) Province near Canton. The Sze Yup, or "Four Districts," were rural areas southwest of Canton. Most of the emigrants from this area were poor peasants who became laborers and domestics in the United States. In the early years, 70 percent of the Chinese immigrants in California were reported to have come from the Sze Yup, 40 percent from one district called Toisan. They spoke rural village dialects considered inferior by the people of the Sam Yup, or remaining "Three Districts." The people of the Sam Yup came from the wealthiest part of the province, north of Canton, and spoke a city dialect. The emigrants from this area were small merchants and laborers skilled in crafts. After the people of the Sze Yup, the largest number were from the Pearl River Delta, in the Chungshan area south of Canton. In the United States, this group dominated the fish markets, women's garment factories, and flower farms of certain kinds on the Pacific coast. Hakka people from this region also immigrated and formed their own district association.

Since the district associations were larger than the family associations, they had more responsibilities and more power. In the early decades of immigration, the district associations met new immigrants at the docks, arranged work and medical attention, supported the unemployed until they could find work, and helped the ailing return to China. Like the family associations, they sometimes decided disputes within the organization. *Sin tongs*, or local village associations, developed within the district association to perform specific duties related to a certain locale, such as returning the remains of the dead to their home villages. At times, the *sin tongs* were used like family associations by immigrants from the Sam Yup and Chungshan areas because their own family associations were dominated by the larger numbers of Sze Yup members with the particular surname in question. In the fiction that specifies immigrants from the Sze Yup and Sam Yup, these terms are used to label the people as well as their districts and dialects, the Sze Yup usually appearing as "See Yup."

At the top of the pyramid, a board was organized to arbitrate disputes. Representatives sat on it from six district associations. The decisions of this board were final. In 1880 the Chinese consul suggested that this board be enlarged and strengthened to gain more prestige and recognition outside Chinatown, and so better resist anti-Chinese legislation and related problems. It was named the Chinese Consolidated Benevolent Association. In other cities, it has continued to be called the Chinese Benevolent Association, but in San Francisco it has been called the Six Companies since the late nineteenth century.

Since China's traditional aristocracy, the landed gentry and scholars, did not emigrate from China as a class, merchants came to dominate the family and district associations and therefore the peak of the pyramid as well. In San Francisco their prosperity began with their acting as contract brokers, arranging work for immigrant laborers who indentured themselves at high rates of interest in return for trans-Pacific passage. The laborers went through a contractor in China or Hong Kong who dealt directly with a contractor in the United States. The merchant contractors usually brought laborers who would belong to their own district associations, which they came to control by virtue of holding the contracts of many of their members. The merchants eventually became speakers for Chinatown through the Six Companies. In all, the merchants both provided community services to, and exercised rigid control over, much of Chinatown. After Chinese exclusion came into effect, when new immigrants were sometimes illegally brought into the country, the community leaders could use the threat of legal exposure and subsequent deportation to enforce their will.

The Six Companies pyramid was the established order in Chinatown. Another system grew up in response to its power and inequities involving tongs. These were patterned after, but were rarely connected to, secret societies in China.

Secret societies have a long history in China, most often appearing on the political scene as revolutionary organizations against oppressive or faltering dynasties. They drew their members from the discontented in society, whether scholars, merchants, laborers, or peasants. In the nineteenth century, one of the strongest was the Triad Society which staged uprisings in the area of Canton in support of the Taiping Rebellion. After the rebellion was put down, the Triad Society turned to illegal activities, including piracy and smuggling. Triad members who reached the United States formed an American branch called the Chee Kung Tong. In addition to its illegal activities, this tong maintained its political aim of overthrowing the Manchu Dynasty in China. At the turn of the century, the Chee Kung Tong supported Sun Yat-Sen's revolutionary movement and so had a hand in the final realization of their goal.

The tongs that originated in the United States had no ties in China. They were similar, however, in offering a haven for the disaffected in society and maintaining a sense of rebellion against the established order. Their members were often drawn from groups with little power in the Six Companies pyramid, such as those whose surname or geographic origin was poorly represented. The family or district associations of such people, if they existed at all, were small and therefore weak; however, in a tong, these men could unite their various surnames and backgrounds in a special brotherhood.

The greatest period of tong activity, which gave Chinatown the lurid reputation it has throughout much of the period between 1882 and 1940, occurred in San Francisco from the beginning of Chinese exclusion in 1882 to the great earthquake and fire in 1906. The failure of the Six Companies to resist exclusion and the confinement of Chinese immigrants to jobs in service or small ghetto businesses lowered the prestige of the Six Companies structure. Illegal activities flourished partly as an outlet for suppressed energy and talent, and partly from the lack of families and the related activities of traditional Chinese society. The tongs paid protection money to San Francisco's law enforcers and they reaped great profits from gambling and prostitution. Many of the tong conflicts involved control of the various rackets; in all cases, they grew out of friction between different interests within Chinatown.

One of the important early tongs, the Suey Sing Tong, was organized in the 1880s to fight the powerful Wong family association. In the late 1880s, twelve tongs of Sze Yup laborers united to fight the Sam Yup district association, which of course represented the minority of wealthier merchants. This violent struggle ended in 1896 in a Sze Yup victory. Some fiction refers to violence between Sze Yups and Sam Yups without other evidence of a deep understanding of Chinatown; one might guess that this prolonged feud reached the authors through the sensational newspaper accounts that white journalists wrote for white readers. Finally, in the rebuilding of the city after the destruction of 1906, the Six Companies joined the Christian missionaries and the San Francisco police in breaking the strength of the tongs. Tong activity continued into the 1930s, but after 1906 the merchants began to join them both for protection and to channel them into directions unharmful to the Six Companies structure.

Tong members were a numerically small element in Chinatown. For most of the residents, life was simply an economic war of survival. Their pay was very poor and those still under labor contracts had to pay their debts out of this small amount. They slept in crowded rooms, sometimes using beds in shifts. In their leisure time, they visited each other to tell stories, play mah jong, and just talk. This Bachelor Society also had two demands in particular for which the tongs provided: prostitution and gambling. Both had always existed in Chinese society, of course, but the lack of family responsibilities and the pressures of Chinatown living sometimes encouraged more participation. The shortage of women not only encouraged prostitution but also created another enterprise. A lively trade was established in bringing Chinese females into the country, legally or otherwise, to be prostitutes or brides. The worst part of this trade was that those being brought over were often the victims of force or deceit and frequently came at a very young age. The management of illegal immigration of both sexes was another lucrative tong business. The illegal activities of the tongs were unsavory and caused much suffering but they were not, as American fiction often claims, normal elements of Chinese culture transplanted in the United States from the old country. They were indigenous responses to the particular situations that prevailed in Chinatown, many of which were caused by the Chinese Exclusion Acts and other forms of legislated racism.

Chinese immigration into the United States did not entirely stop with formal exclusion. Teachers, merchants, students, diplomats, and tourists were allowed into the country since the aim of exclusion was to eliminate those without money or certain skills. On the other hand, many desirable categories were excluded. Under this system, physicians, engineers, editors, and artists were all classified as laborers. At first, the immediate family of legal immigrants could also enter; a legal resident with money might travel to China, marry, and bring in his wife. Chinese Americans born in the United States, of course, were citizens and their offspring would also be citizens and allowed to immigrate, even if born abroad to a mother who was not a citizen. These exceptions to exclusion opened up other possibilities as well.

A thriving trade began for the continued immigration of legally excluded Chinese after the San Francisco earthquake and fire in 1906. All the immigration records in the city were destroyed and many Chinatown residents could claim to be United States citizens now that the authorities had no written proof to the contrary. A man who claimed citizenship could travel to China and upon returning to the United States could report to immigration that a child, most often a son, had been born to his wife in China. This meant that the man could at some point bring in a young Chinese male identified as his son. Once this slot had been opened with the immigration authorities, the "father" would agree to claim a certain individual as his son in exchange for money and, of course, the understanding that in the United States this individual would have to keep up these appearances, including taking on the "father's" surname. Many of these "sons" came as indentured servants and were completely at the mercy of their legal "fathers," who if displeased could expose them for deportation. The tongs, in particular, reaped great benefits from this system.

These paper sons became common during this period that lasted at least until 1943. Less common were paper daughters who came in under the same arrangement, sometimes as part of the larger trade in Chinese females. The immigration authorities responded to this deception with a detailed and hostile grilling of all prospective Chinese immigrants. Their attempts to catch impostors sometimes reached absurdities such as demanding to know the number of steps from their home's doorway to the edge of the village, the number of pigs owned by the family, and the condition of different houses on the street, as though the immigration officials knew the answers themselves. At times, the questions weeded out truly qualified applicants for immigration who had failed to memorize the necessary minutiae.

In the Immigration Act of 1924, the United States made one more attempt to halt the development of an Asian American population. Asian women were barred from entering the country, even if married to United States citizens. Further, a woman who was an American citizen, regardless of her race, would lose her citizenship if she married an alien ineligible for citizenship, such as an Asian national. Later the law was relaxed to allow the immigration of merchants' wives, but the overall effect of this act was to condemn the population of Chinatown to a permanently single life.

From the beginning of Chinese immigration, the Chinese immigrants in the United States had a reputation for accepting their travails from white society without violent resistance. Many events occurred to the contrary over the years, especially when the immigrants were together in significant numbers, but the increase in illegal immigrants lessened the tendency to open conflict with white society. After 1906, the illegal immigrants and their families had a stake in remaining unnoticed by the legal authorities. Any detailed investigation of their relationship to the government could mean exposure; therefore, avoiding the attention of the authorities sometimes became more important than active defense or retaliation against white aggressors. Also, the illegal immigrants could not take jobs outside Chinatown, apply for welfare, or seek legal redress for wrongs suffered inside or outside Chinatown. Their children, too, grew up with the understanding that attention from white society should be avoided at all costs. This attitude continued virtually unchanged until the 1960s.

The inadmissibility in court of Chinese immigrants' testimony had continued, and the legal inequities under which the people of Chinatown lived brought about a certain lack of identification with white society even among the United States-born generations and a corresponding lack of respect for its laws. While fear of exposure haunted the illegal immigrants, none of their neighbors felt compelled by conscience to turn them in strictly because they had broken the white people's law. This increasing psychological isolation from the rest of American society was the last phase of the segregation begun by the physical driving-out process.

Not all the fiction considered in this chapter and the next concerns a Chinatown. These works do constitute all the American fiction about Chinese immigrants and their descendents that appeared in book form during this period, excepting only the Charlie Chan novels, which will be considered in a later chapter. Short stories that appeared only in magazines have been included, as well. Critical sources have been cited on the rare occasions when they are relevant and significant. A few of the works are about Chinese immigrants on the frontier; others are about their small rural communities. Generally, however, this chapter follows American authors into Chinatown to survey the continuing threat of the Yellow Peril that they found there. These stories bridge an important period in history, from the closing of the frontier in the late nineteenth century through World War I, the boom twenties, and finally to the Great Depression. The hostility in the United States toward the Chinese immigrants had been fueled by their unrestricted immigration before 1882; after 1882, naturalism and the sensational activities of the tongs performed this function. At the same time, other authors depicted the Chinese immigrants as helpless victims of racism, usually from a Christian missionary's viewpoint. This fiction will be discussed in two groups. The material in this chapter deals with the period between 1882 and 1908; the following chapter will treat fiction published between 1909 and 1940.

Between 1882 and 1908, naturalism replaces labor issues as the force behind hostility to the Chinese immigrants in fiction. During this time, fiction about Chinatown falls primarily into three categories. The first is fiction by naturalist Frank Norris and others who find support for their white supremacist attitudes in naturalist philosophy. Other important naturalists, such as Richard Wright and James T. Farrell, use a naturalist perspective to oppose racism, but as they do not deal with the Yellow Peril theme they are not represented here. Five authors discussed in this chapter fall into this category. The second category is fiction by muckraking authors whose purpose is to expose urban social ills. None of the five muckraking authors have recognized stature, but all show the influence of the Progressive Era. Naturalist influence is evident here, as well. The third category is that of Christian missionaries writing about Chinese Americans from a Christian perspective. Five authors are in this group. The position of four other novels considered outside these categories will be discussed individually.

The first novel in this section predates 1882, reiterating the arbitrary nature of the date chosen to begin this chapter. It takes place in a rural area where no driving out of the Chinese has yet occurred. In *The San Rosario Ranch* (1880), Maud Howe, daughter of Julia Ward Howe, presents a Chinese domestic servant named Ah Lam working on the ranch. The novel tells the story of the white family on the ranch and an Italian friend who comes to live with them, focusing on the contrast between the manners and romantic notions of the Americans and the Italian. Howe's depiction of Ah Lam is not unlike Margaret Hosmer's depiction of You-Sing, and Howe's New England background is important in this regard. The anti-Chinese feeling of the period, despite the national pressure which had brought about the Exclusion Act, had not yet developed to the same degree on the East Coast as it had on the West. Howe's portrayal of Ah Lam is sympathetic, but not realistic. This is a romantic novel related to the abolitionist fiction of New England in its championing an oppressed racial minority. Here, however, the villains are not the wealthy people who employ Ah Lam, but the working-class whites.

Howe first calls Ah Lam a "white-clad Celestial" without explanation; she next terms him a "white Celestial," though with one of the "coppery faces" of the Chinese.[2] His duties include running errands, bringing tea and refreshments, and doing other household chores. Millicent, the visitor, extolls Ah Lam's virtues.

> Do not suggest a word against Ah Lam; he is the most delightful servant I have ever seen. Our Italian domestics are like great children, who have to be humored and managed with the extreme tact and care. Ah Lam is like nothing but one of the automata described by Bulwer in "The Coming Race," which stand motionless against the wall until roused to action by the vrill wand, when they promptly perform the duty in hand. Ah Lam is only mechanical as far as regularity goes, for he has feelings and deep sentiments beneath his calm exterior.[3]

Howe's attitude toward Ah Lam is protective, represented by the sympathy held by the mistress of the ranch for "babies, Chinamen, and other unfortunate works of God."[4] His travails include crouching behind the seat in a wagon because he is not allowed to sit with the

Mexican driver, who is himself called the "Greaser" by other characters.[5] Howe does not depict Ah Lam as the victim of hardships or attitudes of the harshness described by Harte or Bierce. The enjoyable side of his life includes exchanging Chinese stories and myths for Italian ones with Millicent. Anti-Chinese prejudice appears seriously only after his death.

Ah Lam's death itself is not related to questions of race. During an interlude when Ah Lam is telling tales of China to Millicent, a white man tries to abduct her. Ah Lam defends her, scuffling and scratching the attacker's face with his fingernails. The assailant stabs him repeatedly with a knife and Ah Lam dies in Millicent's arms as the attacker flees alone.

> The closed lids fluttered open, the dimmed eyes looked gratefully for the last time into the face of the girl who had been kinder to him than any other creature in this strange land where he had worked so faithfully, where he had been so cruelly oppressed in life, and so foully murdered. . . .[6]

When the killer is caught and arrested in a crowd, he sees that sentiment runs in his favor and explains, "Wall, boys, you see I am 'spected of having done the business for one of these Chinese vermin. What sort of a town's this as will see a man 'rested for that?"[7] The sympathy of the townsfolk, however, does not lead to their actual interference with the sheriff and his deputies. The killer is eventually tried and convicted of voluntary manslaughter; this conviction is such an accomplishment that the prosecuting attorney becomes famous for the achievement.

This novel is not representative of the post-1882 period. It appears to be a lingering expression of the Eastern attitudes expressed by Margaret Hosmer and Bret Harte. The condescension of the author toward Ah Lam is especially reminiscent of Hosmer's attitude, as Howe describes Ah Lam's virtues entirely in terms of servitude and obedience. His white employers like him because of his similarity to Bulwer's automata; they feel sympathy for him because his social status is low. Where the Abolitionists sought to prove, among other things, that Blacks had normal human feelings and were not brutes, Howe tries to praise Ah Lam by describing his behavior as less than human. He is a shallow character and the gratitude in his eyes at his moment of death is one of the few emotions actually ascribed to him. His hardships in life are not so much shown in the novel as mentioned in general terms; they produce no visible angst. Howe's depiction of Ah Lam, like Hosmer's depiction of You-Sing, fails on two counts: the sympathy expressed for the Chinese immigrant is patronizing and the interpretation of West Coast attitudes toward the Chinese immigrant is filtered through an Eastern sensibility, removed from the emotional climate of the West.

In *Choy Susan and Other Stories* (1885), by William Henry Bishop, only the title story concerns the Chinese immigrants. It is a local color story reminiscent of Bret Harte's fiction in setting, character, and other details. This story also takes place in a rural setting, before the Chinese immigrants have been driven out. It is one of the earliest stories about Chinese immigrants by an American author that neither presents them as a threat nor praises them for being loyal and servile to white Americans. As such, it has no hint of the Yellow Peril in it, and is discussed here as a contrast.

Despite the title, "Choy Susan" is actually about a young Mormon woman, Marcella Gilham, and her efforts to avoid becoming the additional wife of an elderly Mormon whom her father has chosen for her. Choy Susan helps her marry a non-Mormon of her own choice.

Choy Susan is the "bossee-man" of a fishing village called Sloan's Camp south of San Francisco, populated by Chinese immigrants.[8] In antecedent action, she was the wife of a Chinese Christian. After she was scarred by smallpox, her husband dropped Christianity to marry two more wives. All three mistreated Choy Susan, so she ran away. She mentions to Marcella Gilham that she prayed to Jesus for her husband and his two wives to die and nothing happened, but when she dropped Christianity and prayed to Chinese gods for the same result, all three died. She ran away to Salt Lake City where Mormons befriended her; later she worked in the Sierra mines and finally took a partner in fishing and storekeeping in Sloan's Camp. These adventures have shaped her character.

> Choy Susan's bark *was*, in fact, worse than her bite. She was plainly a person much in the habit of being deferred to; and this, together with her need of defending herself against scoffers, of whom she had met with not a few among the 'Melican men, in a long experience, had given her a manner bluff, masculine, and even surly. But she was amenable to kindness, and there were even moments when, under her unsmiling exterior, she almost seemed to appreciate the humor of herself.[9]

As the story opens, Choy Susan has been approached by Marcella Gilham for help on the basis of the aid she had extended to Choy Susan in Salt Lake City. At the same time, a storekeeper named Yank

Baldwin has come to ask Choy Susan about contracting Chinese labor in case his Mexican workers go on strike. Baldwin and Gilham strike up a conversation as they watch a Chinese victim of a white Californian's prank.

> "Oh, he will be hurt; he will be killed, will he not?" she cried, clasping her hands appealingly as the rider disappeared around a turn.
>
> "Yes, I s'pose so; that is, I hope so," replied the storekeeper nonchalantly, taking it quite as a matter of course. . . .
>
> "You talk so about a fellow-being?" said the young girl, turning indignantly upon Baldwin.
>
> "Well, may be they is feller-bein's. I dunno but what they is," he returned, weakening under her glance, and with an apologetic tone. "I dunno's I've got anything particular agin 'em, if *you* hain't."
>
> He apparently admired in her an unusual spirit and originality of ideas, as well as good looks.
>
> "The Chinese has got to *go*, though, I s'pose?" he suggested inquiringly.
>
> "Well, that's no reason for wanting them all to be fatally injured while they're here."[10]

Baldwin also carries a strong prejudice against Mormons which surfaces when he finds out that he has been speaking to one. The heroine's sympathy for the Chinese seems to be derived partly from her own encounters with religious hostility. However, she does not exhibit a consistent concern for the Chinese immigrants.

As a group, the purpose of the Chinese immigrants in the story is to provide a colorful backdrop. Bishop shows the outfitting and sailing of a junk from Sloan's Camp and a Chinese festival in accurate detail, even though they are marginal to the plot, as are all the Chinese except Choy Susan. She helps Gilham locate and marry a man named Easterly, moments before her Mormon father arrives with his elderly colleague. Choy Susan does not represent Chinese immigrant women, but her character and activities are plausibly explained. By combining her characterization with accurate cultural details regarding the Chinese, Bishop portrays the Chinese immigrants with unusual realism.

Alfred Trumble describes a Chinatown in American fiction for the first time in *The Mott Street Poker Club: The Secretary's Minutes* (1889).[11] The club is in the Chinatown of New York, where the members gather in Lee-Tip's laundry. The novel is a farce reminiscent of Damon Runyon's stories of New York four decades later. Trumble exploits the immigrants' broken English and characterizes the Chinese as enthusiastic but gullible poker players for the humor. A brief description of their adventures will adequately indicate the entertaining but shallow characterization.

Hong-Lung, who runs a cigar stand, introduces the game to his cronies. His prior understanding of the game enables him to win easily at first. Lee-Tip wins at the third meeting because he takes the trouble to question the Irish cop on the beat, a champion player himself. The entire club is victimized by a white drunk who sells them phony licenses for playing poker at a dollar each; on another occasion, a Chinese visitor from New Jersey hustles them, pretending at first to be naive and then outplaying them. A white man robs the entire pot at gunpoint and a Chinese player from San Francisco accomplishes the same end by taking the pot and then passing counterfeit money. In contrast to the success of white and Chinese strangers, Trumble presents a Black player with even less skill than the club members. He is a Christian minister who, after losing heavily, rails against paganism and smashes a Chinese idol. In retaliation, the club members beat him up.

For a time, events beyond the poker table affect the club. A member named Gin-Seng gets involved with horse racing and as a result the entire club is hauled into court where they fight raucously among themselves. When Gin-Seng marries an Italian woman, which he can do because New York had no antimiscegenation laws, she objects to his poker playing and the club disbands and reorganizes with nine new members. Hong-Lung and Lee-Tip now plan to clean up on the new members and retire comfortably, but the third original member, Hop-Sam, buys a deck of marked cards and starts winning himself. In response, a brawl takes place, destroying much property and ending the club permanently.

Trumble's handling of Chinese immigrants is new in several ways other than presenting Chinatown for the first time in American fiction. First, he is using them as protagonists and comic relief at the same time. Second, his depiction of their illegal activities is not threatening; their incompetence is too great for them to harm anyone else. Finally, they function in New York City with an ease not seen earlier in the stories of Chinese immigrants on the West Coast or later in the stories of San Francisco's Chinatown. Yet the concept of the Yellow Peril is still in the background here.

Trumble has provided much of the same subject matter presented by writers who clearly depict the Chinese immigrants as a threat to the United States. Their dwellings and places of business are crowded and dirty; they love to gamble and fight; they have no respect for court-room decorum or Christian ministers; one of them marries a white woman. Trumble uses humor to nullify any threat that the reader might otherwise infer from the above, showing that his characters' love of gambling is flawed by insufficient shrewdness and their lack of respect for legal and religious conventions results in buffoonery rather than in escaping legal punishment or in harming Christianity. For the last, of course, a racial hierarchy is presented; the only outsider who fails to get the better of the club is the Black minister who is outplayed, proven a hypocrite, and beaten up. The most surprising development is that Gin-Seng's marriage to the Italian woman is not presented as threatening. In fact, her refusal to let him play poker is a more impor-tant issue than their marriage. The explanation may be that Italian im-migrants in this period were no more respected than the Chinese im-migrants. The Italian and Chinese communities in New York City had grown up next to each other, making contact between them frequent. Trumble disarms the potential threat, but not through any insight into the problems or concerns of Chinatown. He merely suggests that his protagonists lack the intelligence to mount any threat through their gambling or violence.

Stories of Chinatown: Sketches from Life in the Chinese Colony of Mott, Pell and Doyers Street (1892), by William Norr, contains six stories that deal with white women in relationships with Chinese men. The plots involve the decisions of the women to continue or end the relationships. Chuck Conners, the tour guide, appears as a character in several of them. These are muckraking stories intended to illuminate evils the author perceives. Three of them will represent the collection adequately. In the introduction, Norr says that all the stories are based on facts gathered during his many years as a reporter in Chinatown, where he had often patronized opium establishments himself. He also explains why he has written the stories:

> The world in general wonders—when it gives the subject a
> thought—how young and comely women can cast their lot
> with the repulsive Chinese. "He's so good to me," was the
> reply of one girl I sounded on the question, and in "The
> Pearl of Chinatown," one Chinaman's goodness is shown.
> Wah, in "A Chinatown Tragedy," also seems a pretty good

fellow, but it speaks ill for a civilized world when a little kindness will drive our women into the arms of heathen.[12]

In "A Romance of Pell Street," Edna lives with Yee Lip, a known gambler who may deal in opium as well. He "speaks excellent English, dresses in good taste, is always plentifully supplied with money, and plays the mischief with the hearts of the impressionable girls in the Chinese colony."[13] The Chinatown is described as crowded with white women. The opium den in this story also has white male patrons and a Jewish attendant. Edna is considered arrogant by her neighbors, but her reserve actually results from a secret arrangement she has made with Yee Lip. She has a white lover in prison whom she can free with five thousand dollars, and Yee Lip has agreed to pay it if she will first live with him for two years. The tragedy in this story is that, unknown to Edna, her white friend will now have nothing to do with her because of her association with a Chinese man.

"A Chinatown Tragedy" is about the Cavanaugh family. Mamie Cavanaugh lives in Chinatown with Wah Sing, who runs an opium den. She left behind seven younger sisters, their mother, and their alcoholic father in a poverty-stricken home. As the story opens, the eldest sister, Katie, has been locked out of her home by their father and she contacts Chuck Conners in Chinatown. Conners takes her to Mamie's apartment. For a while, Mamie and Wah Sing chaperone her carefully but she finally gets involved in the same element of Chinatown society as her sister. A Chinese sailor gets her drunk and the story ends with their whereabouts unknown. Norr does not blame the environment in Chinatown exclusively for her fate: "Those who know the history of the two handsomest girls in the Chinese colony vaguely wonder whether Tim Cavanaugh will contribute any more to the immoral colonization of Chinatown."[14]

"The Pearl of Chinatown" is a petite young white woman named Pearl who lives with Lee How. His broad and lucrative business concerns are shady but not detailed. Edna, the heroine of "A Romance of Pell Street," describes Pearl's beauty in this story: "she was a picture that made outsiders fortunate or unfortunate to be admitted to the intimacies of Chinatown metaphorically throw up their hands when they saw her with homely little Lee How."[15]

Pearl's life includes much alcohol and opium and she develops tuberculosis. Lee How is unfailingly attentive as she dies.

There were tears in the Chinaman's eyes as he spoke. He was an unusually taciturn fellow, even for his race, and this was the first time he had broken through his habitual impassiveness since they had been together.[16]

Norr ends this story, and so the book, with Pearl's testimony to Lee How:

> "You're only a Chinaman, a poor and despised heathen, whom the civilized world shuns. If the Christians, who think you scum beneath their feet, had only treated me one-half as well as you, one-quarter as unselfish, what a different life I would have had. Only a "dirty Chinaman," they say, but how few of them have such a heart."[17]

Norr fails to tie the situations he describes to the large forces of society such as laws and economics. For this reason his exposés are not completely in the best tradition of Lincoln Steffens and Upton Sinclair. However, he falls into the same general category.

His narrow vision of Chinatown focuses only on the threat its society presents to young white women. These Chinese characters treat their women well but also provide them with liquor and opium. Further, these couples live together without marriage. Norr's underlying assumption is that the lives his characters lead are acceptable for the Chinese but not for young white women. He carefully describes the motives of his white female characters for becoming involved with Chinese men and recognizes that the women's home environments, as in the case of the Cavanaughs, may have as much to do with their presence in Chinatown as the activities of the Chinese. Still, he disapproves of what he sees in Chinatown, where all the Chinese he depicts are gamblers or opium dealers, even if they are kind and considerate to their white women. His perception of these interracial relationships, developed during his journalistic experience, is excellent, but his understanding of Chinatown seems to be limited to this subject.

Edith: A Story of Chinatown (1895), by Harry M. Johnson, is about Chinatown but not about the Chinese residents. Edith is a young white prostitute in the Chinatown of Los Angeles. The novel involves her reunion with her parents.

Johnson explains in his introduction that his purpose is to make his readers aware of social evils. Unlike Norr, he cites the contribution of a corrupt police force in maintaining these evils. He claims that vice in the Chinatown of San Francisco is unsurpassed but that the Chinatown of Los Angeles also has a serious problem with it. However, his concern is not contact between white women and Chinese men; only white men patronize these establishments.

The cribs are located in Chinatown and constitute a part of

that section of the city both in 'Frisco and Los Angeles, but are not patronized by the Chinese; the inmates as a rule consider it "debasing" to receive Chinese patronage, and the policeman on the beat told the writer that he never knew of but two or three instances where the girls would take the Chinaman's money. They are located in the meanest section of the city, and lawlessness and immorality naturally gravitate to such localities and away from clean surroundings and clean moral atmosphere.[18]

The novel begins with Jack Sherwood, a reporter, being assigned to cover Chinatown on Chinese New Year's Eve. He is new to Los Angeles and has never seen a Chinatown before. The Chinatown is decked out for celebrations and crowded with tourists. Sherwood visits a theater, a myriad of small shops, and opium dens.

> [Chinatown] was ablaze with lanterns, brilliant overhead the vari-colored lights of the gay and unique-shaped paper globes. The triangular silk and gold dragon-flag of the wearers of the cue, floating from the mast-head of the brilliantly decorated joss-house; the colors of the various societies, or "tongs," fluttering in the breeze from dozens of staffs; banners of all sizes and shapes, bearing pot-hooked hieroglyphics that put to shame the most elaborate efforts of our own court stenographers; good-luck crowns and ornaments in tinsel-work; paper flowers, blazing candles, and burning tapers of pungent punk—all this display was calculated to make this scene brilliant and animated, to mantle the squalor of the Chinese quarter, to throw a glamour over the picturesque hovels that jostled and squeezed and crowded each other in Chinatown.[19]

As Sherwood heads home, he walks past a block of prostitution houses where the windows are well lit and prospective patrons walk by to survey the women on display inside. As he wonders if the legal authorities know about the situation, a police officer asks him to move along to keep the flow of onlookers from backing up. Sherwood's objection to this block is not that prostitution exists but that there is "no need to flaunt it in the very eyes of all the world, where children, young boys, and innocent women may be thrown into contact with it."[20]

Edith is on display in one of the windows. The Chinese had nothing to do with her becoming a prostitute; as the daughter of a wealthy Eastern family, she had been thrown out of her home when she became pregnant out of wedlock. The baby was stillborn and she had immediately left the man, who had refused to marry her. However, her attempts to support herself by ordinary means all failed and she turned to prostitution as a last resort.

After Sherwood sees her in the window, she becomes the focus of the story—Chinatown and the Chinese have no further role to play. Sherwood is acquainted with Edith's parents, who have long since regretted casting her out. He finally arranges a reunion which allows all the parties to maintain their dignity.

Johnson blames Edith's parents for her fate, not the Chinese. In muckraking fashion, he points out that slum areas like Chinatown always have poor law enforcement. The impression he conveys is that the Chinese immigrants are victims of their environment just as Edith is.

Robert W. Chambers was one of the most popular American writers in the United States from the mid-1890s to his death in 1933. Though his popularity did not outlive him by much, he wrote fiction about a variety of subjects that were well-received in his lifetime. His work includes historical fiction, stories of high society, and occult fantasies. One of the last is a novella called "The Maker of Moons" (1896), an allegory of Chinese invasion that combines the Yellow Peril, a Chinese myth, and occult features of Chambers's own creation.[21]

The story is about mysterious events taking place at the Lake of the Stars in the Cardinal Woods, somewhere north of New York City. The narrator, Cardenhe, goes north on a hunting trip into the Cardinal Woods with two friends, Pierpont and Barris, and two white personal servants. On the train north, the narrator learns that Barris, a colonel in the Secret Service, is using the hunting trip as cover for a professional mission. The government has discovered that gold is not an element, but a composite metal, and that the discoverer of this secret is up in the Cardinal Woods manufacturing it. Gold sculptures have been gradually entering the galleries and museums of New York, and of course eventually the monetary base for American currency will collapse. Barris's mission is to stop the manufacturers of the gold and kill them if necessary.

Pierpont is especially distressed, because his income is derived from a gold mine. Cardenhe has already had some exposure to this phenomenon, since he had seen one of the strange gold sculptures in Tiffany's the same day he boarded the train. A man at Tiffany's had shown him a magnificently textured gold serpent, but Cardenhe was more struck by a mysterious live creature, crablike with soft yellow fur, that the jeweler found clinging to the box the sculpture came in.

I shrank back as he held the repulsive object dangling before me, and he laughed and placed it on the counter.

"Did you ever see anything like that?" he demanded.

"No," said I truthfully, "and I hope I never shall again. What is it?"

"I don't know. Ask them at the Natural History Museum—they can't tell you. The Smithsonian is all at sea too. It is, I believe, the connecting link between a sea urchin, a spider, and the devil. It looks venomous but I can't find either fangs or a mouth. Is it blind? These things may be eyes but they look as if they were painted. A Japanese sculptor might have produced such an impossible beast, but it is hard to believe that God did. . . ."[22]

The reference to Japanese art foreshadows the appearance of other Asians, the Chinese, later in the story. Dividing God from the origin of the creature, and suggesting it has a relation to the devil, prepares the reader for the occult forces that surface in the Cardinal Woods. Cardenhe's reaction to the creature is one of revulsion and horror, which also helps to set the tone for his experiences to come. The crablike creature gives off an odor in Tiffany's and Cardenhe says, "I hated the thing. It was the first living creature that I had ever hated."[23]

In the Cardinal Woods, several discoveries take place. One of the servants spies a "Chinaman" in the woods but the likelihood of this is so slight that Cardenhe convinces him that he was mistaken.[24] Shortly after, Cardenhe spends a day wandering alone in the forest while Barris and Pierpont actively search for other people. Cardenhe stumbles across a beautiful and strangely naive young white woman at a forest pool. Her name is Ysonde and she has carved dragonflies, fishes, shells, and butterflies on a semicircle of stone around the basin. Cardenhe's first meeting with her is one of enchantment but little else, and it ends when she vanishes almost before his eyes. The next morning at the camp, Barris and Pierpont show Cardenhe a ball of gold they found that has intricate carvings all over it. Cardenhe takes the carved figures for dragons. Barris identifies the ball as the symbols of

> the terrible Kuen-Yuin, the sorcerers of China, and the most murderously diabolical sect on earth. . . . Why, Roy, I tell you that the Kuen-Yuin have absolute control of a hundred millions of people, mind and body, body and soul. . . . But you never before heard of Kuen-Yuin; no, nor has any European except a stray missionary or two, and yet I tell you that when the fires from this pit of hell have eaten through the continent to the coast, the explosion will inundate half a

world—and God help the other half.[25]

As they look at the ball, however, they realize that the carvings are not dragons, but the yellow furry crabs, which briefly writhe and squirm.

The entire hunting party sets out in search of the Chinese in the forest and the mysterious glade that holds Cardenhe's pool, half believing that Cardenhe dreamed of the place. The glade remains elusive, however, until the group gives up and Cardenhe goes alone to shoot game for dinner. In only a few moments, he stumbles into the glade where Ysonde is waiting for him.

At this meeting, the mystery of the gold begins to unfold. Ysonde has a gold carving that she has made herself, being the sculptor of the mysterious carvings in New York. Her stepfather gives her gold, which he makes himself. She knows that he takes much more gold to strange men, but does not know what they do with it. Further, she says that she is eighteen and has lived in the forest for two years. Before that, she grew up in Yian, "a city across seven oceans and the great river which is longer than from the earth to the moon."[26]

Cardenhe tries to find out if Yian is in China, but Ysonde has no understanding of nations or geography. However, when he asks about the people, she replies, "The people of Yian? I could see them in swarms like ants—oh! many, many millions crossing and recrossing the thousand bridges.[27] Cardenhe suddenly sees the small golden ball at her waist, the symbol of the Kuen-Yuin, and he realizes that her stepfather is Yue-Laou, a mysterious Chinese sorcerer Barris has mentioned. Cardenhe and Ysonde fall in love in a rapturous momentary swirl of fantasy, but then Ysonde seems to disappear again. Actually, the moment they kiss, she turns into one of the small yellow crabs and falls to the ground. Cardenhe collapses, to wake up in the darkness with Barris and Pierpont standing over him.

Barris continues his investigation and finds that three men are making the gold: two white men, one of whom is caught and expected to confess, and an unidentified ringleader. A great malignant force seems to be gathering in the forest and one night Cardenhe is drawn out of his tent into the forest by a whispering in the trees. As he wanders the forest toward Ysonde he sees that all the animals of the forest are moving rapidly across his path in the same direction. When he reaches Ysonde, who is lonely for him, she identifies the leader of the Kuen-Yuin, according to what her stepfather has told her.

Yue-Laou is Dzil-Nbu of the Kuen-Yuin. He lived in the Moon. He is old—very, very old, and once, before he came to rule the Kuen-Yuin, he was the old man who united with a silken cord all predestined couples, after which nothing can prevent their union. But all that is changed since he came to rule the Kuen-Yuin. Now he has perverted the Xin—the good genii of China—and has fashioned from their warped bodies a monster which he calls the Xin. This monster is horrible, for it not only lives in its own body, but it has thousands of loathsome satellites—living creatures without mouths, blind, that move when the Xin moves, like a mandarin and his escort. Yet if one of these satellites is injured the Xin writhes with agony. It is fearful—this huge living bulk and these creatures spread out like severed fingers that wriggle around a hideous hand.[28]

These satellites, of course, are the curious yellow crabs. As Cardenhe talks with Ysonde, the yellow beasts are on the move through the forest with a dark shape that is the Xin and with headless dogs that, Ysonde says, are the spirits of murdered children. Finally Cardenhe sees Ysonde's stepfather and as he and Ysonde watch him create gold and then the symbol of the Kuen-Yuin she realizes for the first time that he himself is Yue-Laou.

Standing on the shore of the lake, a stone's throw away, was a figure, twisted and bent—a little old man, blowing sparks from a live coal which he held in his naked hand. The coal glowed with increasing radiance, lighting up the skull-like face above it, and threw a red glow over the sands at his feet. But the face!—the ghastly Chinese face on which the light flickered—and the snaky slitted eyes, sparkling as the coal glowed hotter. Coal! It was not a coal but a golden globe staining the night with crimson flames—it was the symbol of the Kuen-Yuin.[29]

A seemingly endless wave of the yellow crabs swarms over the forest. Yue-Laou falls at the lake's edge from Barris's gunshots as the dark shape looms over Barris. Then it causes him to disappear, presumably dead. After this, the story cuts to an epilogue.

In this epilogue, Barris's will reveals that he had dealings with Yue-Laou many years earlier. Yue-Laou had made a woman out of a white water-lotus bud and had given her to Barris. After a child was born, Yue-Laou took away both wife and daughter, earning Barris's undying hatred. He believes that Ysonde is his missing daughter. Cardenhe and Ysonde remain together, safely so far, though Pierpont and Cardenhe still fear the threat from China.

Now the world knows what Barris thought of the Kuen-Yuin and of Yue-Laou. I see that the newspapers are just becoming excited over the glimpses that Li-Hung-chang has afforded them of Black Cathay and the demons of the Kuen-Yuin. The Kuen-Yuin are on the move.[30]

Though Yue-Laou only appears once in the story, his presence pervades the story after the narrator reaches the Cardinal Woods. Chambers's description of sorcery seems to be derived from the European concept of magic, not from the Chinese Taoist or folk magicians. More importantly, the Xin and the blind, mindless yellow crabs are metaphors for the American fear of Chinese invasion. The Xin is an evil presence that represents the unknown in China, those qualities usually termed exotic or inscrutable. The yellow satellites that move with it in a great mass, under one mind but in many different bodies, of course represent the imagined unending horde of Chinese on the march to North America, as in the novels described in chapter 2. This sort of invasion is also symbolized by Yue-Laou's gradual flooding of the United States with gold, yellow in color. The strange vermin also are a part of the vision of the Chinese as filthy and subhuman. The role of Ysonde is less clear symbolically, though Yue-Laou's magical creation of her mother and control over her might be seen as a threat to white women.

Chambers overlays his descriptions of Yian and China, which are clearly fantasy, with just enough derivation from Chinese culture to lend a sense of credibility to the whole. The name Yue-Laou, now usually anglicized Yuè Lau (Yueh Lao), does refer to a Chinese mythological old man in the moon who links those destined to be married, but Chambers brings him to earth. Kuen-Yuin appears to be an approximation of Guan Yin (Kuan Yin), the Chinese goddess of mercy. The sorcerers Chambers describes have nothing to do with the goddess of mercy, but their name does have the appearance of a Chinese name. Similarly, the city Yian is probably derived from Sian, a city in western China.

This story is a transition of sorts between two types of fiction dealing with the Yellow Peril. Its relation to the early novels of Chinese invasion is obvious, with the mindless mass of yellow crabs threatening the United States, but this story has two elements which are developed much more by later authors. One such element is the mysterious but immensely powerful old Chinese man whose power is ultimately personal rather than political; this kind of figure reaches its height in Fu Manchu. The second element is the use of weird, grotesque beasts as part of the threat which the Chinese pose to the United States. This device is also developed most fully in Sax Rohmer's stories of Fu Manchu.

Edward Townsend includes the Chinese immigrants in New York in one novel and two short stories. *A Daughter of the Tenements* (1895) is about the ghetto communities of Irish and Italian immigrants and their first American-born generations. A Chinese character named Chung from Chinatown has a small but crucial part in the plot. The villain of the novel, a financier named Waters, has letters that incriminate him of embezzlement. Chung steals them by accident when he takes Waters's pocketbook for the hundred dollars in cash it contains. He is only in the financier's building because he is paying the rent his uncle owes for his store in Chinatown; when he spies Waters's empty office, however, he recognizes the opportunity to increase the money he can take to his gambling sessions. His cloth-soled Chinese shoes allow him to walk noiselessly and his "cunning" keeps him from suspicion, as he calmly pays his rent elsewhere in the building after the theft.[31]

When Waters discovers the theft, he learns that Tom Lyons, the hero of the novel, has just left the building. He comes under suspicion while Chung is ignored. Chung's manner of dealing with white people includes repeated smiling and bowing which Townsend considers further evidence of a cunning and deceitful nature. Chung learns that the letters have value when he hears of a reward for their return, and he hides them pending a better grasp of the situation. He uses part of his stolen cash to buy an interest in an opium den that masquerades as a lodging house in Chinatown. This interest requires the payment of protection money to the police. The patrons of the den include both Chinatown residents and white derelicts from the tenements of the Irish and Italian ghettoes.

> On the third floor, in the front, with windows opening on an iron balcony overlooking the street, is what is called a "Joss temple." In the rear of this room is a hideous, squat grimacing figure before which incense sticks are always burning. The priests (if they are priests of the temple who appear out of some half-lighted corner of the room, noiselessly and stealthily, and startle sight-seeing visitors) make a revenue by selling a cent's worth of the incense sticks for twenty-five cents. Back of the temple a door leads from this hallway into a little-cubby-hole of an office. In this office there is a counter extending from wall to wall, and behind that is a door leading to a dark room beyond. Back of this counter and in front of the second door, from eight or

nine o'clock in the evening until nearly daylight, a
Chinaman sits in a space which allows only room for him
and a narrow passage to the room beyond when he lifts a
gate in the counter to admit a customer. The customers of
that Chinese functionary are opium-smokers, and their occupations, honest and otherwise, keep them abroad late at
night; in some instances until the awful craving of the habit
drags them to the den, even though their occupation may be
no less exciting than trying to escape from the police.[32]

One of the den's regular patrons is Bill, a foster brother of Tom
Lyons. He has been down and out for some time when one day he
overhears an arrangement between Chung and a city detective in the
den itself.

"If you can catch lewad mebbe Chung can catch papers,
then you and me devide lewad."
    "You're a pretty slick Chink. I'll see about that reward."[33]

Bill manages to steal the papers from Chung and return them to Tom.
Tom clears himself and Chung is sent to prison, ending his role in the
novel.

In this story, Chung is a stereotyped figure whose theft of the
papers is merely the result of an unexpected opportunity, but whose involvement with opium comes easily and without concern for morals.
Townsend uses Chinatown as local color, taking the reader briefly into
a sleazy criminal environment as one of the plot twists. He does not
make much of a social comment, accepting as normal the detective's
presence in the opium den. By contrast, his short stories are stark
melodrama with attempts at social messages.

Two short stories concern the victims of Chinese opium pushers in
Near a Whole City Full (1897).[34] In both, Townsend presents a more
dangerous threat from the Chinese than Chung constitutes. These
stories involve white women who have been enslaved with opium and
kept as prostitutes in Chinatown. "By Whom the Offence Cometh" is
the story of Lena, daughter in an immigrant family from Europe. To
avoid the endless day labor of her existence, Lena runs away and joins
a sneak thief. With him she develops an opium habit and when he is arrested, she goes to a Chinese restaurant. A man named Chung runs it
and supplies her with opium. She becomes one of his prostitutes and he
keeps her until she is about to die. He then sends her away and she dies
on the steps of a building where a missionary board is gathering to
discuss sending more missionaries abroad.

"The House of Yellow Brick" is about Kate, a white prostitute in a Chinatown whorehouse. No Chinese characters actually appear, but the opium habits of Kate and the other women in the house are blamed on the environment of Chinatown. Kate is already dying of the habit and observes that whites die from opium but the Chinese seem to smoke it for years without visible harm. Finally she dies on Easter Sunday with a moral victory behind her; she refused to smoke after church for fear she would forget the one prayer that another churchgoer had helped her remember. The story is simplistic and heavy-handed in conveying its message.

Chester Bailey Fernald (1869–1932) lived in California from 1889 to 1894 and from 1903 to 1906. He traveled between these periods, including China on his itinerary. In 1907 he moved to England. His first book was *The Cat and the Cherub and Other Stories* (1896), which contains six stories about San Francisco's Chinatown. These comprise slightly over half the volume. *Chinatown Stories* (1900), published only in England, includes all the stories about Chinatown in *The Cat and the Cherub and Other Stories* plus four more.

The title story to the first book involves a five-year-old named Hoo Chee and his pet cat, One-Two. His father is a merchant suspected of having been a traitor to his tong. The father expects that tong vengeance will not be aimed directly at him, but at this son, who will someday perform the traditional rites of what is sometimes called ancestor worship. Therefore Hoo Chee is not allowed to play outside and must remain home alone.

One day when his parents are out, he runs off with One-Two, following a white art student whom he has noticed walk by his house before. She invites him into her home, models his bust in clay, and gives him lunch as well as a bath. In the meantime, the family servant in charge of him is afraid she will be punished for losing track of him. She tells his father a story about tong kidnappers. At the same time, the art student's Chinese cook has recognized Hoo Chee but is afraid to report his whereabouts for fear that he will be accused of kidnapping him. These two clearly fear irrational and cruel behavior on the part of Hoo Chee's father. Finally, the cook learns that Hoo Chee's father belongs to the same tong as he. Knowledge of their tong association dissolves his fears and he goes to inform the father personally of Hoo Chee's whereabouts.

When Hoo Chee's father arrives, he first sees the clay bust and fears that his son has been killed. In particular, he believes that his eyes have been destroyed in order to make photographs. The origin of this momentary belief is not explained, but appears to be a device of Fernald's to show how little of scientific matters a Chinese immigrant supposedly understands. Hoo Chee is found hiding in a chimney and is taken safely home.

"The Cruel Thousand Years" takes place after Hoo Chee's family has moved. They have a fenced backyard where Hoo Chee can play outside. Hoo Chee's father is now the head of his tong, which traffics in women slaves. Their neighbors, the Sum family, oppose this activity. Because they have a daughter, Sum Oo, who is Hoo Chee's age, his father orders his son to avoid her or be kept inside his house "for a thousand years!"[35]

Hoo Chee disobeys once again, being especially interested in Sum Oo because she has a pet cat. The two children make friends, and play in a large packing crate. For a while, Hoo Chee's father believes that Sum Oo's father has kidnapped his son. The two children eventually come out of hiding and the story ends with Hoo Chee expecting to be kept inside the house for a thousand years.

Chinatown Stories includes three more stories about Hoo Chee. In "The Cherub Among the Gods," Hoo Chee finally is kidnapped, by an enemy of his father within his tong. Hoo Chee is carried into a tunnel that leads to a room thirty feet underground, next to a joss room containing the gods mentioned in the title. Hoo Chee's father dies from shock at the kidnapping. A soothsayer named Dr. Wing Shee, who made a brief appearance in "The Cruel Thousand Years," rescues and adopts Hoo Chee. In the previous stories, tongs and women slaves have been mentioned along with potential violence, but none of these was actually depicted in the stories. Here for the first time, villains kidnap and threaten to kill Hoo Chee and the description of the evil manner of the gang contains a racial aspect: "In an ugly Oriental way all the members laughed."[36] Fernald is now dealing with familiar Chinatown figures who fight tong wars and deal in organized criminal activity. Even Dr. Wing Shee, a protagonist, smokes opium. The lurid reputation of Chinatown and Fernald's imagination produce fictional devices such as the room thirty feet underground. At the same time, Fernald knows enough about the community to mention social and political divisions between Chinatown men who speak Sam Yup dialects and those who speak Sze Yup dialects, and to describe Guan Yin, the Goddess of Mercy. His accurate portrayals of this type unfortunately lend credence to the false presentations in his stories. The remainder of Fernald's stories about Chinatown similarly depict violent, shallow stereotypes and sometimes a naiveté that approaches stupidity.

Fernald's melodramatic and highly imaginative stories of Chinatown received favorable critiques. Citing his supposed realism, Arthur

Hobson Quinn praised him for his renditions of Chinese culture and life in the United States.[37] May Lamberton Becker credited Fernald with acquainting the East Coast with the Chinatown of San Francisco and gripping the American imagination with "tales of the Orient established in the West."[38] Unfortunately, Fernald's stories are more fantasy than reality, though they are interpreted as realism. The critics' enthusiasm suggests a scarcity of knowledge of the topic on both their parts.

The Californians (1898), by Gertrude Atherton, offers a brief but interesting look at the viewpoint from which some wealthy Californians regarded the Chinese immigrants. Chinatown remains at a distance from the reader, as this romantic novel deals with high society in San Francisco. While it touches on the Chinese San Franciscans little, the ones who do appear function as an integral part of the city's life. The heroine, Magdaléna Yorba, is descended from both Spanish and New England ancestors. Her home has some pieces of Chinese furniture, works of Chinese art, and Chinese servants, but her sheltered life conditions her to stay away from unfamiliar environments.

> [Chinatown,] which began a block to her right, was out of the question, although she would have liked to see the women and the funny little Chinese babies that she had heard of: the fortunate Helena had been escorted through Chinatown by her adoring parent and a policeman.[39]

Her only personal contact with the Chinese occurs with servants, who have minor but numerous roles. Atherton mentions "the catlike tread of Chinese butlers,"[40] and Magdaléna, when frightened, reflects that "the only man in the house beside her father was the Chinaman, and Chinamen are as indifferent to the lives of others as they are to their own."[41] When she goes to a house her aunt and uncle maintain but no longer use, she finds a Chinese majordomo in charge. She rings and "the Chinaman answered in his own good time. He looked a little sodden; doubtless he employed much of his large leisure with the opium pipe. . . ."[42]

On occasion, Magdaléna does see the Chinese on the street from a distance, such as "a row of Chinese washhouses, in whose doors stood the Mongolians, no less picturesque than the civilisation across the way."[43] Another time, she sees "blank-faced Chinamen" on Kearney Street.[44]

Atherton's Chinese immigrants are a clear threat to Magdaléna in their own community, but only a vague one in their capacity as employees, where they are under some control. Importantly, they do not present a threat merely on racial and cultural grounds. Magdaléna's circle of family and friends views all working-class people as dangerous, especially foreigners, including European ones. Her sheltered existence has been designed to isolate her from everyone not at her social and economic level, and the Chinese immigrants are a part of this category. Neither, however, does Atherton give her Chinese characters any individuality or sympathy.

Frank Norris's naturalism is evident already in an early novel, *Moran of the Lady Letty: A Story of Adventure off the California Coast* (1898), although this is also clearly a kind of romance. In it, six Chinese characters more or less on the side of good are ranged against a comparable crew of Chinese pirates and scavengers; two white characters oppose them both. While the story is set on the ocean rather than in Chinatown, the two ships have sailed out of San Francisco and their differences originated in the Chinatown there. The protagonist, Ross Wilbur, is a young white sophisticate who is shanghaied aboard the first ship, the *Bertha Miller*. This ship has been sent out by one of the Six Companies to catch sharks for their fins and livers. The crew is led by white Captain Kitchell, who was hired to circumvent a law forbidding "coolies" from taking a ship out of San Francisco.[45] Captain Kitchell dies and a woman named Moran is found alive on a derelict ship. Ultimately, she and Wilbur take over the crew of the *Bertha Miller*. They are soon approached by the Chinese pirate ship. After the pirate ship is shipwrecked, a battle develops between the two crews over the *Bertha Miller* and a treasure of ambergris. The animosity goes deeper, however. The pirates belong to the See Yup tong, bitter enemies of the *Bertha Miller*'s crew of Sam Yup tong members. Norris is actually naming two dialects of southern spoken Chinese rather than real tongs, but he is accurate in ascribing them to competitive organizations of Chinatown.

This novel distinguishes three levels of human value, the first being the white race. The most careful distinction is between the Sam Yups and See Yups. Wilbur meets the Sam Yups first, beginning with the cook, known as Charlie.

> He spoke pigeon English fairly. Of the balance of the crew—the five Chinamen—Wilbur could make nothing. They never spoke, neither to Captain Kitchell, to Charlie, nor to each other; and for all the notice they took of Wilbur he might easily have been a sack of sand. . . . The absolute indifference of these brown-suited Mongols, the blankness of their flat, fat faces, the dullness of their slanting, fishlike

eyes that never met his own or even wandered in his direction, was uncanny, disquieting.[46]

The Sam Yups are all habitual opium smokers, as well, who go about their chores "with the extraordinary absence of curiosity which is the mark of the race. . . ."[47] They can be assertive, however; when Moran, a Norwegian, has become captain of the ship, the Sam Yup crew refuses to let her and Wilbur return to San Francisco. They still have sharks to catch in Magdalena Bay. At the end of this project, however, when the scraping of a sulfur-bottom whale against the hull of the ship causes it to lurch and rise, the Sam Yups become superstitious cowards.

> Forward, the coolies were already burning joss-sticks on the fo'c'sle head, kowtowing their foreheads to the deck. . . .
> "Feng shui! Feng Shui!" they exclaimed with bated breaths. "The feng shui no likee me."[48]

Norris does not indicate that he knows the meaning of "feng shui." Literally "wind water," this term refers to the balance of natural elements and ether in the cosmology of Chinese folk religion. Wilbur and Moran simply guess that the term refers to local deities. At any rate, after a second brush with the still-unidentified sulfur-bottom whale, the crew takes the only dory and rows for the nearby shore in fear, leaving the two white characters alone.

At this stage, the See Yup Chinese appear in a junk, at first merely to arrange a deal. They will share part of a dead sperm whale they have found if they can use the equipment aboard the *Bertha Miller* to strip the carcass. The appearance of the junk's See Yup crew compares unfavorably with even the Sam Yups.

> Her crew were Chinamen; but such Chinamen! The coolies of the *Bertha Miller* were pampered and effete in comparison. The beach combers, thirteen in number, were a smaller class of men, their faces almost black with tan and dirt. Though they still wore the queue, their heads were not shaven, and rats and mops of stiff black hair fell over their eyes from under their broad, basket-shaped hats.
> They were bare-foot. None of them wore more than two garments—the jeans and the blouse. They were the lowest type of men Wilbur had ever seen. The faces were those of the higher order of anthropid apes: the lower portion— jaws, lips, and teeth—salient; the nostrils opening almost at right angles, the eyes tiny and bright, the forehead seamed

and wrinkled—unnaturally old. Their general expression was one of simian cunning and a ferocity that was utterly devoid of courage.[49]

When the work with the whale is finished, the See Yup leader, Hoang, confronts Moran, the Norwegian, to conclude the deal. Norris provides a spectacle of racial confrontation through Wilbur's Anglo-Saxon eyes and reminds the reader again that although the characters are on the high seas, they represent the American West Coast.

At length, on the afternoon of the third day, the captain of the junk, whose name was Hoang, presented himself upon the quarterdeck. He was naked to the waist, and his bare brown torso was gleaming with oil and sweat. His queue was coiled like a snake around his neck, his hatchet thrust into his belt. The man, the Mongolian, small, wizened, leather-colored, secretive—a strange, complex creature, steeped in all the obscure mystery of the East, nervous, ill at ease; and the girl, the Anglo-Saxon, daughter of the North-man, huge, blonde, big-boned, frank, outspoken, simple of composition, open as the day, bareheaded, her great ropes of sandy hair falling over her breast and almost to the top of her knee-boots. As he looked at the two, Wilbur asked himself where else but in California could such abrupt contrasts occur.[50]

Despite Norris's unfavorable characterization of the Chinese, and the See Yups especially, he acknowledges one good quality in them: "Like all Chinamen, Hoang was true to his promises," and he closes the deal without treachery.[51] Open conflict only occurs after Moran discovers a lump of ambergris in her portion of the whale and tries to keep it all herself. Her refusal to share this treasure angers the pirates, who then take it all. Moran and Wilbur are forced ashore by a leak in the *Bertha Miller*, but the pirate ship is completely destroyed by the same sulfur-bottom whale that damaged the first ship. This leaves the white characters and both Chinese crews stranded separately on the same stretch of Baja California. Norris brings all the characters together for a final confrontation that ranks the three groups according to their human value as he measures them.

The first step toward this confrontation is the reunion of the Sam Yup crew with their former officers. Charlie approaches their camp and conducts his negotiations in a classic pattern of inscrutability and the passive resistance associated sometimes with Black slaves or servants as well as Asian American domestics.

"I come buy one-piece bacon. China boy no hab got."

"We aren't selling bacon to deserters," cried Moran. . . .

"No hab got bacon?" he queried, lifting his eyebrows in surprise.

"Plenty; but not for you."

" . . . I buy um nisi two-piecee tobacco."

"Look," said Wilbur deliberately; "don't you try to flim-flam us, Charlie. We know you too well. You don't want bacon and you don't want tobacco."

"China boy heap plenty much sick. Two boy velly sick. I tink um die pletty soon to-molla. . . you gib me five, seven livel pill. Sabe?"

"I'll tell you what you want," cried Moran, aiming a fore-finger at him, pistol fashion; "you've got a blue funk because those Kai-gingh beachcombers have come into the bay . . . and now you want us to take you home."

"How muchee?"

"A thousand dollars."

"You no hab got livel pill?" inquired Charlie blandly.

Moran turned her back on him. . . .

". . . I gib you ten dollah fo' ten livel pill," said Charlie.

"Will you give us a thousand dollars to set you down in San Francisco?"

Charlie rose. "I go back. I tell um China boy what you say about livel pill. Bime-by I come back."

"That means he'll take our offer back to his friends," said Wilbur, in a low voice.[52]

Charlie's behavior contrasts unfavorably here with Hoang's man-ner when he approached Moran to clinch their deal. Hoang appears with the marks of an active man, sun-bronzed, muscular, sweaty, with his hatchet in his belt and his queue out of the way around his neck. He finishes his business quickly and honestly and then leaves. Charlie is superficially cordial but actually uncooperative, talking in riddles and resisting attempts to make him speak plainly. Though Hoang is more dangerous because of the open and direct threat he poses, Charlie presents the hidden danger of an unknown ally, and a subordinate who retains his own secrets. Ironically, the villain has more admirable qualities than the ally of the protagonists. This is another careful distinction Norris makes to separate the mere undesirables who are on the side of the whites from the truly villainous Chinese who are in-dependent.

Charlie offers one reassuring fact as the Sam Yup crew and their officers stage their attack on the pirate crew. He tells Moran, "One time I fight plenty much in San Flancisco in Washington Stleet. Fight um See Yups."[53] While this is good news at the time, it reiterates the criminal nature of even the Sam Yups. Norris has established that the two groups of Chinese are distinct, with the See Yups lower on the scale of humanity. Now he reminds the reader that the leader of the Sam Yups, while a cook and certainly no pirate, not only can be untrustworthy and deliberately obtuse, but also has a background of street violence. Since Charlie has been presented as the least undesirable of the Chinese, the reader assumes that the others have even worse personal traits and histories.

Moran, Wilbur, and the Sam Yups are victorious in the hand-to-hand battle, but Charlie is mortally wounded. He asks that his $1,500 share of the loot go to an elaborate funeral with four horses, a silver-detailed coffin, a six-piece Chinese band, seven hundred firecrackers, a roast pig, and an abundance of rice and Chinese brandy, "all same Mandarin—all same Little Pete."[54]

Little Pete was the first notorious tong leader, a racketeer in the Chinatown of San Francisco. Charlie's respect for Little Pete and his assumption that Little Pete's funeral was the equal of a mandarin's result logically from his experiences as a tong fighter and opium smoker. These qualities make him a stereotyped Chinatown figure and because he is the leader of the Sam Yups, this image includes them by association.

As a result of the battle, the three groups have established a pecking order. This situation reflects the value judgements that Norris earlier placed on them all: the Sam Yups are superior to the See Yups and the whites are superior to both. Wilbur chastises the captive Hoang:

> I hope this will be a lesson to you. Don't try and get too much next time. Just be content with what is yours by right, or what you are strong enough to keep, and don't try to fight white people. Other coolies, I don't say. But when you try to get the better of white people you are out of your class.[55]

These statements are significant for two reasons. The first is the clear division between the Chinese and the whites, which has been indicated consistently throughout the novel. The two races represent inherently opposed forces as Norris, the naturalist, interprets them. The second is the refusal to criticize the Chinese for fighting among themselves. This lack of concern over intra-Chinese conflict reflects the assumption that the Chinese are mysterious beyond understanding, and that their own affairs can only be left to them. This is the final message of the novel about the Chinese, when Hoang frees himself, kills Moran, and flees into San Francisco with the ambergris.

> Chinatown was his lair; once there and under the protection of his tong, Hoang knew that he was safe. He knew the hiding places that the See Yup Association provided for all its members—hiding places whose very existence was unknown to the police of the White Devil.[56]

In two other early novels by Norris, references to the Chinese appear as a part of life in San Francisco. *Blix* (1898) includes a walk by the two main characters through Chinatown, where they linger for lunch.

> They were in a world of narrow streets, of galleries and over-hanging balconies. Craziest structures, riddled and honeycombed with stairways and passages, shut out the sky, though here and there rose a building of extraordinary richness and most elaborate ornamentation. Color was everywhere. A thousand little notes of green and yellow, of vermilion and sky blue, assaulted the eye. Here it was a glint of cloth or hanging, here a huge scarlet sign lettered with gold, and here a kaleidoscopic effect in the garments of a passer-by. Directly opposite, and two stories above their heads, a sort of huge 'loggia,' one blaze of gilding and crude vermilions, opened in the gray cement of a crumbling facade, like a sudden burst of flame. Gigantic pot-bellied lanterns of red and gold swung from its ceiling, while along its railing stood a row of pots—brass, ruddy bronze, and blue porcelains—from which were growing red, saffron, purple, pink and golden tulips without number. The air was vibrant with unfamiliar noises. From one of the balconies near at hand, though unseen, a gong, a pipe, and some kind of stringed instrument wailed and thundered in unison. There was a vast shuffling of padded soles and a continuous interchange of singsong monosyllables, high-pitched and staccato, while from every hand rose the strange aromas of the East—sandalwood, punk, incense, oil and the smell of mysterious cookery.[57]

This account of the prefire Chinatown in San Francisco is the most descriptive one located for this study. The rich and striking details seem to indicate a firsthand familiarity with the scene on Norris's part,

which would be consistent with his knowledge of his material generally. The sympathetic lyricism of this description does, however, seem at
odds with his treatment of the Chinese as people. It also marks a growing emphasis in American fiction on the exotic view of Chinese culture
as well as on the filth and vice that had been showcased since the early
novels about invasion.

The other references to the Chinese come from a supporting
character named Captain Jack. On one occasion he had hunted sharks
with a Chinese crew in Magdalena Bay, as depicted in Ross Wilbur's
experiences; on another he had smuggled Chinese immigrants across
the Canadian border for thirty dollars a head. Chinese characters are
not a part of the story.

A handful of references to Chinese Californians also appear in
McTeague: A Story of Chinatown (1928), keeping them in the reader's
mind as a part of San Franciscan life. McTeague's mother had worked
with a Chinese cook in a mining camp. Chinese market gardeners appear on the streets every morning, and on the edges of town Chinese
ragpickers go over the refuse heaps. The sentiment toward them, of
course, is still sharply negative, especially on the labor question. One
white character, concerned about the cigar makers' problem, says of
the Chinese, "It's them as is ruining the cause of white labour. They
are, they are for a *fact*. Ah, the rat-eaters! Ah, the white-livered
curs!"[58] Another character, formerly a French laundress, has been put
out of business by Chinese competition. None of these references is important alone, but in a group they constitute an expected part of Norris's San Francisco.

In *Ti: A Story of San Francisco's Chinatown* (1899), Mary E.
Bamford reaches a new level of perception and accuracy in her efforts
to depict the Chinese immigrants. The novel includes detailed descriptions of Chinese clothing, homes, and other cultural materials with frequent illustrations. Her account of the Chinese relating to each other is
anchored on solid characterization that presents individual Chinese as
having their own attitudes, concerns, and beliefs. She perceives them
as a threat only because they are not Christian. The story tells of the
conversion to Christianity of Ti, an eight-year-old Chinese boy living
initially with his father in a Chinese fishing hamlet on the San Francisco Bay.

Bamford refers to Ti's father, aunts, uncles, and friends by name;
the white missionary school teachers are nameless, emphasizing the
division existing between the two groups of people. Ti's white mission
teacher sincerely cares for Ti and her other Chinese students, and Bamford accurately depicts the kind of personal strain and suffering of both

those who convert and their loved ones who do not. Bamford's clear and unquestioned conviction that conversion to Christianity is worth the painful price is perhaps admirable in its faith, but from a neutral standpoint, it seems unfortunate in an author whose understanding of Chinese culture is deep and generally sympathetic.

The relations among the Chinese in the fishing hamlet are generally good, and Ti loves his father and misses his dead mother. One of Bamford's few apparent failures in depicting the Chinese immigrants accurately is her presentation of numerous Chinese families and their children in the hamlet and in San Francisco's Chinatown. In 1900, the ratio of Chinese males to females in the United States simply did not allow families to constitute a major sector of their communities. They played a lesser role in these societies than a reader of Bamford's novel might believe. However, her positive and informed depiction of relationships in extended and nuclear Chinese families is more understanding of the Chinese than the prevailing attitudes of this time and so marks significant progress toward accuracy.

In subtle ways, Bamford introduces her religious bias, her awareness of the antipathy toward the Chinese current in her time, and her knowledge of the problems the Chinese faced in this period. She mentions Christian sayings and values on several occasions, noting that "hither and thither went the ignorant, hard-working Chinese people, who did not know the meaning of them."[59] When white immigration officers arrive in the fishing hamlet, Bamford's unassuming Chinese do not exhibit the hostility or violence that one sees in the work of Atwell Whitney or Frank Norris. She is careful to explain that they do not threaten anyone.

> None of the dwellers in the little hamlet seemed outwardly
> to object to the white men's seeing all they wished to see.
> The Chinese were peaceful, but they did have a desire to
> know what was coming. They knew this unexpected visit
> meant something.[60]

The officials are checking immigration certificates among the Chinese which prove that they have entered the country legally. Ever since 1882, periodic checks for illegal Chinese immigrants had been a fact of life for these communities. This particular investigation requires that all the adults in the fishing hamlet present their certificates if they have them. At this, the Chinese become annoyed and restless. Both their animosity and their reluctance to express it outright to legal authorities are realistic reactions in this time. In addition, Bamford has tied their anger to an event common to their actual experience, in contrast for instance to the See Yup Chinese of Frank Norris, whose viciousness came only from their supposed low status on the evolutionary scale. Norris showed no understanding of their social, economic, or legal concerns. In Bamford's novel, events and behavior have clear logical connections, producing the depth of characterization in her Chinese which is so lacking in works about them by most of her predecessors and contemporaries.

Ti's father has left his immigration certificate in San Francisco, where he thought it would be safer than in the hamlet. The immigration officer places him under arrest and accompanies him and Ti to the city to inspect the certificate. When all is declared well, Ti and his father remain with relatives for Chinatown's festival of "Kwong Goon." This is the Chinese god of war, literature, vengeance, and, most importantly here, of travelers such as immigrants. His name has often been spelled "Kwan Kung" according to the Wade-Giles system of anglicizing Chinese, and is spelled "Guan Gung" in the Pinyin system. In the United States at this time, he was the most important figure in the Chinese pantheon. He is a stern and strict god, in this way more resembling the Jehovah of the Old Testament than a forgiving Jesus. Bamford sees him as the representation of heathen evil.

> Those Chinese who had relatives that had died since the last Kwong Goon festival, brought prayer papers and joss sticks to the altar. Candy, tea, cigars, and dried fish were laid before Kwong Goon. Well might the Chinese fear him, according to their religious belief, for he is the deity who is supposed to devour the bodies of irreligious Chinamen.[61]

Ti is given good reason to be afraid of Guan Gung. His cousin Whan contracts diphtheria and other Cinese claim that this is the punishment of Guan Gung for Whan's mistaking an offering of fish to the god for something to eat. Whan's brother Hop and Ti also catch the disease, however, and Whan and Hop die. Ti questions Guan Gung's judgement for apparently punishing Hop and himself without reason.

Ti's father returns to the fishing hamlet, leaving Ti with his aunt and uncle, who are disconsolate without their sons. Ti becomes caught between a well-meaning white mission teacher and the insistence of his uncle that he pray in the traditional Chinese manner. Ti's uncle is depicted as stubborn and strict, determined that Ti not convert. Ti's father is drowned while catching fish, and when word of this arrives, Ti's uncle convinces Ti that he must worship before the ancestral tablet and make sacrifices or else deprive his father in the spirit world. So far, the uncle is still honorable and considerate and his insistence is clearly derived from his own religious beliefs.

Bamford next develops the uncle's character along lines that do not follow with complete logic what she has already presented. The uncle gambles in Chinatown, losing heavily, and he begins smoking opium. As a result of these dissolute habits he goes bankrupt, loses his store, and sends his wife and Ti to the fishing hamlet to live with another of Ti's uncles. Bamford fails to relate gambling and opium smoking to social and environmental pressures or to have any sympathy with those who have such habits. She only explains that a Chinese gambler, being superstitious, will never read the Bible or any book, because the Chinese word for book, "shü," is a homonym for the word meaning "to lose."[62] She does not specify dialect. This tells the reader why a Chinese gambler may be unlikely to convert to Christianity, but does not back her implication in this part of the novel that non-Christian Chinese are naturally gamblers and opium smokers, whose only chance for recovery from these habits is through conversion to Christianity.

Bamford's description of the Chinatown in San Francisco contains extensive, well-researched details of cultural behavior as well as physical appearance. Her accounts of a gambling den, a raid by the police, and an opium factory are all convincing. She also describes long passageways under and through the buildings, with locked gates to prevent unwanted visitors. The image of Chinatowns as urban mysteries with secret catacombs and hidden grottoes is prevalent during this period, to be challenged later as sensational rumor. While Bamford's description is convincing, the work is a novel and makes no claim that she actually saw such passageways.

In the fishing hamlet, Ti and his aunt find life very difficult. The uncle with whom they now live beats Ti into worshipping the traditional gods. His aunt, who has been leaning toward Christianity, burns her picture of the Goddess of Mercy and other materials for traditional worship. She loses the goodwill of her neighbors for this and when a fire breaks out in the community six months later, she is blamed for bringing down the retribution of the Goddess for burning her picture. Ti and his aunt flee to the protection of missionaries in San Francisco, where Ti's former mission teacher arranges for Ti to learn a trade from a Christian Chinese shoemaker. Ti decides to take after his teacher and carry the word of Christianity to all the Chinese American children in California when he grows up. His teacher concludes,

"The poor little Chinese children! Often the parents won't believe us teachers when we tell them of Jesus and his love, but sometimes they will believe their children when they carry home the gospel we have taught them. Oh, if only there were more teachers to tell the story to the poor little Chinese children! Dear Lord, send forth more laborers unto this, thine harvest!"[63]

Bamford's novel presents the most realistic and sympathetic fictional view of the Chinese in the United States so far since the early work of Bret Harte. Unlike Harte, she investigated Chinese cultural values and attitudes, which was probably easier for her in a time when the frontier was closing and becoming less violent. Also, the passage of time had brought about increased contact and accommodation among people of different cultures who had entered the West Coast. Only her missionary bias prevents her novel from being a wholly perceptive and honest account of the Chinese communities in the San Francisco Bay area. That bias, however, remains firm, even though she sees how much personal suffering the efforts of missionaries caused.

The Shadow of Quong Lung (1900), by Dr. C. W. Doyle, can be viewed either as a series of five short stories, or as a composite novel of episodes related through the featured villain of the book, Chinatown crime lord Quong Lung. The author, who lived from 1852 to 1903, was born and raised in India before studying medicine in England and practicing there for thirteen years. He lived in Santa Cruz and San Francisco from 1888 until his death.[64] He has created a prototypical Fu Manchu like Robert W. Chambers's Yue-Laou; the stories, or episodes, involve the activities of Quong Lung from the viewpoint of his victims. The Chinatown residents here are more carefully characterized than those of William Norr, but they are more cruel and ruthless than even those of Chester Bailey Fernald. Doyle's attitude toward the people of Chinatown is expressed clearly in the preface, where he says prophetically of San Francisco's Chinatown, "Of course the best thing to do with Chinatown would be to burn it down; but the scheme is too Utopian to be discussed in a mere preface."[65]

Quong Lung is a graduate of Yale, a barrister of London's Inner Temple, and the greatest force in Chinatown's tongs and crime in general. In "The Illumination of Lee Moy," Lee Moy is the blind son of a mother who keeps him drunk to disguise his blindness from others, who believe he is clumsy from alcohol. When she learns that his blindness is a prelude to death from a rare disease, she kills him herself in order to be merciful. At this juncture, Lee Moy's father wants to return to China, but he is deeply in debt to the stern and ruthless Quong Lung. He pays his debt by selling both his store and his extremely attractive wife to Quong Lung. She is a well-paying investment for him, and when a young white female acquaintance asks her whereabouts, he warns her not to interfere.

> Suey Yep is one of my chattels; never forget that fact! Any interference with my property by you, or by anyone else, would result in the sudden and irreparable depreciation in value of that property. Whatever my shadow falls on withers—and besides being a Master of Arts, I am a Master of Accidents![66]

"The Shadow of Quong Lung" is next. Quong Lung exploits the skill of a scrivener who not only owes him money but is implicated in a past murder of which Quong Lung has knowledge. Their attention is turned to the attractive wife of Ho Chung, a Chinatown goldsmith. She is still in China with a newborn son. They learn of her only when Ho Chung enlists the scrivener's services because, except for some spoken phrases, he and his wife speak different dialects. The scribe agrees to translate their letters. From San Francisco, Quong Lung arranges to have the child murdered and then the scribe forges a letter from Ho Chung directing his distraught wife to join Quong Lung's wife in Shanghai. They arrange for her to come to San Francisco with Ho Chung's knowledge, but the scribe alters the date of her arrival in his translation of her letter to Ho Chung.

Doyle refers to the multitude of Chinese dialects and establishes that Ho Chung must rely on the scrivener for translations of letters from his wife. Doyle is apparently unaware that the dialects represent differences in the spoken language; written Chinese is basically one language. If Doyle had made Ho Chung illiterate or semiliterate, his use of the scribe's skill would also have allowed the plot to proceed along the same line; however, as given, the story indicates a lack of knowledge on Doyle's part about the Chinese language.

Quong Lung's influence insures the wife's entry into the United States; she is given an identity as the Californian daughter of the scribe, thereby satisfying the requirements of the Chinese Exclusion Act. In a description of Quong Lung's tong and henchmen, Doyle identifies the worst criminal element in Chinatown as See Yups, as Frank Norris did, though, like Norris, Doyle does not indicate whether or not he understands that the term refers to a group of dialects and those who speak them.

Ho Chung's wife is imprisoned by Quong Lung's underlings when she reaches San Francisco. Ho Chung learns the truth of the situation and knifes the scribe. He then locates his wife but cannot free her. They express their love for each other before Ho Chung stabs her to death to keep her from Quong Lung. He then attempts to kill the villain, but fails and dies as a result.

Ho Chung and his wife are the only Chinese characters in the book who exhibit the normal, decent human qualities of affection and responsibility. They are average Chinese immigrants who fall victim to Quong Lung in complete innocence. They are unfortunately the exception to Doyle's characters; all the rest are criminals in conflict with one another.

"A Civil Death in Chinatown" refers to a silent treatment invoked as punishment against an alleged, but framed, traitor to Quong Lung's tong. The traitor is completely ignored; any who break the code are marked for death. Quong Lung's reason for framing him is to separate him from his lovely young wife. She is told that her husband has left her for another woman and is lured to Quong Lung's home in her grief. Her husband searches for her frantically but falls dead of a knife wound just as he finds her. Though wronged in the story, he is a criminal informer for Quong Lung and as a See Yup tong member is counted in the ranks of Chinatown's dregs.

In "The Wings of Lee Toy," Quong Lung assigns an underling named Lee Toy to kidnap the small son of Captain Loomis, the city police officer officially in charge of Chinatown. He has offended Quong Lung, who now seeks revenge. The first step is to replace Captain Loomis's regular Chinese domestic with Lee Toy, who soon runs away with the child. However, before he gets very far, he is struck down by a cable car. Captain Loomis, who does not realize what was happening, takes Lee Toy into his home to take care of him. His kindness causes Lee Toy to change sides and become the child's faithful guardian. Eventually, Quong Lung burns the Loomis home and Lee Toy falls to his death while saving the child. He dies a hero, representing an evil figure in whom good finally triumphs.

The final story, "The Seats of Judgement," contains the death of Quong Lung. He has a white classmate from Yale, an electrical engineer, build an electric chair in order to kill a traitorous tong brother. His classmate, whom Quong Lung introduced to opium, is suffering from the debilitating effects of the drug to which Doyle says the Chinese are immune. He decides to turn Quong Lung over to the law. As a result Quong Lung is surprised by the entry of his old classmate and a police detective just as he is preparing to remove the body from his electric chair. He accidentally falls against it himself and dies. Quong Lung has had his way with all the people of Chinatown, but dies as soon as a white man moves against him.

Many of the criminal activities that Doyle presents in his Chinatown are matters of historical record. The practices of the criminal element were acknowledged symptoms of the ghetto economy in the Chinatowns. However, excepting only Ho Chung and his wife, Doyle presents a Chinatown exclusively inhabited by the cruel, ruthless, and sly, without balancing images of positive qualities. Historically, large social and economic forces influenced Chinatown life, but Doyle does not concern himself with these. This book exhibits strong naturalist influence in its assumption that race and behavior are inextricably connected, but it contains no clear expressions of this belief.

A children's book, Hezekiah Butterworth's *Little Sky-High or the Surprising Doings of Washee-Washee Wang* (1901) is not about a Chinatown or the Yellow Peril, but both lie in the background. Sky-High is a Chinese boy who has been sent by his father from China to Boston to learn about life in the United States. He is sent by an American consul to the home of the Van Burens, a wealthy American family with generations-old involvement in the China trade. His courtesy, intelligence, lavish gifts, and fancy Chinese clothes win him affection and high regard in the family, where one of the two children address him as "wang," or king, because of his reserved but friendly demeanor and his obvious wealth. Butterworth's positive tone toward him, however, is also patronizing. Sky-High is introduced more in the manner of a doll than a person, as young Lucy Van Buren says,

> "Oh, mother! Where did you get him? His eyes are like two almonds, and his braided hair dangles away down almost to the floor, and there are black silk tassels on the end of it, and kitty is playing with them . . ."[67]

The term *Chinaman* is used casually through most of the book as the accepted term for the Chinese, but the first reference of this sort is an odd amalgamation of words: "He's a little Chineseman!"[68] Sky-High is a heathen, but little attempt is made to convert him. He is taken to church, has Christmas explained to him, and is allowed to keep a "wan," or charm against evil spirits, over the door to his room. The mistress of the family concedes this last point when he asks about a charm over the stable.

> "Yes," said Mrs. Van Buren, "while the horseshoe remains over the stable to keep witches out, you may let the wan stay. You have just as much right to your superstitions as we do to ours."[69]

Sky-High does face initial hostility from strange white children, even in Boston. His activities with the family are those of a houseboy, and his ironing all the laundry earns him the name "Washee-Washee Wang." The Irish cook Nora is first ornery, then civil, and finally kind to him, the last change occurring after he gives her an expensive Christmas present. The white boys throw dirt and sticks at him, but Lucy and her brother Charlie protect him from them and eventually win them over to a friendly attitude. This is the only evidence Butterworth gives of the hostility that created and maintained the Chinatowns in this period. Sky-High is the rich offspring of a mandarin in Manchuria who shares nothing on a personal level with the laborers of Guangdung (Kwangtung) and their descendants. Butterworth's lack of understanding about the realities of Chinese life and American working-class life in general comes clear in one line: "No doubt a working-boy can rise in China the same as in our land!"[70] The story has a fairy-tale ending, when the Van Buren family travels to China at the same time Sky-High returns home. He returns their hospitality lavishly and they find that his father is a true prince of the Manchu Dynasty, making Sky-High a real *wang* after all. His father is pleased with the closeness between the Van Burens and his son, apparently not caring that a scion of the Imperial House has been a domestic servant for a family of commoners. On the surface, Butterworth's treatment of Sky-High is culturally accurate and affectionate. At the same time, an assumption of white racial superiority and a resulting condescension toward the Chinese are faint but unmistakable, suggesting influence from missionary writers like Hosmer and Bamford.

William E. S. Fales, author of a short-story collection titled *Bits of Broken China* (1902), apparently lived in China for a time, as his book is dedicated "To my friends of the China coast, where I passed many happy years. . . ."[71] His stories about the Chinatown of New York contain an unusual mixture of sympathy for the viewpoint of his subjects with stereotyped depictions of them and their activities. Two of the stories will be discussed here. In his introduction, he argues against the established symbols of the Yellow Peril by emphasizing similarities.

> The grotesque pictures of Western writers which represent the Chinese as monsters of iniquity and marvels of Machiavellian craft are about as true to fact as the concept of the little Chinese girl in Chao-chao-fu who asked an American consul: "Won't you please spit fire at my naughty cat?". . . When it comes to the last analysis, the mandarin is indistinguishable from the university man, the Canton merchant

from his New York confrère and the good fellow of the Celestial Empire from his colleagues of the great republic.[72]

The metaphor of the title, suggesting that American Chinatowns are simply transplanted shards of the mother country, reveals an important assumption behind these stories: Chinese immigrants and their offspring are not Americans, but still foreigners.

The protagonist in "Temptation of Li Li" is the first of Fales's Chinese characters who is not a crook. Li Li is a clerk in a Chinese lottery who does not like his work. He is learning English from a white woman,

> an old maid, named Miss King, whose chief dream was to make Li into a devout Christian. Once she had invited him to her house, far up on Madison Avenue, where she lived with her bachelor brother. Li called and was warmly received by his teacher, but was snubbed and almost insulted by Mr. King himself. The poor woman apologized to the Chinaman for her brother's discourtesy and almost cried when Li, with an expressionless countenance, asked if her brother was a Christian.[73]

Li Li happens to live in a room near the quarters of two white thieves. When they steal an immense booty from the Kings, Li steals it himself and prepares to go to China, where he could live comfortably until his death. However, he recognizes the loot and returns it to his teacher instead, saying, "Miss King, I bring you back your jewels and your bonds because you are a very good woman and a good Buddhist, just the same as a Chinaman."[74] Mr. King apologizes for his earlier treatment of Li and gives Li a gift of jewelry and cash which allows him to retire to Canton after all.

The last story, "The Turning of the Worm," involves an interracial marriage. A white couple, Bella Tillman and Diamond Harry, lead a fast and exciting life in the Tenderloin until Harry deserts her, leaving her broke. Bella takes a job sewing piecework near Chatham Square and moves into a building nearby. One of her neighbors in the building is Lee Yu, an employee in the Wang Hi Chong & Co. banking house. Lee Yu woos her with generous gifts and kindness, and she accepts his eventual marriage proposal without hesitation. Even his generosity, however, cannot hold her interest.

> He was a devoted husband, manifesting his affection by a steady stream of gifts. Before a year had rolled by, Bella was better off than she had ever been in her life. She had a fine

wardrobe, plenty of jewelry and at least a hundred dollars in cash. She ought to have been happy, but her nature was a mass of contradiction, and, in spite of her surroundings, she looked yearningly back to the old days when she and Diamond Harry burned the midnight oil in the Tenderloin district.[75]

Bella runs into a destitute Harry on the street and runs away to live with him again. However, she is supporting them with the money and gifts from Lee Yu, and after three months, Harry absconds a second time, taking all her valuables. Bella, sick with typhoid, returns to Lee Yu. He cares for her dutifully, brings her gifts of fruit and flowers, and mystifies her with his kindness. When she is well, however, he dismisses her:

> "I used to love you very much, Bella, but that was a long time ago. . . . You may be in need, and you may be in trouble, so now that you are going away and you will never come back, you will take this money, so as to be happy until something happens.". . . Then, clasping his own hands, he bowed with that unfathomable dignity which marks the Oriental, and remained with his head bent and his eyes fixed upon the floor until she had crossed the threshold and passed out of sight.[76]

Lee Yu is the only Chinatown resident in the book with no activities or interest in the world of crime. Fales's other Chinese figures are always portrayed with some realistic human traits and with sympathy for their viewpoints. However, all but Lee Yu and Li Li are thieves, killers, or traders in illegal drugs or alcohol; Li Li is ready to steal, stopping only when he realizes that his prospective booty belongs to his friend and teacher. Lee Yu alone is an honest, serious member of society. Fales does well by him, contrasting his standard of behavior sharply with those of Bella and Diamond Harry; unfortunately, the rest of the book's characters represent only partial progress, where the criminals of Chinatown are seen sympathetically, but still as evil and pervasive in Chinatown. The stories do not connect the pressures of racism, both legislated and social, to the kind of lives these people of the Chinese ghetto are leading. Like Fernald's fiction, these stories have the qualities of fiction in the realist school, but with unreliable information.

In *A Chinese Quaker: An Unfictitious Novel* (1902), Nellie Blessing Eyster offers a rambling account of San Francisco's Chinatown through the eyes of a Quaker woman from Indiana. The author, born in Maryland in 1836, lived in San Jose, San Francisco, and Berkeley from 1876 until her death in 1922 and was herself involved in mission work as well as in other reform causes like the WCTU.[77] Her novel includes both the evil, sensationalized aspects of Chinatown and the finer members of the community. The viewpoint character, Wilhelmina Proctor, arrives in San Francisco in 1884 and is appalled both at her first sight of a Chinese scavenger and by a newspaper account of Chinatown crime.

> Her repugnance was involuntary and natural, for her gaze was fixed at that moment upon a Chinese scavenger with his two huge baskets suspended at either end of a long bamboo pole which was balanced across his shoulders. With a long-pronged fork he deftly piled some city rubbish into the basket—then turned to pastures new. He was an uncanny object to the eyes of a cultivated woman—there was no denying the fact. His queue was wound around his head, and covered with an old black felt hat from beneath whose rim strands of long, wiry, black hair straggled in uneven lengths over his thin, yellow and collarless neck. His dark blue cotton blouse was patched and dirty, and his small, thin hands, like claws, prodded here and there in ash-heaps and in gutters for bits of paper, strings, rags, and small bottles. His face, though young, was as devoid of expression as that of a wooden doll, and as placid as the surface of a stagnant mill-pond. . . . By a singular coincidence her eyes fell immediately upon a four-column article, profusely illustrated, headed: CHINESE SOCIETIES. THE HIGH-BINDERS IN SAN FRANCISCO. It seemed a contribution ready to be emptied into the channel of her present thought. She read, at first, with a curiosity to know its meaning, and then was led on through its entire length by the fascination which the horrible often has over the most sensitive minds.[78]

Wilhelmina's newfound prejudice is assailed by her brother Abner, who urges her to meet the residents of Chinatown herself.

> "Thee is, like so many others, measuring what is perhaps the most ancient civilization in the world by the standard of Christianized America. As for the tirades of the newspapers against the poor Coolies, who have sought and found a home on this Pacific Coast, and who are aiding by their

> honest and incessant labor to develop it, thee knows that in
> the main, political ambition, and ignorance just such as
> thine, lie at the root of it all.[79]

Wilhelmina rapidly changes her opinion of many of the Chinatown
residents, partly through her meeting and teaching of a young boy
named Tong Sing Wing, as well as through knowing a young Christian
Chinese merchant named Li Jue, who may be the first adult Chinese
immigrant male in American fiction to receive a complimentary
physical description.

> At that moment there approached with rapid step another
> young man, about eighteen years of age, whose face was as
> beautiful as an octoroon girl's. His complexion was a rich
> blending of the rose and olive, and his skin as fine in texture
> and as smooth as ivory. His eyes were large, soft and dark,
> and his nose and mouth beautifully shaped and expressive of
> great refinement. . . .
> "A Chinese Adonis!" she mentally exclaimed.[80]

The early plot involves Wilhelmina's instruction of Sing in English
and Christianity, in exchange for closer friendship with him and his
Chinese friends, who are taken aback at being treated by her as equals.
She learns both about the more respectable Chinese, including merchants, a Christian reverend, and students, and about the unsavory,
such as traders in slave women and opium. Eyster associates the prostitution with traditional Chinese polygamy, recognizing neither that
such polygamy was only for the wealthy, nor the unbalanced sex ratio
in American Chinatowns. Eyster also has Sing tell Wilhelmina that the
Chinese certainly do eat rats, supporting an old rumor about the
Chinese in the United States. Eventually Sing comes to live with his
tutor because, according to Eyster, Chinese families have no concern
for affection but only for obedience and respect, enforced through
punishment.

The plot gradually moves from Wilhelmina's education about
Chinatown to the specific plight of one slave girl and the efforts of
Wilhelmina and her friends to rescue her. Wilhelmina learns that
unscrupulous highbinders are behind the trade in Chinese females.

> The object of nearly all Chinese slavery is to keep the victim
> in a life of shame when womanhood is reached. If the slave
> resists her fate, all the tortures of the Inquisition are
> resorted to by her cruel masters, till she yields herself, body
> and soul. Hundreds of Chinese women, in California alone,

to-day, deceived by the promise of getting rich husbands in that fabled America of which many have heard, reach here only to be sold and re-sold into situations from which only death, or violence, can release them.[81]

After the rescue, Wilhelmina and her brother move to a rural area, far from the ghetto. Sing later studies mining engineering at Berkeley, where he learns of an effort by Chinatown merchants, the Chinese consulate, the Six Companies, and the city police to destroy the tongs. Finally, he goes to China to work as an engineer, associating with mandarins and intellectuals with Western educations. While Eyster's final vision of China is one of optimism and respect for the high culture, she writes of the Chinese Americans through Sing when he observes, "how the cultivated Chinese of my native land are misrepresented by the poor peasants who come to America and there display their ignorance and poverty!"[82]

This novel wanders in its attempt to include a general education about Chinatown as well as a specific story about Sing and the rescue of the slave girl. The mixed attitudes of the missionaries who have learned about the Chinese are shown well in Wilhelmina's exposure to the good elements of Chinatown as well as the bad. A new respect for the Chinese is emerging here, but unfortunately it is associated primarily with the aristocracy of China and China itself, not with the broader spectrum of Chinese and Chinese Americans. Eyster's criticism of the people of Chinatown also seems to justify the Exclusion Acts to some extent, though some of her information about them is false. Two such items are her assertion that they eat rats and that Chinese families feel no affection. Her most valuable contribution is that the concern Wilhelmina and her brother have for the Chinese is informed and genuine, not a combination of affection and condescension.

Jack London wrote two stories about Chinese immigrants in the San Francisco Bay area in which his kind of naturalism is apparent in his racism. First published in *Youth's Companion*, these stories are included in his collection *Tales of the Fish Patrol* (1905). London also wrote a short story dealing with the threat of invasion by China of the rest of the world, and two short stories featuring Chinese immigrants in Hawaii.

The villains in the two stories in *Tales of the Fish Patrol* are Chinese shrimp catchers. They are pictured as wild and nasty, sailing around the San Francisco Bay in their junks. Their nets not only bring in shrimp but also tiny fish. The fish patrol is supposed to protect these fish to insure a future supply of adult fish and so they sometimes try to catch and arrest the crews of the junks. In "White and Yellow," the narrator and one white friend arrest several crews but have to sail an overcrowded ship across the Bay in rough weather. The villain is an evil-looking, pockmarked captain called Yellow Handkerchief by the narrator. Yellow Handkerchief and his fellows are depicted as cowards in a balanced confrontation but as vicious if the situation favors them. Yellow Handkerchief feigns honesty and attemps to escape, but fails. In "Yellow Handkerchief," the fish patrol again captures him. This time, however, he escapes with the narrator as his prisoner. Yellow Handkerchief attempts to kill him, but the narrator escapes unharmed. When the narrator is being carried off by Yellow Handkerchief and his crew, his fears are dictated by his racial beliefs.

> What was to happen next I could not imagine, for the Chinese were a different race from mine, and from what I knew I was confident that fair play was no part of their make-up. . . . It was very evident that he advocated doing away with me and that they were afraid of the consequences. I was familiar enough with the Chinese character to know that fear alone restrained them.[83]

London's Chinese shrimp catchers are villains whose violent tendencies are racial traits. The stories are short adventure tales, neither complex nor very interesting except as indicators of London's attitudes toward the Chinese at the time. A year after these appeared, he wrote a short story called "The Unparalleled Invasion," (1906), which presents once again the idea of China invading the rest of the world. His socialism is not evident here and he spends no more time than Oto Mundo did discussing the dangers that Chinese labor poses for the white worker. Perhaps, writing two decades after Whitney, Woltor, and Dooner, London considered the argument to be common knowledge. Also like Mundo, London does not spend much time discussing the Chinese in the United States, being content to establish the imminent danger that China presents to the U.S. militarily. Character traits involving morality are ignored altogether; London's thesis is simply that China has become, by 1976, a military threat invincible to all conventional methods of war, by virtue of a gigantic population.

In recounting the transformation of a decrepit, agricultural China of the nineteenth century into the powerful, highly technological China of the twentieth, London gives his one acknowledgment to Chinese labor, in terms of value to China: "The Chinese was the perfect type of industry. He had always been that. For sheer ability to work, no worker in the world could compare with him."[84] In large numbers, such workers are an even greater asset.

China becomes a world power through a combination of Chinese diligence and the technological ability that Japan had already brought to Asia at the time of London's writing. Neither moral nor economic issues are raised, being immaterial. China now poses a tremendous migratory invasion threat to the rest of the world merely on the basis of population.

> There was no way to dam up the over-spilling monstrous flood of life. War was futile. China laughed at a blockade of her coasts. She welcomed invasion. In her capacious maw was room for all the hosts of earth that could be hurled at her. And in the meantime her flood of yellow life poured out and on over Asia.[85]

The conventional methods of war against China all prove ineffective, being unable to kill fast enough. So an American scientist named Jacobus Laningdale devises a method for killing faster. Sealed glass tubes contaminated with every known form of plague are dropped from balloon ships and shot onto the coasts from warships. The Chinese might survive one plague, but not scores of them. Disease, disorder, and famine prevent the Chinese from acting with strength and decision. The West masses huge armies on the borders of China and traps the Chinese and their plagues within their own boundaries. A year later, careful expeditions into China find only a few roving survivors, who are immediately executed. The Chinese people are completely eliminated.

Perhaps in recognition of the American bicentennial, though it is not mentioned, a concert of Western nations organizes the resettlement of China, filling it with a mix of European immigrants in the manner that they had settled the Western Hemisphere, only this time with no fear of competing with Chinese immigration. The conflict between the races which began at Atwell Whitney's Yarbtown ends in genocide for the Chinese and a substantial tribute to the Americans, in the formation of a newer version of the United States where China used to be. London's perception of the threat China mounts in this story and his willingness to destroy all the Chinese follow logically from the attitude he expressed toward them in the stories of the fish patrol.

London wrote two stories about Chinese immigrants to Hawaii, however, that are surprisingly sympathetic toward them. In these apparent palinodes, both protagonists are poor laborers who prosper in Hawaii. Originally published in *Woman's Magazine*, "Chun Ah Chun" is included in *The House of Pride* (1912), one of several collections of

London's stories about the Pacific Islands.[86] Chun Ah Chun comes to Hawaii as a contract laborer, and after serving out his term under the contract goes into a variety of businesses for himself. He begins by investing in an import firm, taking a job as a cook until the firm prospers. His wealth grows quickly when he begins to import Chinese contract labor himself. Eventually his millions are beyond reckoning and he has a hand in dealings of all kinds. He marries a Hawaiian citizen who has not only ancestors from Hawaii, but also from England, New England, Italy, and Portugal. With her Chun Ah Chun produces fifteen children who are, London calculates, one-thirtysecond Polynesian, one-sixteenth Italian, one-sixteenth Portuguese, one-half Chinese, and eleven thirty-seconds Anglo-Saxon. Chun Ah Chun carefully introduces his three sons into his businesses and arranges grand marriages for his daughters by providing sizeable dowries, the largest of which is three hundred thousand dollars for the oldest. Eventually Chun Ah Chun, content with peace and quiet, retires alone to his home city of Amoy, China, which London mistakenly identifies as a province. Meanwhile, his wife and offspring quarrel and sue each other over their respective fortunes.

London includes two concerns in this story which indicate a greater understanding of the Chinese immigrant experience than his earlier stories revealed. The first is Chun Ah Chun's concern over communicating with his children. He does not mind that they are Christian and he gladly pays for their educations at Oxford, Harvard, Yale, Vassar, Wellesley, and Bryn Mawr. The result, however, is that they have values and habits he does not share and so he feels alienated from them in Hawaii, where they are more at home than he. The phenomenon of immigrant parents not completely understanding their children raised in a new land is a common one, and London describes it effectively. His second concern is racism against the Chinese, which he himself seems to express in the earlier stories. At the end of this one, Chun Ah Chun returns to Amoy through Macao, where he is rudely refused a room at the fanciest European hotel for racial reasons. Chun Ah Chun has a means of responding that most Chinese laborers and ex-laborers lack: he leaves, buys the hotel, and returns to fire summarily the offensive management. This incident is unrealistic, or at least very uncommon, but the important point is that London's sentiment is now with Chun Ah Chun.

"The Tears of Ah Kim," reprinted from *Cosmopolitan*, is included in another collection of London's tales of Hawaii, *On the Makaloa Mat* (1919).[87] Ah Kim is a towing laborer on the Yangtze River before coming to Hawaii as a contract laborer. The story has two distinct subplots from this point. One follows Ah Kim's economic progress from a laborer's wages for five years to modest prosperity, at which time he brings his mother from China to join him. Now that he has money, marriage is a desired and possible step, but remains a point of contention with his mother, who disapproves of his choice. He marries only after his mother dies, when he is past fifty. The second subplot is actually a retold Chinese fable that begins after Ah Kim's mother joins him. She frequently canes her son for various mistakes to teach him to live better. The beatings are extremely hard and continue as the two of them grow older. The neighbors marvel not that Ah Kim accepts it as a filial son should but that he never sheds tears, no matter how much he suffers. Finally, on one occasion, he begins to cry as his mother strikes him but he refuses to explain why this time is any different. His mother dies soon after and he reveals that he cried not from pain, but from sorrow; the caning no longer hurt because his mother was too old and weak to strike forcefully. The fable exhibits filial devotion and London recreates it faithfully. At least one critic has psychoanalyzed London on the basis of this relationship between son and mother, apparently unaware of the story's origin in fable.[88] In both of these stories, London depicts the Chinese immigrants as intelligent, decent individuals with a cultural background distinct from those of the white and Polynesian people of Hawaii, but not evil in itself. Two possible reasons may lie behind the difference between his depictions of these characters and the shrimp catchers he presented as such villains.

One possibility, of course, is that London's attitudes toward the Chinese, especially as immigrants, had fundamentally changed. If he had become more understanding of the racism Chinese immigrants faced and also of them as thinking individuals, he might logically write of them with more sympathy. Possibly in addition to this, or even instead, London may have seen Hawaii in an entirely different light from the West Coast of the United States. He may have felt no threat from the economic success of Chinese immigrants in Hawaii because it was not part of the United States proper in his time, and was still largely populated by native Hawaiians. The success of the Chinese there would not rock the establishment of white plantation owners and traders nor displace any white workers, since there were very few. London was at times a follower of Herbert Spencer, and critic Earle Labor gives a concise summary of London's pertinent attitudes: "A humanitarian with profound compassion for the underdog, regardless of color or race, he nevertheless believed in the supremacy of the Anglo-Saxon race."[89]

E. Spence de Pue's *Dr. Nicholas Stone* (1905) is a detective novel that epitomizes the exploitation of Chinatown's lurid reputation.[90] Three white protagonists visit the Chinatown of San Francisco because the white villain has apparently hired some underlings from Chinatown. Chinatown itself is a "world of dreadful odors and scurrying coolies. . . . A long narrow hall stretched before us. On either side, at short intervals doors were open, others shut, and everywhere was the odor of opium and punk."[91]

Two of the white characters end their first visit by escaping a cleaver attack and climbing through a window. The two male protagonists undertake a second visit in search of revenge which ends in the temple of the Sam Yups. One of the white heroes is slashed by a knife here in a violent confrontation, intensified by great billows of smoke in the temple as it seems to burn. Chinatown and its residents have no purpose in the story except to provide some easy suspense and violence through the use of stereotyped tong killers.

Helen Green's *At the Actor's Boarding House* (1906) is a collection of short stories that first appeared in *The Morning Telegraph*. It contains sixty stories, all of which are no more than a few pages long. Six of the stories deal with New York's Chinatown, though its residents play only marginal roles. The stories are intended as exposés similar to the fiction of William Norr. Green was twenty-six when the book was published, with a life of adventure and action behind her that already had included horse breeding, mining, prospecting, and writing. She had firsthand knowledge of Chinatown, but it was the knowledge of a hostile outsider. Most of the stories in the volume concern vaudeville troupes at the Maison de Shine, and the stories set in Chinatown are about white Americans, some of them actors. Two of them will characterize the whole group.

"The Finish of Daffy the Dip" takes the reader into an opium den. A couple of white tourists, certain that they cannot see the real Chinatown without a guide, offer the opium addict Daffy two dollars to show them an opium den. He takes them to a partitioned-off section of a laundry run by Canton Willie and his employee, Charlie Lee. "Canton Willie was very polite. He wore American clothes and much jewelry and had a familiar, sociable air that shocked the female visitor."[92] Daffy promptly lies down for a smoke, but the man he brought in offers to buy him food and tell him where he could go to be cured. Daffy is not interested and, in anger, the tourist tells Canton Willie to throw him out or be raided. Daffy is ejected, soon to be arrested for vagrancy and to die in prison. Green offers the moral that "charity applied with the axe is bad business."[93]

"The Emperor's Pipe" begins with a group of white tourists

following a guide through Chinatown. Some of them, from Kansas City, leave the group to explore on their own. In a saloon, a white lookout for a Chinese opium den offers to take them for a visit to the place above a Chinese restaurant. He has them watch another white employee of the den smoke, who afterward spins a tall tale about the pipe he has used. Claiming that it once belonged to the emperor of China, he declares that it is worth at least fifty dollars. The tourists bargain him down to twenty and the story ends with him ordering another pipe from the Chinese doorkeeper for the next mark.

Green's presentation of Chinatown and its influence on white Americans is a clear assertion of the dangers of allowing Chinese immigration and settlement. Her images of Chinatown and Chinese Americans are not at all original, but her emphasis on white drug addicts and petty crooks who are part of this community indicates a belief that the influence of Chinatown is noxious and spreading. She is consciously muckraking, but her work is flawed like Norr's by her failure to relate social conditions to politics and economics. All the many tales of drugs and violence in Chinatown by other authors suggest a less serious threat to white society than Green's handful of short pieces.

A novel entitled *Ah Moy: The Story of a Chinese Girl* (1908), by Lu Wheat, details the life of a girl in China, born in 1880, who at age twenty is sold into slavery and taken to San Francisco.[94] Of the novel's 154 pages, only the last 30 take place in the U.S., though the most important events occur there. The bulk of the novel describes Ah Moy's childhood in the northern province of Honan, China, with a particular emphasis on the hardships caused by the role of females in traditional Chinese society. Ah Moy's parents clearly love their three daughters and Wheat is careful to cite the social system, and not individuals, as the cause of their suffering. This suffering includes female infanticide and the selling of daughters among the poor, the binding of daughters' feet among the wealthier, and the general preference of parents for sons over daughters.

Wheat dedicates the novel to Wu Ting Fang, a Chinese diplomat who spent many years in the United States, and to Herbert Giles, professor of Chinese in Cambridge, England, who had a part in developing the Wade-Giles system of romanizing the Chinese language. Her novel is full of social and physical details within China, including many footnotes explaining customs to the American reader. She apparently knew something of Chinese society as well as of Chinese American society, though one might guess that Wu and Giles aided her research. At the same time, Wheat views Chinese social customs through unmistakably Western eyes; while the pain and crippling discomfort of foot-binding, for instance, is unarguable, the comments on the subject from Ah Moy's mother seem oddly pedantic for a character raised within Chinese society.

> The same questions, and many more, Ah Moy put to her mother, who answered with sadness in her tone,
> "Yes, yes; it is the custom, and women have little voice in the matter."
> "Women must obey the man of their family, whether they wish to do so or not," she again continued. . . .
> "Yes, yes; she is strong and if it must be done—it must be done," and casting a pathetic glance at her own crippled feet, she hobbled out of the room.[95]

Later in the novel, Ah Moy's father comes into contact with the efforts of Europeans and Americans in China to discourage the practice of foot-binding. He also meets other Chinese fathers who doubt its desirability. The above scene, however, takes place before non-Chinese values have reached the family. Traditionally, this practice was considered a sign of prosperity, since working women needed normal feet to do their labor, and it indicated the economic and social status of the women who had it done.

Famine and the Boxer Rebellion threaten to destroy Ah Moy's family. Her two older sisters have already married and left home, but her parents find that they can only support one child. Since Ah Moy's brother can continue his father's line of descent, they decide they must sell Ah Moy, whose beauty and bound feet will bring a good price. Wheat presents this decision as difficult and painful for all concerned.

> With slow and faltering step, Ching Fo approached his daughter, whom he found seated upon a bench at the side of the monastery. When he reached the spot, he laid his hand almost reverently upon her head, and said, with painful emotion,
> "Daughter, all my life I have revered the gods and have believed in the spirits of my ancestors. Yet, at this moment, I can see but one malicious monster ruling the world. Driven by his evil hand, I am compelled to say that while thou art my beloved daughter, and thy mother and I bless the day that thou didst enter our unworthy home, I see no other way to tide over the distress into which we have fallen than to sell thee to a slave-dealer."[96]

A merchant and slave dealer named Quong Lung buys Ah Moy.

Her father disconsolately explains that he has not been able to obtain the usual clause guaranteeing that she will only be sold as a wife to a rich man. He gives her a prized family knife for protection.

Quong Lung takes Ah Moy and a Eurasian girl named Wing on his ship first to Shanghai, but the end of the famine has lowered prices. He takes them aboard a ship for San Francisco where prices will be higher due to the unbalanced male/female ratio in the Chinatowns. Ah Moy is given a fake passport and coaching to get her through immigration; Wing, being half-white, is expected to enter without serious trouble. However, on board with them are American missionaries, driven out of China by the Boxers, who suspect Quong Lung of dealing in slavery. At San Francisco they arrange to have Ah Moy and Wing held by immigration officials while Quong Lung hurries to Chinatown to consult his attorney and his fellow tong members. At the same time, one of the missionaries has returned to his home mission to consult his own colleagues and attorney. Ah Moy's fate is decided in court where she follows Quong Lung's direction in order to avoid the missionaries. She was taught in China to distrust missionaries and they cannot find anyone in San Francisco who speaks her northern dialect. Ah Moy believes that Quong Lung has arranged for her to marry a rich man.

While Wheat places the missionaries in the role of trying to rescue Ah Moy, which is historically accurate, she also acknowledges the critical and condescending attitude of many missionaries toward the Chinese. In the following conversation, a missionary is comparing Eurasians with Asians, beginning with the latter.

> "As a class, they are hard to manage," said the matron, still doubtfully, "we have them occasionally at the home, and they are apt to make trouble; the other girl is easier saved."
>
> "The other one is already saved," responded the doctor, rather tartly; "she has behind her ages upon ages of virtuous ancestors, and she does not need any help from us."[97]

Ah Moy soon finds herself in a Chinatown house of prostitution, far from the station of her once-prosperous family in China, while Wing inherits a million dollars from her dead white father. Ah Moy uses her father's knife first on a prospective client and, after writing a letter to her father, kills herself.

Wheat tells a potentially melodramatic story without falling into melodrama. She is the last of the missionary novelists to write about Chinese Americans, and has the least amount of condescension toward them. The events at the end of the novel are told in a straightforward manner, relying on the adequate characterization of Ah Moy to convey the sense of tragedy. Despite occasional turns of phrase which remind the reader that Wheat is writing from a white American perspective, her depiction of the female slave trade in American Chinatowns is realistically handled.

Frank Norris is the most important naturalist to write about Chinese Americans. His descriptions of the Chinese, Scandinavian, and Anglo-Saxon traits of his characters are detailed presentations of his belief in the natural animosity and incongruity of the Asian and Caucasian races. The sense of elemental conflict between the two in his fiction is similar to that in the early novels of Chinese invasion. Other authors in this chapter do not argue or present naturalist tenets so much as they assume them. Fernald, Doyle, de Pue, and Fales accept the vices of Chinatown as normal and accept Norris's naturalist vision of human races as fundamentally different in values such as courage, honor, and intelligence, with whites at the top of the evolutionary scale. They are naturalists by implication more than by clear argument. At the same time, their fiction contains cultural inaccuracies and deletions that together create a misleading picture of Chinatown rather than a realistic one. This tendency is developed further by authors who are discussed in the following chapter, but the distortions about Chinatown begin with the authors considered here. Jack London clearly sees the racial confrontations in his stories about the Fish Patrol through naturalistic eyes, but his later stories set in Hawaii do not exhibit a belief in inherent racial differences.

The category of muckrakers is heavily influenced by this type of naturalist attitude toward race, as well. William Norr, for instance, believes that the Chinese Americans and white Americans have different basic natures and have no reason to mix. Simultaneously, he blames the fact that they do mix in New York on social ills, thereby combining exposés with naturalist assumptions. Helen Green writes with this viewpoint, as does Edward Townsend in his short stories about Chinatown, though they are perhaps not fully muckrackers because of their failure to show that the social conditions they deplore result from economic pressures and political corruption. By contrast, Harry M. Johnson points out these relationships and finds the people of Chinatown innocent victims of these forces. This makes him a true muckracking novelist, though a minor one.

The first priority of the missionary authors is to develop sympathy in their readers for the Chinese Americans. Sometimes the Chinese American characters are converted to Christianity and sometimes not, but they are consistently portrayed as undeserving victims of racism. Maud Howe is writing out of the New England tradition that produced the Abolitionists, but later missionary writers find themselves responding in part to the naturalist vision that considers the Chinese as biologically inferior to whites and inherently opposed to the culture and institutions of white America. Mary Bamford, Nellie Blessing Eyster, and Lu Wheat explicate the trials of Chinese immigrants in the United States from the criminal element of Chinatown, from white law enforcement officials, and from their own Chinese traditions. In doing so, they create a variety of individual Chinese immigrant characters. This breadth of character never appears in the naturalist interpretation of Chinese immigrants' lives, since the naturalists emphasize the race and what they consider an ancient and effete society over individuality. The missionary authors are not actually concerned about the issues raised by the naturalists per se. However, the strain of naturalist influence represented by Frank Norris becomes during this time the mainstream of thought about Chinese Americans. While Hosmer and Howe must depict characters representing hostile white labor in their descriptions of the frontier life of the Chinese immigrants, Bamford, Eyster, and Wheat must instead present these naturalist attitudes in their attempts to generate sympathy for the Chinese immigrants. Both the naturalists and the missionaries, however, disappear from the list of fiction about Chinese Americans after the first decade of the twentieth century. Naturalist influence remains, of course, but in the second decade of this century, fiction about the Chinese Americans develops some new qualities.

V
Chinatown, 1909–40:
Fantasy and Diversification

The authors discussed in this chapter fall into three categories, of which the first two are narrowly defined. One includes authors of fiction about Chinatown that are so distorted as to be fantasies. The second includes the first two Chinese American authors of fiction. The third category is a catchall listing four authors whose work represents a new diversification of the treatment of Chinese Americans and a lessening of importance of the Yellow Peril theme.[1]

In the fiction about Chinatown considered in this chapter, the influence of naturalism and muckracking are taken selectively. Both schools were part of the growth of realism in the late nineteenth century, but their application to Chinatown was flawed from the beginning by authors who tried to interpret Chinatown society without a solid education in Chinatown life. In the second decade of the twentieth century, the realism of these schools is forgotten in fiction about Chinatown and the result is the presentation of Chinatowns that never existed anywhere.

The two Chinese American authors have a unique position from which to view the Yellow Peril theme. Their characters are Chinese Americans who are considered part of the Yellow Peril by the white characters they face in their daily lives. They function in Chinatown societies that are accurately portrayed and deal with the real concerns of Chinatown residents.

To a degree, the remaining four authors expand the depiction of Chinese Americans beyond the accustomed boundaries of class, occupation, and character. At the same time, the racist attitudes expressed by the naturalists who wrote about the Yellow Peril still linger. These authors do not write about Chinatown, but their work emerges from a background dominated by Chinatown fiction and so are included in this chapter.

The plot of *The Flame Dancer* (1908), by Frances Aymar

Mathews, is a variation of that of *The Moonstone*, by Wilkie Collins, taking place partly in highly imaginative Chinatowns of New York and San Francisco. A millionaire named Reginald Stevens has stolen sacred jewels from an Asian religious cult and the villain, a Chinese scholar named Struh-La, is attempting to get them back. Stevens has made his fortune through thefts of this kind in Asia. Struh-La is described as a Lolos man from North China whose coloring is sufficiently pale that he can sometimes pass for a white man who merely resembles an Asian. His tool for effecting a conspiracy is called See-foo-tee, an unrealistic depiction of hypnotism. With this he dominates the minds of three American women very easily. The ancestry of one of the women, Luliani, is half-French and half-Lolos. Eventually she breaks the power of Struh-La's will by falling in love with Stevens while Struh-La has fallen for her. Before this occurs, however, Luliani is taken into the legendary maze beneath Chinatown where, forty feet underground, she dances a flame dance wearing the sacred jewels.

The entrance described to the catacombs of Chinatown is revealed by swivelling aside a square of mosaic set in the street. Steps have been carved out of solid rock that lead to three lower levels with landings from which six passages extend. The first level is not very different from the Chinatown above ground; it has

> huddling houses, jutting verandas, projecting windows, quaint signs, bloused and trousered women pattering back and forth; restaurants, joss-houses, a theater, bazaars, fish-markets, all the teeming antlike life of the Orientals, whose nature is to burrow when they inhabit the white man's land.[2]

The second level is similar, though more wealth is evident from the appearance of the buildings and people. The lowest level is a haven primarily for women and children. Struh-La is happiest here.

> To him, with all his veneer of white civilization, white learning and white dissipation, this alone gave enjoyment; the mystery and safety of its forty feet underground; this acme of the burrowing instinct was delectable.[3]

Finally, after Luliani has rejected Struh-La, he confronts her and Stevens, addressing the latter:

> "Take her, she is your blood and breed. I give her to you. I give you also all the jewels she wears. You stole them from me years ago. I am the man who came and begged you not

to rob the sacred temple of my ancestors. You laughed. I told you I would regain them. I have. I wanted the woman. I attained her. I no longer want her. But this one thing," he looked down at the talisman in his hand, "I keep. I go back to the East. Take the woman and her jewels, and go away from here in peace."[4]

Stevens and Luliani leave all the jewels with him, laughing and humiliating him further, before walking away together.

The reference to Struh-La's Western veneer suggests to the reader once again the idea of Chinese cultural unassimilability. At the climax, Struh-La has the jewels back at a substantial price: his dignity has not only been lost by receiving the jewels in this casual manner, but also by the preference of the half-white and half-Lolos woman for a white man over a Lolos man. In all, this novel is an adventure fantasy without being labeled as such. Mathews has freely created not only the underground levels of Chinatown and all their detail, but also the immense power of See-foo-tee and the religious cult itself.

The first Chinese American author of fiction was Edith Eaton (1867–1914). She wrote under the pseudonym Sui Sin Far, which is the name of a kind of Chinese water lily. Eaton was born in England to an English father and a Chinese mother. Her family moved to the United States while she was a child and she lived in Seattle as an adult, working as a reporter and short-story writer. Many of her stories were collected in *Mrs. Spring Fragrance* (1912).[5] Though she writes about a variety of subjects, all her stories feature Chinese American protagonists struggling with problems peculiar to their immigrant and/or minority status. As one might expect, a number of her stories depict interracial marriages between Chinese and white Americans and their offspring.

Eaton is included here because her vision of Chinatown and Chinese Americans is that of an insider. Her characters are considered part of the Yellow Peril by white characters and deal with this as an integral part of life. One of her more melodramatic stories, "The Chinese Lily," was discussed in chapter 3.[6] Considering other stories more representative of her work as a whole will provide a contrast to the stories of Chinatown written by white authors.

Most of Eaton's stories take place in San Francisco, but the first two are set in her home city of Seattle. In the title story, Mrs. Spring Fragrance and her husband are an immigrant couple. She has picked up fluent English in only five years and also taken on enough white American customs to cause friction with her husband, who has remained more traditional. He has established himself in business after working his way up from being an immigrant boy without a formal education. The second story reveals that he has been successful enough to contribute money to China for the building of a school in Canton and a railway to his home village, which is probably in Toisan.

The Spring Fragrances were married through the traditional arrangement by their parents, without their meeting ahead of time. They have had two children die in infancy, and the combination of their childlessness with their arranged marriage, which is nevertheless happy, causes Mrs. Spring Fragrance to involve herself in the affairs of their neighbors, the Chin Yuens. The Chin Yuens are trying to arrange a marriage for their daughter Mai Gwi Far, or Laura. Laura has grown up in Seattle with white American values, however, and has an American-born boyfriend named Kai Tzu who does not fit into her parents' plan. Laura and Kai Tzu have little interest in certain Chinese traditions such as arranged marriages. In one early scene in the story, Laura plays the piano and Kai Tzu sings "Drink to Me Only with Thine Eyes."[7] Kai Tzu's own social status is enhanced by his being a noted baseball pitcher on the West Coast.

The prospective groom whom Laura's parents have selected also has another match in mind. For the sake of romance over social obligation, Mrs. Spring Fragrance spends much time in various intrigues until Laura's prospective groom decides to take a stand and marry the woman of his choice. This leaves Laura similarly free. Meanwhile, Mr. Spring Fragrance has become concerned about the amount of time his wife has been spending on unexplained trips around town and begins to worry that she is having an affair. When his wife finally explains, he even accepts her new way of thinking and agrees that young people should choose their own mates.

Eaton writes with well-defined characters and a clear understanding of bicultural pressures. This first story is understated and evocative, describing the process of acculturation experienced gradually by a middle-class Chinese American couple. Some of her stories depict working-class families in the grip of economic pressures, and other tales present immigrants with intolerant attitudes about cultural behavior. In "The Wisdom of the New," a wife arrives from China with her young son to join her husband after a long separation. She finds that she despises American culture. Just before their son is to enter an American school, his mother poisons him to prevent his cultural contamination. Her husband abandons his successful laundry business and takes her back to China. "Its Wavering Image" features a woman like Eaton, half-Chinese and half-white. A white reporter courts her in

order to get an insider's description of Chinatown. After he publishes
an account of some of her private observations, she suddenly decides to
live as completely Chinese. This surprises the reporter, whose belief in
white supremacy caused him to assume she would unquestioningly lean
toward her white heritage. His desire to get a story about Chinatown is
one result of the belief in the Yellow Peril that was rampant in these
years. The fact that his exploitation of her Chinese descent drives her to
identify more strongly with the Chinese Americans is an indication of
consciously developed racial and ethnic pride which white authors
never approach in their stories of Chinese Americans. Eaton herself
seems to have made a similar choice, in view of her chosen subject
matter and pseudonym.

Eaton also writes stories about more melodramatic situations. "In
the Land of the Free" is about a young mother who is separated from
her child by the immigration authorities for ten months, after which
the child no longer recognizes her. Other stories involve the smuggling
of illegal alien Chinese and corrupt immigration officials who require
bribes. Whatever the plot, however, her characters have Chinese
American cultural and social concerns that rarely include tongs,
opium, or revenge. Even those with violence have an underlying
realism of character and background absent from earlier fiction about
Chinese Americans.

Java Head (1918), by Joseph Hergesheimer, deals with an unusual
Chinese immigrant in unusual circumstances. Gerrit Ammidon, a New
England sea captain, returns to his family home called Java Head, in
Salem, Massachusetts, bringing a Manchurian wife of noble ancestry
and personal background, named Taou Yuen.[8] Not only is she neither
from South China nor of the laboring class, but instead of entering the
American West she immigrates to New England, the home of the
liberal tradition in the United States. Even so, she faces pronounced
racial prejudice from the time she arrives at Java Head and when she
dies, her husband reflects that her presence in the United States killed
her.

Hergesheimer characterizes Taou Yuen fairly well and was
familiar with some of the clothing, jewelry, literature, and customs
which were a part of life for Manchurian women of her rank in China.
She does seem to represent all such women, as the influences on her
personality Hergesheimer discusses are nearly all general cultural
forces; he makes very little mention of her particular childhood or experiences as an individual. Her motives are clear and reasonable,
though, and she is sympathetically treated.

The Ammidons and their neighbors in Salem have a long history in the China trade and are familiar with many Chinese works of art, styles of clothing, and pieces of furniture. They also have an understanding of Chinese history unusual in white Americans; instead of talking about the Chinese as inveterate opium smokers and dealers, they are quick to deny any participation back in the opium trade from India which the British forced on China in the Opium War. At the same time, a sense of possible contamination from the Chinese also exists, as expressed when one family members says, "It's curious about the China service . . . anyone out there for a number of years gets to look Chinese. Edward is as yellow as a lemon, but nothing like as pleasant a color."[9]

When Gerrit first returns from Asia with Taou Yuen, his marriage is a complete surprise. All his family and friends are appalled, angered, and insulted by his choice of a noble Manchu as a wife. He defends her vigorously at first, but the lines are clearly drawn against her from the moment she arrives.

> At the same time that he had felt no necessity to apologize for his marriage he had known that Taou Yuen must surprise, yes—shock, his family. She was Chinese, to them a heathen: they would be unable to comprehend any mitigating dignity of rank.[10]

Gerrit also finds that his wife's entry into Salem society is more difficult than he had hoped.

> In China he had hoped that in the vicinity of Washington Square and Pleasant Street she would appear less Eastern; but, beyond all doubt, here she was enormously more so. The strange repressed surrounding accentuated every detail of her Manchu pomp and color. The frank splendor of her satins and carved jades and embroidery, her immobile striking face loaded with carmine and glinting headdress, the flawless loveliness of hands with pointed nail protectors, were, in his room, infinitely dramatized.[11]

In addition to her foreign appearance, she also must resist the prejudices of the other seafarers who have had some slight contact with the Chinese. One such man is certain that she was "a common woman of the port who had made a fool of the dull sailor. . . ." This man is attracted to her, not as an individual, but as an exotic figure.

> He wanted to embrace her satin-shod feet, to cling to her odorous hands. . . . Not only her bodily charm intoxicated

him, but the thought of her subtle mind added its attraction, its shadows never to be pierced by the blunted Western instinct, the knowledge of pleasures like perfume, the calm blend of the eight diagrams of Confucious, the stoicism of the Buddhistic soul revolving perpetually in the urn of fate, and of the aloof Tao of Lao-tze.[12]

The desirability of Asian women for white men is contrasted sharply with the attitude of white Salem women toward Asian men.

"Most of the Captains like China," Taou Yuen said. "They are so far away from their families—" she made a brief philosophical gesture. . . . "It would be the same," she continued, "if Chinamen came to America." Mrs. Wibird shuddered. "A yellow skin," she cried impetuously; "I can't bide the thought."[13]

Salem does not accept Taou Yuen, despite her efforts and her defense by Gerrit. Eventually, he becomes discouraged, and begins to see the differences in a more serious light himself. He soon feels a renewed interest in a white woman he had known before his last trip to China, and she returns his attention. At the same time, Taou Yuen rejects with finality the advances of the other man interested in her and he responds,

"With all your Manchu attitudes . . . yes, your aristocratic pretense of mourning and marks of rank, you are no different from the little pleasure girls. . . . I forgot you were yellow, I had forgotten that all China's yellow. It's yellow, yellow, yellow and never can be white. I shut my eyes to it and it dragged me down into its slime."[14]

Taou Yuen collapses when she realizes that Gerrit, her mainstay in Salem, has turned away from her. She dies mysteriously, apparently from shock and disappointment but, within Gerrit

a perception, yet without base in facts, convinced him that Taou Yuen had been killed by America. It was a fantastic thought, and he attempted to dismiss it, waiting for more secure knowledge, but it persisted. She had been killed by unfamiliar circumstances, tradition, emotions.[15]

In Hergesheimer's view, the antipathy of New England toward a Chinese immigrant could be nearly as great as that on the West Coast if the immigrant in question moved in next door instead of into California. This parallels in some ways the accusation that Northern liberals championed Black civil rights in the South more than in the North. In addition, this intolerance arises specifically from the differences of race and culture. Taou Yuen's nobility and wealthy background do not count for anything.

Beggar's Gold (1921), by Ernest Poole, is a novel that touches only marginally on Chinese Americans. Its central theme is that China has an exotic aura which offers a lifelong fascination to a white American farm boy in New York State. The visions of China that Peter Wells carries throughout his life change over the years to include the mystic lure of China at the turn of the century, a growing concern for the problems of the people of China, a recognition of China's potential threat to the world, and finally, in the liberals' disillusionment after World War I, a solace in Chinese philosophy. This last development reflects Poole's own experience, though he visited Russia after the war, not China, to observe the socialist experiment.

In most of the novel, the attitude of Americans toward China and the Chinese is heavily patronizing. The earliest lure for Wells, though, comes through the charm of adventure and the exotic.

> Out of those subconscious depths, where all he had ever heard or seen, read, hated, loved, desired, dreamed, was stored as in a house of gold, up came marvelous pictures now. Golden idols, tinkling bells, sinister priests on murder bent, lurking in dark temples with long gleaming knives in their hands; enormous brightly painted junks attacked by swarms of river pirates; camels in long, weird processions winding over the desert at night; mandarins in shining robes watching their dozens of gorgeous young wives dance before them in the light of tossing paper lanterns; harem loves, escapes and murders; fields of poppies, opium dives![16]

As a young man in New York City, Peter teaches in a public school and befriends Katherine, a young white woman born and raised in China, and a boy named Moon Chao, the son of a Chinatown actor. As a child, he represents China to them, being mysterious, clever, cute, and helpless. Peter studies China with Katherine, and they marry with plans to go to China and work. When Moon Chao's father is killed in a tong feud, they plan to adopt him and take him to Peking with them.

Moon Chao is well developed as a character but his father is not, and the description of Chinatown is limited to a brief paragraph about the ghetto dive where the frightened Moon Chao flees after his father is murdered. The Wells' plans are disrupted by the return of Moon Chao to China to live with an uncle, and the birth of a daughter to the Wellses. Moon Chao's uncle later offers them teaching jobs in Peking, but financial problems prevent their going. Katherine's suggestion that Peter go alone causes a burst of frustrated rage which is taken out on the Chinese in the novel's only expression of direct hostility and contempt.

> "How the devil could I make a start over there? It's been you we've counted on from the start—you and your knowledge of Chinese—and of the whole country, and how to get on. Send me traipsing over there all by myself—to teach a lot of little Chinks, in a language I don't even know? What do you think I am? A god?" He marched over to the Buddha in the corner and held out his hand. "We're regular fellahs, you and I! . . . All I need is a pigtail and a dressing gown! They'd take me for a native then!"[17]

Even though Peter's anger is largely at his own helplessness, his readiness to use racial slurs and to mock Chinese cultural symbols is significant. Despite Katherine's early youth in China, the image of China both Peter and Katherine hold is an abstraction. This is emphasized by Peter's fear of actually carrying out his fantasy alone.

Moon Chao returns eighteen years later to study the school system in New York. Speaking excellent English, he tells his American friends of China's bright new future as a republic. He leaves, to pass through again during World War I, with more enthusiasm about the place of China in the developing world. Peter is impressed and profoundly touched by the imminent success of the country of which he has always been fond. Moon Chao's words suggest a clear Yellow Peril in the new China which he envisions after Chinese laborers leave their wartime work in France:

> As these few hundred thousand boys come home and scatter far and wide over the farms of China, four hundred million people there will waken slowly—slowly feel a sense of what their lives might be—and the power of the East![18]

In Poole's view, however, and so Peter's, the potential strength of China is no threat to the United States. After the war, Peter joins a radical political demonstration and loses his job as a school principal. Moon Chao invites him to China where his sense of loss as a liberal after World War I is replaced by a feeling that he can contribute to the emerging modern nation. Moon Chao convinces him that "In the East, we think not only of what is outside a man's body but of how it will affect the man's spirit life within. . . . The people of America are not thinking of that now."[19]

Poole combines in this novel many important elements in the American image of China. Much of Peter's concept of China is fantasy formed from vague lifelong impressions, hearsay, and reading. Poole describes well the fascination with what is considered exotic, the combination of patronizing affection with expressions of racial contempt, the awareness of China as a growing power, and finally true affection for the Chinese and a belief in the spiritual value of Asian culture. For the image of Chinese Americans, he conveys a more oblique message. Chinatowns and their inhabitants exist only as unsavory outposts of foreigners, some of whom are good, as is Moon Chao, and some of whom are bad, as are the tong assassins. This balance of good and bad elements is a positive and unusual step for its time, but Poole's failure to deal with Chinese Americans as part of the American people is a major flaw.

The exploitation of Chinatown's lurid reputation by American authors reaches its height in fiction by Hugh Wiley and Lemuel de Bra. Wiley has two short-story collections, *Jade: and Other Stories* (1922) and *Manchu Blood* (1927). He is second only to Sax Rohmer, the English creator of Dr. Fu Manchu, in creating imaginary customs and behavior of a cruel and vicious nature in Chinese and Chinese American societies. Writing well after the San Francisco earthquake of 1906 and its fire that destroyed the Chinatown there, he "resurrected an exotic past that did not exist in order to satisfy our thirst for romance and adventure."[20]

Three stories in the first volume will represent that collection. In "Jade," a jewelry store owner named Sun Kee befriends an Irish American cab driver named Lingo Riley, who brings his Chinatown tourists by the shop as part of his routine.[21] Sun Kee goes to great lengths to sneak a prospective bride into the country illegally, and though Riley helps him, Riley's wife brings in the police because of her dislike for the Chinese, causing the woman to be deported. Sun Kee does not blame Riley but gains his revenge by gassing Riley's wife and pouring molten gold down her throat. He returns to China on the same ship as his deported bride-to-be.

"Joss" involves a wealthy Chinatown figure named Ming Sun Tai who makes a point of donating heavily to charitable causes. These include Christian concerns, though he still worships the traditional gods of China. He appears to be an average, decent pillar of his community. A wealthy senator antagonizes him, however, by desecrating the ground where his father is buried, in search of gold. Ming Sun Tai strangles him with a necklace he has given to the senator for that purpose. As an indication that greed has no part in the killing, he gives the senator's daughter a donation to her Christian mission equal to the value of the gold found with the senator at the time of his murder.

In "Junk," the main character is a red-haired Chinese boy who is driven out of his home in China because of his hair color, for which no explanation is offered. He wanders, joining a travelling troupe of actors as a musician because a red-haired Chinese man adopts him. He finally roams to California. His music is not popular there, though, and so he opens a junk business on the side. When someone leaves yet another red-haired Chinese boy on his doorstep, he adopts the boy and runs the junk store full-time. He loves this foster son very much and apprentices him to a Portuguese grocer. However, the grocery business is a front for opium smuggling. When the authorities find this out, the foster son takes a fall for his employer, who goes free. After serving some time in prison, he dies of a lung disease. His foster father, taking revenge in equal measures, had already captured and imprisoned the Portuguese drug dealer; when the foster son dies, the father has the Portuguese prisoner eaten alive by his two great pet turtles.

"Tong" is about a poet and his beautiful sister, both of whom become involved with the Ling Yip Tong because of financial problems. The poet is hired as an assassin and he learns to use a revolver well. However, tong leader Yut Gar assigns him to kill the intended husband of the poet's sister so that Yut Gar himself can marry her. The poet kills Yut Gar instead, making the bullets strike his body so that the Chinese word for everlasting life is ironically written on him. Then the poet arranges the wedding of his sister and his assigned victim before he must flee the vengeance of the tong.

Wiley's Chinatowns are classic representations of the Yellow Peril. Though some of his characters are not eager criminals, such as Sun Kee and the poet, they are depicted with an exaggeration of exotic qualities, as in Sun Kee's draught of molten gold and the poet's shooting the outline of a Chinese word into his victim. Most of Chinatown appears to be a world of crime and cruelty, and its more decent members still, when pressed, exhibit a flair and affinity for violence and murder. Even though the protagonists are also residents of Chinatown, their lack of depth and realism prevents the reader from developing much sympathy for them and identification of them as individuals. Wiley's own imagination played too great a part in their creation.

Wiley's second collection, *Manchu Blood* (1927), contains two parts. Of the ten stories, six in the middle deal with a Dr. Holland and his aged and loyal Chinese cook, Jim Sin. Jim is intended as a positive figure. The first two and last two stories in the book stand independently and are similar to the Chinatown stories in his first volume.

"Manchu Blood" is about an elderly immigrant of Manchurian descent named Sang How. He conducts his grocery business in the Chinatown of San Francisco, stubbornly maintaining his identity amidst his Cantonese neighbors. He decides at the age of sixty to marry Gay, a seventeen-year-old Chinese American born in San Francisco who works as a cashier in his store. To cement the engagement, he purchases an expensive ring once worn by the empress of China. When he hears that Gay has been engaged for a year to Ling, a native Chinese American, he has only contempt.

> "Ling!" he interrupted. "I will tell you who he is. He is a product of Chinese blood and American customs. . . ."
>
> "He is more than that, Uncle Sang. He has tenderness and sweetness and education, and he will be a great musician."
>
> "He is a college-bred tinkler on a child-sized guitar—and makes a living selling fish."
>
> "A master of the violin," Gay corrected. "A composer whose work is known to all the American musicians in San Francisco. Selling fish is an honest business, Uncle Sang. . . ."[22]

Sang changes his tack and Gay accepts his engagement ring when he declares,

> "In this tray there is five thousand dollars in gold. There are three larger trays in the safe deposit of the Anglo Bank, all of them filled with gold. I own this building and the building across the street and another one on Grant Avenue. Even your American business men would call me rich if they knew what I possess."[23]

Greed has changed Gay's mind, but when she sees Ling, his enthusiasm for their own engagement overwhelms her. Before she can explain, he takes away her ring from Sang and replaces it with his own diamond ring. He hurries to his concert with Sang's ring on his little finger, believing it to be a minor bauble of hers.

A concertgoer recognizes the empress's ring on his finger and word of Ling's wearing it spreads quickly. Sang retrieves it by paying henchmen to chop off Ling's finger after the concert. Sang spends the night in an opium sleep and in the morning Gay, sleepless in worry over the missing Ling, goes to Sang. In his opium room, he smokes again and gives her back the ring, still on Ling's finger. He then drifts into another drugged sleep. Horrified, she turns on the room's gas jet and locks him inside. Running out on the street, she meets the wounded Ling, whose earlier whereabouts are not mentioned. They are reunited to the sound of Sang's room exploding as the flame of his opium lamp ignites the gas in the room.

"The Patriot" deals explicitly with a Chinese American born in the United States. The first portion of the story describes the early life of his father, Fong Lin, who wanders aimlessly until his wife from a childhood marriage, Spring Moon Flower, catches up to him. They fall in love and remain together.

> They starved for a while. Then in a great port where ships from the western seas assembled to trade the products of far lands for the treasures of China, Lin listened to a labor contractor's lure, and within the week, in company with a hundred other deluded slaves he and Chun Yuey, who was dressed as a man, were battened in the foul slave-pens of a ship bound for Callao.[24]

They land in San Francisco and Wiley gives a much more sympathetic account of their travels in the United States than the stories in his first collection even approached. Their experience is not representative of their fellow immigrants, though, as they make a huge gold strike and have wealth assured for the rest of their lives after a relatively short time. Still, the anti-Chinese hysteria of the 1870s and 1880s is presented clearly and Fong Lin reflects,

> "The human race consisting largely of beasts . . . the use of opium will no doubt cease in the same millennium that sees an end of drunkenness and theft and murder among the superior moralists native to this Christian land. For that matter, if these western lords of the Orient would for a little while cease to thrust the black drug down China's throat, our reform might be accomplished at an earlier date."[25]

A son named Fong Lee is born to the couple and becomes the focus of the story from this point. He is educated at the best schools, including a university on the East Coast, and he speaks without an accent. In the process, he learns much of the prejudice against the Chinese and Chinese Americans but little about business that he had not already learned from his father. He is capable of taking over his father's many businesses but refuses to associate with the gambling houses and opium dens he has read about. His father informs him that the family businesses do not include any of these.

> "More than half of those dens of death were owned by white men and the proprietors of the balance were renegade dogs tutored in the foreign concessions of our Chinese seaports. Let your heart be at ease. The path of virtue is plainly marked, and at some cost in worldly goods I have followed it."[26]

Fong Lin returns to China, leaving his business affairs in his son's hands. Fong Lee becomes involved in the efforts of Sun Yat-sen to unify China as a republic. In World War I, he organizes Chinese Americans to support the United States, but at the same time he begins to feel discouraged about American life.

> "I am sick of their jazz and of their verbal democracy, their cash and carry religions, their boosterism, their big business, their little theatre and big movies, their pseudo-philanthropies . . . and of their hypocrisy."[27]

Inaccurate and exaggerated accounts of Chinatown's gambling, tong wars, and opium traffic further discourage him. Finally, Fong Lee decides to visit China. He makes two public statements before going which his confidential secretary releases to the newspapers:

> "I love this country, and even as my people, when they die, cannot sleep with tranquility except in the soil of China, neither could I contemplate resting elsewhere after life is done save in America, my native land. . . .
>
> "It has been a sanctuary for the oppressed peoples of the earth, and while my education and my training have been accomplished under the guidance of Occidental teachers and methods, I still respond to the essence of my origin, the instinct of my race, in feeling that this land of my birth must finally be my resting place."[28]

These two statements of American patriotism appear on the front page of San Francisco's newspapers and elicit tremendous enthusiasm on the part of San Franciscans. Therefore, when word of Fong Lee's death in China comes back, elaborate arrangements are made for the return of his remains to San Francisco, including speeches, a parade with seven bands, and Chinese aviators flying over the city. Colleagues of Fong Lee from his activities supporting Sun Yat-sen receive the casket.

The story ends with a twist. Fong Lee is alive in China and has sent a huge shipment of opium in his supposed casket. In San Francisco, his colleagues sell it for a quarter of a million dollars in gold, targeted for the military activities of the Kuomintang. Fong Lee says, "Our Southern Armies are in the field. The war chest is none too heavy . . . this makes me regret, in a way, that I have but one life to sell for my—for China."[29]

In this story, Wiley has directly confronted the issue of assimilation by Chinese Americans. Fong Lee is born and raised in the United States; he is given the best education his father's money could provide, the sharp business acumen that kept their wealth accumulating, and no visible problems caused by white racism or his status as a minority citizen. Even so, he turns away from the United States because he is dissatisfied with certain parts of white American culture and the depiction of Chinatown in the newpapers. His decision is not made lightly because he faces greater problems in China, where civil war rages. Wiley rejects the notion that Fong Lee would be, or would want to be, truly and reliably American. Fong Lee's decision to leave, which has no more motivation than indicated in the quotes above, has also removed his qualms about dealing in opium. His publicly proclaimed patriotism is a lie; in short, he has reverted to type.

"Manchu Blood" again presents the Chinese immigrants as people involved with crime and not at all as law-abiding Chinatown residents. "The Patriot" begins with such residents, but ends with a reaffirmation of two familiar traits, the willingness to deal in opium and cultural unassimilability.

In the six stories about Dr. Holland and Jim Sin, the latter is an immigrant who works as a cook and a servant. A continuing theme is his desire to save ten thousand dollars in order to retire to China. The plots indicate Jim's loyalty and skills. In "The Rebate," Jim returns two thousand dollars to his mistress which she had lost when a Chinatown merchant sold her a fake Chinese antique which she dropped and broke. He gets the money back by playing poker with the merchant and skillfully cheating. To his mistress, however, he says only that the merchant was sorry the vase broke so easily and so returned the cash. "The Survival of Sin" involves Dr. Holland's request that Jim find "a Number Two boy" to aid him in his domestic duties.[30] Jim deliberately arranges the coming of Wing Fat, a young man with "a veneer of Western learning" whose interest in caring for small animals and experimenting with a kite and crystal set guarantee his being fired by Dr. Holland.[31] In this way, Jim survives by eliminating a potential threat to his job. In "Sin Vigilant," Jim and Dr. Holland invest in shares of a gold mine. Jim carefully sells out just before the value drops, saving not only his money, but his master's as well. "Salt Cured" is about a gold-panning Chinese immigrant, an old friend, who asks Jim to aid him up in the mountains where he lives. Jim captures a stagecoach robber and receives a thousand-dollar reward, but instead of adding it to his retirement fund, he takes it in gold dust and salts the panned-out river where his friend has been working. His motive is to keep his friend in the peaceful mountains he enjoys rather than have him quit the area for San Francisco. At the beginning of "Gold Filled," Jim needs only three thousand dollars to complete his fund. This story involves his successes in cheating his close friends at poker. To make this acceptable in his protagonist, Wiley explains that cheating among them is expected, the only sin being that of getting caught. Jim makes a killing, but the exact amount is not mentioned. In the final story of the series, "Minted Gold," Dr. Holland hires a Number Two boy himself, named Yut, who proceeds to steal whiskey from his master. Jim returns the stolen barrels and convinces Yut to return to China. Perhaps more important than the theft to the depiction of the Chinese in this story is the hypocrisy revealed in Yut's informal resumé. In response to Jim's criticism of his service to Dr. Holland, Yut declares,

> "My heart is pure and its purity protects me from the filth of thy tongue. I am a brave soldier and a Christian, and I attend church on Sundays and Wednesdays, while you no doubt are indulging your evil desires for gambling and for drinking the nauseating beverage you and your kind call Chinese gin."[32]

For all of his self-righteousness, of course, he is still a thief.

Wiley presents Jim and his contacts in Chinatown consistently in the series with cultural details that are not related concretely to the plots. "The Rebate" opens with Jim trying to knit a sweater and giving up; his decision is couched in a proverb, as are most of his important comments: "Wisdom is bought with the coin of experience and time is money. I will buy a felt jacket and what it costs in cash I shall gain in precious hours."[33] While Wiley's knowledge of traditional Chinese culture and the Chinatown of San Francisco seems greater in this book than in his first, one fundamental flaw is repeated. He seems to believe that the Mandarin and Cantonese dialects have a separate written language, as well as spoken, and so he makes suspect the depth of his understanding. In any case, Jim's proverbs are all Wiley's.

Wiley does show Jim's encounters with racism. Because these incidents involve dialogue, Jim is usually speaking in heavy dialect in response. Wiley sometimes uses it even in the narrative to indicate Jim's thoughts.

To the scion of the Bishop family, he dealt a single crate and upon the Franklin twins, as a penalty for a song beginning Ching Chong Chinaman, he bestowed three crates and a difficult problem wherein good boy ketchum two box bad boy ketchum one.[34]

This use of dialect is prominent in the story, as the young residents of Chinatown with whom Jim deals normally speak standard American English unless they converse with him. This phenomenon is part of an overall quality Wiley has presented in the Chinese, expressed in the phrase "veneer of Western learning."[35] Not only did Wing Fat have a silly and shallow personality beneath that veneer, but Yut proves to be a thief beneath his exterior as a good Christian. Wiley has more sympathy for Jim than he has for most of his protagonists, but even Jim fits the mold of certain stereotypes: the rule at his poker game is cheating, and frequent gambling is assumed to be natural. The same loyalty Jim has for his master is exhibited toward his gold-panning friend, but this must be measured against his cheating his other friends at cards. Wiley's affection for Jim is that of a master for a loyal and clever domestic, genuine but limited to the traditional expectations of his role in terms of both race and class.

In the 1930s, Wiley created one more Chinese American character, who does not appear in the collections. James Lee Wong is a young Yale-educated Chinese American who works as a secret agent for the federal government and uses his scientific training to solve crimes. Called both James Lee and Lee Wong, he appeared in three short stories between 1934 and 1936 in the *Saturday Evening Post*.

Wiley seems to have changed his position on the unassimilability of Chinese Americans with this character. Wong is neither evil nor a working-class servant to a white master, but a dynamic and sophisticated individual. Yet he seems to have turned his back completely on his heritage, suggesting that as a Chinese American he must choose between being Chinese American culturally, and therefore similar to Wiley's earlier Chinese Americans, and being completely acculturated into the Anglo-American world, and therefore having neither interest in nor involvement with his Chinese heritage. Wong is not a Chinese American who represents an American ethnic culture but a converted, or even coopted, former member of the Yellow Peril who has now become a functionary solely in white American society.

In the first story about Wong, "In Chinatown" (1934), this conversion is described by a former classmate:

He was six feet tall. . . . After the first drag at his cigarette he let a cloud of smoke drift through the thin nostrils of his aquiline nose. . . . His face was suddenly the face of a foreign devil—a "Yankee."[36]

Though Chinatown figures in the story, Wong's task has nothing to do with this community. A mysterious Russian woman has been murdered and Wong finds that a Japanese agent used mercury to kill her. This crime is part of an international conflict over Manchuria occurring at this time between Russia and Japan. That Wiley has made Wong suave and confident while operating in white society is a surprisingly forward step considering Wiley's earlier handling of Chinese Americans. However, the cost is high—Wong is never involved with Chinese Americans in any substantive way.

The second story about Wong is "The Thirty Thousand Dollar Bomb" (1934), in which Wong prevents an international incident.[37] A United States senator has purchased shocking documents suggesting that in the event of war, the United States would join Russia and Germany against France and Japan. Wong operates in the highest levels of government in this story, and determines through scientific analysis that the documents are forgeries.

In the final story, "No Witnesses" (1936), Wong takes a vacation in the Sierra mountains at a resort.[38] When another guest is murdered for the large amount of cash he is carrying, Wong deduces on very small evidence that a young student committed the crime. Wong tricks him into revealing himself. The most interesting part of this story is the interaction between the Chinese cook at the resort, Hong Yet, and the other characters. When Wong speaks to him in standard English, Hong Yet replies the same way. When white characters address Hong Yet, he speaks in broken, heavily accented English. Before being caught, the murderer habitually teases Hong Yet and taunts him with many different racial insults. Hong Yet responds in kind, once even playfully reaching for his cleaver in simulated anger. This is the first time Wiley has depicted a white man who taunts the Chinese Americans with racial insults unequivocally as a villain, and shown a working-class Chinese American as an ordinary individual who deliberately adheres to racist stereotypes when he chooses to amuse himself this way.

Many of Wong's traits are positive, such as his education, his demeanor, and his social status. He is not a fully drawn character, however, because he does not have a personal life or personal concerns of any kind. Wiley has eliminated the unpleasant characteristics of his earlier Chinese American figures, but has failed to replace them with more than the most rudimentary characterization of Wong as a secret agent. This blandness may explain why James Lee Wong lasted only for three short stories while visions of Chinese Americans as quaint, exotic, or evil continued to flourish during and after his time. If Wiley had characterized him more fully, he might have enjoyed more success.[39]

Lemuel de Bra's collection of short stories, *Ways That Are Wary* (1925), contains familiar plots, characters, and behavior in San Francisco's Chinatown. Writing about Chinatown in a manner now familiar, de Bra depicts a world of opium, vice, tong violence, and gambling. The title story is a novelette about the betrothed of Ah Chee, daughter of a wealthy merchant. She and Lee Quan, an artist trained in an American college, want to marry but he does not have the two thousand dollars required by her father for her hand. A well-to-do butcher, Bo Ch'at, also wants to marry her and her father favors him. Lee raises the money when he learns of an embargo on Chinese brandy. Ah Chee's father imports it, but Lee manages to gain a shipment intended for him and then sells it to him for the betrothal price. At the same time, Bo Ch'at attempts to eliminate Lee by having a servant plant morphine in Lee's room. However, the servant is distantly related to Lee and leaves quinine instead. The story ends in Bo Ch'at's secret underground room, where he oversees the hiding of morphine in sausages he will sell. His servant, who will otherwise be killed by Bo Ch'at when Lee is not arrested for having morphine, takes a cleaver to Bo Ch'at's head.

Three related short stories comprise the middle of the book. They tell the story of a scholar named Mock Don Yuen, which follows a variation of the same plot as the preceding story. In "Mock Don Yuen Meditates," the scholar is nearly framed for smuggling opium by his cousin and rival Ah Yut. However, he arranges to have Ah Yut arrested instead. Ah Yut is eventually released, but not before he has signed over his son, Ah Din, to Mock Don Yuen as a slave and his foster daughter as a wife. The scholar ignores the term *slave* and allows Ah Din to follow his ambition of attending an American business college. The story ends with the scholar praising the wisdom of Confucius. In "The Wedding of Chan Fah," Ah Yut ignores the fact that Chan Fah, his foster daughter, has been signed over to his cousin and he betroths her to a man named Lee Bow Art for $1,750. Mock Don Yuen sweeps into the presence of Lee Bow Art just as Chan Fah is being taken to him and he presents a marriage license obtained at a pawnshop. This convinces Lee Bow Art of a prior claim, due to his quick glance and limited English. After all is settled, Ah Din returns home exhibiting the influence of his youth in the United States. "'Lo," he sang out, flinging his school cap at a peg. " 'Lo there, sis!' "[40]

"Mock Don Yuen and the Tongs" tells of the final resolutions of this conflict. Lee Bow Art shoots and kills Ah Yut because he lost Chan Fah. Mock Don Yuen has Chan Fah draw Lee Bow Art to their home, where the scholar holds him at gunpoint. He has Lee Bow Art write a confession in order to free Ah Din, who has been arrested for killing his father. Mock Don Yuen then poisons Lee Bow Art to avenge his cousin's murder and prevent a general war between the tongs.

In both the first novelette and the stories about Mock Don Yuen, the more virtuous people of Chinatown prevail in their struggles with the villains. On the other hand, even the protagonists utilize deceit, violence, and murder to accomplish their ends. This vision of Chinatown continues in the eight remaining stories in the collection.

The last story in the book is "The Queer Fortune of Duck Yoan," which presents the most positive character in all the stories. According to his father's will, Duck Yoan must pass a test of worthiness in order to inherit all his father's substantial holdings. Duck Yoan is an earnest but untried young man who chooses to marry Lau Sin, the woman he loves, and thereby relinquish all claims, he believes, to his inheritance. However, Lau Sin has been betrothed against her will to another, and Duck Yoan must not only carry her off, with her consent, but fight her betrothed on the waterfront. He does both successfully.

Duck Yoan's father had lived a success story on the Horatio Alger pattern:

> "My father came with neither money nor learning, nor friends; he died the richest man in Chinatown, praised for his scholarly attainments, mourned by a host of loyal friends. His countrymen call him "Rich and Noble." The foreign devils call him "The Whitest Man in Chinatown."[41]

Because Duck Yoan had been spared the trials of economic hardship, his father had left a will which contained an unread codicil. The executor of the will informs Duck Yoan that his decision to forego his inheritance in favor of Lau Sin and his courageous efforts in taking her from her betrothed have fulfilled the conditions of this last codicil. Duck Yoan comes into his full inheritance without restriction, having passed through trials of courage and violence. Taken alone, this story does not present Chinatown or its inhabitants in a particularly bad light, as the fight on the waterfront is brief, realistic, and reluctantly undertaken. However, the resolution of the conflict in this story is a link to the others, where crime is the rule in Chinatown society. Perhaps the fact that this last story does not rely completely on the negative images of Chinatown is the greatest indictment of the other stories; apparently, when de Bra wished, he was capable of presenting admirable traits and high morals in his characterization of Chinatown residents. He preferred, however, to use imaginative plots and settings, substituting stereotypes for real knowledge about Chinatown.

The commercial value of the Yellow Peril was well established by this time. An advertisement in *Sunset* magazine says:

"Ways That Are Wary" gives us a dozen ripping stories with situations enough to please the greatest literary sensation hunter. . . . It supplies thrill and romance . . . and it gives a rich and vivid insight into the customs and lives of a most picturesque people . . . dim interiors where opium is smoked and flageolets pipe—ornately carved balconies where lanterns glow and Cantonese daughters quaintly sing "The Ballad of Unapproachable Maidens."[42]

An anonymous reviewer in the same issue apparently believes that de Bra is writing informative realistic fiction and praises both the supposed realism and the so-called characterization, claiming that the stories

give you the Chinaman in America as no other stories we have read have ever done. . . . The Chinese attitude, the incomprehensible Oriental slant which is a mystery to the Occidental is splendidly caught . . . these types walk, sip tea, plot or amuse themselves . . . without being "types" at all. . . . Mr. de Bra's book . . . does interpret the Chinatown of San Francisco, delicately, fully, unforgettably.[43]

Actually, of course, de Bra's interpretation of Chinatown is simply a fantasy.

One "Occidental" who did not find the "Oriental slant" incomprehensible is Henry Milner Rideout. Rideout's collection of nine short stories called *Tao Tales* (1927) is dedicated to a Chinese friend named Pon Kwai, who apparently told the stories to Rideout. Within each story, a humble Chinese cook named Yi Tao relates anecdotes from his village in China, in the course of conducting his business of cooking, gardening, laundering, and cleaning. The stories themselves are enjoyable, involving reincarnation, fortune-telling, revenge for murder, love, and finally Ming pirates off the Fujian (Fukien) coast. Since these tales are set in China, their particulars do not involve a Yellow Peril that threatens the United States. However, Yi Tao and his concern with his stories conceivably might.

Yi Tao is a garrulous individual who speaks with an extremely heavy accent early in each story, until the author shifts into standard

English to make the flow of the story smoother. Yi Tao is unconcerned with the affairs of his employers:

> Who knows what they talked of? Not Yi Tao; for though his table near his cook stove became at such times the only convenient place for man or boy, he was too busy to think of any but that spiritual thing, the honor of the house, embodied in food borne quietly through a swing-door into the dining room. What they talked of, does not signify . . . for the point is, that what did signify was Yi Tao's own conversation.[44]

His environment is mundane and businesslike, while his concerns are often abstract.

> In white jacket unbuttoned round the throat, black trousers, and black cloth shoes with padded soles, he moved like a neat ghost, flipping his towel round the plates and laying them away dry and clean. A brew of thoroughwort tea wafted strong medicine about the room, and this with Chinese potatoes and plenty of good spring water taken before sleeping, would cure his malady. . . .
> ". . .Joss house, what is fo'? S'pose you going there, all same you' chu'ch for askee de Got to do somet'ing welly nice. Is de Got in he's house?"[45]

This interest in the higher aspects of life explains Yi Tao's desire to tell stories, most of which see justice triumph over wealth and power. They offer a variety of characters with many different and colorful problems, in contrast to Yi Tao's steady and quiet duties as a domestic servant. Yi Tao's image gradually comes into focus until the reader sees that his stories are the impressions of his homeland which he carries as the last link to the country that he gave up as an immigrant. They not only offer the familiar culture and social environment with which he was raised, but also the solace of triumphs by common individuals over the rich in contrast to his menial duties in reality.

Rideout's tales represent an extreme rarity in the American fiction of this period by having no concern with the Yellow Peril at all. Yi Tao neither constitutes a threat to white Americans nor a patronized supporter of white supremacy. His work as a domestic servant, while not ground breaking, is historically probable. In addition, the depth of his character and his interest in religion, love, and politics prevent him from being a stereotype. The significance of this book in regard to the Yellow Peril lies in the scarcity of such works that show no sign of its influence.

After Edith Eaton, or Sui Sin Far, the next American writer of Chinese descent to write fiction in English about Chinatown is H. T. Tsiang, or—in the Library of Congress's romanization—Chiang Hsi-tsêng. The question of national identity arises here because he was an immigrant from China who seems to have come to the United States to study.[46] If so, his youth was spent in China. This distinction is not raised to separate him arbitrarily from the other authors considered here, but to suggest that an inherent difference may already exist. In considering the influences on a particular artist, one must include the social and cultural environment; in the case of immigrants to the United States, questions of ethnicity and age at immigration also contribute to the formation of the artist's identity. Two of Tsiang's novels involve American Chinatowns, *China Red* (1931) and *And China Has Hands* (1937), and his concern with his native country is as clear or clearer than that with his adopted one. Both novels are about Chinese immigrants to the United States; in considering them, one must remember that his viewpoint does not reflect that of Chinese Americans born and raised in the United States any more than it reflects that of white Americans. Nor, as one who came as a student, did he have the laboring background so common in Chinatown. As an immigrant himself, however, he writes of the immigrant experience eloquently.

Tsiang contributes two new elements to fiction about the Yellow Peril. As in the work of Edith Eaton, the reader sees in Tsiang's novels interaction of white Americans and Chinatown residents from the viewpoint of an author who is a member of the supposed threat. Unlike Eaton, Tsiang is an immigrant and a part of the Bachelor Society. Secondly, Tsiang was a supporter of the Communist Revolution in China and so introduces for the first time the red scare in association with the Chinese and Chinese Americans.

China Red, which opens in 1926, consists of letters from a female college student in China to her fiancée who has gone to study at Stanford. They are both involved in the political events of China between Chiang Kai-shek's Kuomintang and the Chinese Communist Party. The novel has little to do with the United States, as even the Stanford student's activities revolve around Chinese politics among other Chinese and Chinese Americans. Later he begins to work in the United States and by surrendering his student status he is on his way to becoming an immigrant. When he first arrives, however, he does offer some observations about the United States to his betrothed, who responds:

We say that when Chinese girls have their feet bound so as

to please the male sex, it is inhuman; and we are trying to do away with this barbarous custom. But our sisters on the other side of the ocean, instead of binding their toes, lift up their heels. When old-fashioned Chinese girls powder their faces and paint their lips, we laugh at their artificiality. But our sisters on the other side of the ocean do this even in public. . . . The word "China" is a proper noun, just the same as the word "America," so why should not a man who lives in China be called "Chinese"? I see so often in print, "Chinaman," "Chinaman"! Somebody said that this word is used to make fun of us.[47]

The one unforgettable experience for any Chinese immigrant or foreign student in the United States was passing through immigration. She reflects on his account of this with irony:

Some of our people could not afford to buy first-class passage and they were therefore confined to the lower deck of the ship. When they arrived in America, a commission was already waiting to take them to Angel Island to be entertained. The "Angels" on the island entertained our poor brothers there for many weeks and months and made them forget to go ashore to pick up the gold. Sometimes the "Angels" were so hospitable that they even gave some free tickets for the home voyage, much against their will. American capitalists are surely men of justice![48]

Political activity destroys both main characters. The Stanford student is deported ostensibly for losing his student visa, though his left-wing activities are a major consideration as well. When he returns to China, the Kuomintang executes him. His fiancée is seduced by a Kuomintang official and abandoned, after which she dies from an attempted self-induced abortion. This is really a novel about Chinese society and the characters' concern with the United States is marginal.

And China Has Hands deals entirely with the everyday life of a Chinese immigrant and his struggle to establish himself in the Chinatown of New York City. His name is Wan-Lee Wong and Tsiang opens with the explanation that "Wan-Lee" means "ten thousand fortunes." The novel is written in short episodes, some of which are no longer than a few sentences and recount Wan-Lee's concerns in a simple manner.

Since his father had been a citizen of the United States, Wong Wan-Lee was an American citizen through him, although he was born in Canton, China.

On his arrival in America, Wong Wan-Lee had been troubled by the Immigration Officer, and it cost him two thousand dollars to fight the case.

Wong Wan-Lee won, and here he was.[49]

Wan-Lee first works as a waiter in a Chinese restaurant, but buys an established laundry as soon as he can for four hundred dollars. The work is hard, long, and not very rewarding financially, but he has no bosses restricting him. He dreams of returning some day to the restaurant as a wealthy patron and flaunting his money in front of his boss and those he dislikes, but inviting out the Black dishwasher whom he had befriended.

Wan-Lee faces racism in several forms, but his first encounter with hostile white children presents him with a puzzle. On a holiday, they stand in front of his laundry repeatedly taunting, "Where is your pigtail? Chin, Chin, Chinaman!"[50] He first attempts to scare them away by gesturing and stamping his foot on the ground, the way he used to chase away annoying dogs in China. This accomplishes nothing, so he tries throwing them lichee nuts. One boy is at first afraid Wan-Lee is throwing opium to poison them, but they soon decide the lichees are delicious. However, they continue shouting and taunting him, now in the hope of getting more fruit. Wan-Lee is saved by a newcomer to the scene.

> "What are all you kids doing?" asked a smartly dressed Chinese girl who passed by. "Don't think you are wise! Do you think you can put something over on one of my fellow-countrymen? I was born right in this country and I'm not afraid of nobody! You rascals, I'll call the cop or I may break your neck myself."[51]

The speaker is Pearl Chang, who has recently come from the South. Tsiang explains that the Chinese Americans in the South are mostly grocers and more successful than those of the West. Therefore, they are more likely to have families. Since their families produce children of both sexes, he says, "there is no girl scarcity among the Chinese in the South as is the case in the North."[52] However, Pearl's father is a Chinese American and her mother is Black, suggesting that Chinese American women were scarce only a generation earlier. Tsiang also explains the delicate social position of Chinese Americans in the South between the two more numerous races, noting that because they are put in the middle, "some Chinese think they are better than black men."[53]

Pearl Chang has come North to pass for being completely Chinese. The reason is that she feels Chinese on the inside and so she hides her curly hair under a hat and uses makeup in such a way as to make her lips look thinner. Wan-Lee is only the second man of Chinese descent she has met, the first having been her father.

Pearl's thoughts before meeting Wan-Lee are important as they represent the experience of Chinese Americans, and other Asian Americans, who grew up isolated from others of their racial and ethnic heritage. Even in isolation, she has been affected by the Yellow Peril concept through the movies.

> What she could not understand was why this laundryman cut off his pigtail, so that he looked like most Americans. Would it not be nice if he kept his pigtail as she saw all her countrymen with pigtails in the movies? If he had, then when those kids had come for Lee Chee nuts, he could have whipped them with the pigtail and certainly they would have fled like dogs, and there would have been no need for her to help.
>
> She had seen things about China in the movies and read things about China in novels. She had heard things about China from her white teachers and white schoolmates. She had a general idea of how a Chinaman looked. But she felt she would learn more if she could have a chance to see a Chinaman herself, with her own eyes, and to feel one with her hands. That would be something original.[54]

Wan-Lee and Pearl carry on a disjointed romance that proceeds with irregularity and is interrupted through misunderstandings, some of which involve a difference in cultural values. At the same time, Wan-Lee's solitary life in the laundry continues. He is approached by a white prostitute, a white detective seeking protection money, a city health inspector looking for a bribe, and a Chinese immigrant working as a tailor. Wan-Lee buys a new overcoat from the last, and learns that he holds an M.A. from Columbia University and is a doctoral candidate as well. His laundry is robbed by a masked man whose voice resembles that of the detective. Perhaps the oddest character to approach him is the author Tsiang himself, who appears in the novel as a minor character. He attempts to explain his Communist books to Pearl and Wan-Lee with varied success and provides a sort of dry comic relief.

Wan-Lee's companionship with Pearl includes the discovery that she has never used chopsticks, and periods of awkward silence when the two observe each other with a lack of understanding. After Pearl loses much of her dinner to a cat through fumbling with chopsticks and then begins dancing around the room whistling to amuse herself, Wan-Lee wonders if she is a "Mo No," a phrase meaning "no brain" in Cantonese that is applied by Chinese immigrants to their United States-born cousins.[55] He decides that she is not, concluding his thoughts with what she can do with her appearance that he would not see in China.

> The high-heeled shoes made Pearl Chang's feet small without foot-binding.
> The high-heeled shoes made Pearl Chang shake her body from left to right and back to front.
> The high-heeled shoes made her two tennis balls jump around on her chest, and yet they were there always.[56]

Later, however, they go to a Chinese New Year festival and in the crowd they see a tiny baby with her parents. Pearl, not understanding the term she uses, touches the baby's cheek and says, "You little Chinky!"[57] The baby girl cries until Wan-Lee comforts her and he decides that Pearl is a Mo No after all. They leave the festival later, aware of white tourists following Chinatown guides in search of hatchet men and tong wars.

Wan-Lee develops Pearl's identity as a Chinese American by telling her stories of China, giving explanations of Chinese regional cultures, and teaching her Chinese history. He moves from the selling of opium by the British to the racism he faced in New York. In the middle of the talk, Pearl discreetly discards a small picture of a white movie actress she has been carrying. When their relationship develops a physical element, she is the aggressor, but the situation does not last long. Through a series of mistakes and misunderstandings, they stop seeing each other for a long time.

Wan-Lee goes to a dance hall and dances with a white woman called Darling, who explains that she moved from a hall frequented mainly by white men to this one, where men of Asian descent predominate, because more customers were there. This reflection of the sex ratio among Asian Americans reaches its culmination when Wan-Lee buys coffee for Darling and asks to take her out. She tells him to wait for her outside the hall when it closes.

> He saw many yellow-faced fellows like himself wandering around impatiently.
> A white-faced fellow stepped up to Darling and said gaily, "Honey, are you tired?" Let's take a taxi!"
> And Darling said to Wong Wan-Lee: "Good night,

Chinky!" and the fellow said to him: "Hello, Charlie, where's your laundry?"[58]

Finally Wan-Lee goes to a Chinatown brothel. The woman there is mainly concerned with the tip he will leave. She had been bought as a slave in China and belongs to a tong man.

Wan-Lee and Pearl are reunited after a sequence of further developments. Pearl gets a job as a waitress in a Chinese restaurant in Chinatown, but she loses it on account of her mixed ancestry. She finds work in a Chinese cafeteria with white waitresses and busboys on Broadway where she looks sufficiently Chinese to lend the desired atmosphere. Having lost his laundry to a loan shark and his money in a Chinese gambling establishment, Wan-Lee becomes a busboy in the cafeteria where Pearl works. He is now more interested in politics than before and is happy that two laundry associations have merged to fight corruption better, and that the Nationalists and Communists in China are resisting Japan together; he himself pickets the Japanese consulate.

Finally, the cafeteria workers strike for better wages and shorter hours. Wan-Lee is not afraid of his employer as such, but because he belongs to a tong. Even so, Wan-Lee joins the multiracial strike and Tsiang reappears as a character to help picket. Wan-Lee is shot, however, by a Japanese agent who remembers him from the protest at the consulate and wants both revenge and to make white Americans believe that the Chinese are shooting each other and will be poor allies. Wan-Lee dies in Pearl's arms, claiming that China will defeat Japan because "China Has Hands."

Tsiang displays the concerns and observations of Chinese immigrants as only an immigrant could do. The details of Chinese culture can be learned, but not the emotional responses of the immigrant or the misunderstandings with people born in the United States, such as Pearl. The events of Wan-Lee's daily life have the mundane detail of truth, as do Pearl's interest in her Chinese heritage and the misunderstandings she has with Wan-Lee. The gamblers and tong members are presented as real people with whole lives, functioning as a part of the ghetto community, rather than constituting the major portion of it. While they are not developed much as characters, the touch of an author writing about his own people is unmistakable. Tsiang's characters live in a Chinatown just a few years after the characters of Hugh Wiley and Lemuel de Bra do the same, but their experience has almost no similarity to that of the characters described by those two authors. Wan-Lee and Pearl Chang are seriously developed characters who must operate within the ghetto society, aware that they are part of the Yellow Peril.

Charles R. Shepherd wrote *Lim Yik Choy* (1932) from his experience as the superintendent of the Chung Mei Home for orphaned Chinese American boys in El Cerrito, California, a position that he held for twenty-five years. This novel is the biography of the boy for whom it is named, commonly referred to as Ah Choy, who spends crucial years of his orphaned childhood in Morrison House, which represents the Chung Mei Home. The fictional superintendent, George Douglas, represents Shepherd himself. Ah Choy immigrates from China with an adopted uncle, who dies in the United States. Ultimately, he overcomes his handicaps as an orphan and a young Chinese immigrant and graduates from college. Shepherd presents a straightforward account of the racism Ah Choy faces as well as his efforts to deal with it.

Ah Choy's entrance to the United States in the company of his uncle brings about the first problems. The immigration officer grills the youngster heavily to establish his identity, asking how many windows are in his house, who his neighbors in China were, and other bits of trivia. This was standard procedure toward potential Chinese immigrants in those days of exclusion, to make sure that immigrants fulfilled the requirements of the few legal openings that existed.

Ah Choy's confrontations with racism primarily involve Irish Americans, the descendents of the railroad workers who built the Union Pacific and produced the demogogue Dennis Kearney. In spite of its Christian orientation, Morrison House is burned down when the organization moves into a building in a residential community where the Chinese are not welcome. Shepherd distinguishes between two of the agitators, one of whom is a vicious and unthinking individual, while the other is an honest and sincere man who has simply been taught that the Chinese immigrants constitute an immoral and uncivilized threat to his family. As one might expect, the latter changes his attitude after becoming acquainted with the well-behaved orphans, most of whom have already been converted to Christianity by patience and a soft-sell approach within the orphanage.

Shepherd does not, however, depict the children solely as martyrs. They do have conflicts among themselves, one of which arises because one orphan is envious of Ah Choy's successes. While not extremely important in itself, this incident adds to the realism of the story.

Ah Choy passes successfully through high school, where he quarterbacks a championship football team, and goes on to college on a scholarship. He rooms with Bob Douglas, son of the superintendent of Morrison House. At first Ah Choy faces more racism there in the form of objections to his participation in sports. During the initial hazing days, a white wrestling opponent named Richardson has to be talked into wrestling Ah Choy. Ah Choy beats him, but when he decides to try out for football, Richardson objects: "For my part, I come from a family that has lived in California since the Chinese first came over here. They make splendid servants; but I've not been brought up to mix with them socially."[59]

When Ah Choy gets his football tryout, he dazzles the onlookers with perceptive strategy, awesome elusiveness, and speed. In high school his playing had earned him the name "China-baby," while in college his lack of weight brings him the label "Bantam."[60]

As a sophomore, Ah Choy becomes interested in Ah Laan, a female student one year behind him in school who has come from San Francisco. Each welcomes the chance to speak Cantonese and share their Chinese cultural values with the other. However, as interest develops, Ah Choy's Christianity becomes an obstacle. Ah Laan is not Christian, nor does her father approve of her marrying one. Their educations proceed while the romance develops.

Shepherd makes Ah Choy's social ostracism from much of the college clear by two points. One is that he befriends a young Black who shines shoes; the other is that Richardson and Ames, a friend of his who is the substitute quarterback behind Ah Choy, plant liquor in Ah Choy's room and testify that they witnessed his carrying it into his room against college regulations. The authorities, who are unaware of Richardson's grudge against Ah Choy, suspend judgement for two weeks so that Ah Choy can try to prove his innocence. However, they clearly believe him guilty. Ah Choy responds,

> "Since you refuse to believe me innocent, I will not wait for you to declare me guilty. I am leaving this college today. I am through trying to get an education in an institution where a man is at a disadvantage because of the color of his skin. I have put up with slights and insults from students because I considered them irresponsible; but, this is more than I can stand."[61]

Ah Choy stalks out, pausing only to declare that he is finished with Christianity, as well. He returns to Morrison House and speaks to George Douglas, who urges him to continue arguing his innocence. Ah Choy then goes to San Francisco to speak with Ah Laan, who advocates the same course. He returns and finds that Bob Douglas has been investigating on his own. Douglas learns that Richardson is behind the frame and sees that his father informs the college authorities of Richardson's attitude toward Ah Choy.

In the meantime, Ah Choy finds that his missing a week of football practice before the championship game has meant being relegated to the bench. Ames starts the game but guilt interferes with his playing ability. Finally, in tears, he confesses to Ah Choy that he planted the liquor, and he urges that Ah Choy try to salvage the game, which they are losing, twenty to zero. Led by Ah Choy, their team comes back to win twenty-one to twenty. At the end of the novel, Ah Choy and Ah Laan marry, as her father has finally agreed to allow her to marry a Christian, and they go to Canton to run an orphanage.

In this novel, certain white characters clearly see Ah Choy as a threat. Shepherd presents both their treatment of him and his attempts to deal with the treatment as the basis of the novel. He includes both hostility and sympathy on the part of white characters, making this novel one of the most balanced in that respect. Further, the Chinese orphans are also presented as normal children with faults as well as virtues. Shepherd's account of his characters and events has a kind of realism that may result from his actual experience with such situations. This is a rare and valuable contribution to the fiction on this subject. Only two developments in the novel should be raised as points for caution. The first is that Ah Choy does not represent Chinese American youths of his time in that he wins great popularity through sports and he meets and marries a Chinese American woman. Both undoubtedly happened at times, but Ah Choy's experience should be considered that of a hero and role model like Frank Merriwell, and not that of an average Chinese American boy. Second, his placement in an orphanage run by a white man meant that he and the other orphans had a white representative in their dealings with a sometimes-hostile society. This provided solutions to certain situations that would not have existed for Chinese American nuclear families.

Idwal Jones was a Welsh immigrant who moved to California in 1911. His collection of short stories, *China Boy* (1936), includes four stories about Chinese immigrants on the frontier and two about the first Japanese immigrants to the Pacific Coast. Chinatowns are not prominent in his stories, but his return to frontier settings at this date, after the popularity of stories about Chinatown had been established, signals the end of this first period in American fiction that showcases Chinatown. His view of the Asian immigrants is sympathetic and his characterization is sound. However, a penchant for crime and violence remains an important quality in their behavior.

The title story is an exception. Its protagonist, Pon Look, is a soundly characterized and entertaining figure. He is a wanderer who comes from China at about the age of ten in the 1850s, whose first job is in the stable of a San Francisco circus. Next he roams the Sierra foothills with a Shakespearian troupe. After the company leader absconds with all the money, Pon Look apprentices himself to a Chinese cobbler in San Francisco until he learns the craft. He takes up wandering again and falls in with a party of fifteen Cantonese prospectors captained by "a harsh giant, a hairy Manchurian."[62] They make a huge gold strike, but abandon it through ignorance. When their mistake is discovered, the party disbands after the "Cantonese, screaming like magpies, beat their captain with staves, and he crawled away, out of his wits with chagrin."[63]

Pon Look settles down on the Summerfield ranch as a caretaker and general hired hand. To confine the cattle, he builds a stone wall around the entire spread—a project requiring forty years. This is a monument to his patience, diligence, and industry. As a realistic activity, it is not well presented; he lacks a driving motive, having started simply because a bull escapes him one night when he is on watch. This is the weakest part of the characterization. Jones suggests that the character traits necessary to complete this task are representative of Pon Look's race and ancestral culture in that his wall is an analogue of the Great Wall of China. Despite the depth of his character, some traits also correspond to stereotypes, such as his passive method of resisting Mrs. Summerfield's order to wash the dishes.

> He said no. Whereupon she rushed at him with a broom and smote him violently as he stood in the yard. Pon Look took the blows without a murmur, and remained like a statue, with hands folded, while his mistress, still plying the broom, waxed hysterical.[64]

Pon Look is not a shallow, stereotyped character, but the fact that certain stereotypes—like a passive-aggressive and even tolerant nature—are a part of his makeup is important. His patience pays off after his employers die, as their heir retains him as caretaker but does not live on the premises or interfere at all.

A new mine shaft sunk nearby cuts the water supply to the ranch, leaving it dry. Pon Look, now aged, is given a pension by a banker who manages the estate, paying him corn, flour, bacon, ammunition, and a quart of fine whiskey each week. He retires to a tremendous grove of trees including sugar pines, sequoias, manzanitas, and redwoods. He lives as a happy hermit, journeying occasionally into San Francisco's Chinatown for entertainment. There he sells wildcats, cougars, or bears, which he sometimes captures through unknown means, to Chinatown merchants who use them to draw crowds. Finally, an accidental fire is started by strangers that destroys his woods. Pon Look, now around eighty-five, drives away in his buckboard and disappears.

"Marsh Duck" is about Quong Lee, owner of a restaurant and opium joint for farm workers of Portuguese, Native American, and Chinese descent or origin. He wants to provide women, too, but cannot arrange it. When searching for a delayed opium shipment one night, he is framed by a white police officer and is sentenced to six months in a mental institution. After his release, he goes to great lengths for his revenge. He becomes a cook at the favorite restaurant of the man who framed him and slowly befriends the man, who does not recognize him. Finally, Quong Lee invites his victim to a fine duck dinner, hooks him on opium, and eventually hires him as an impoverished addict to work for him.

"The Hanging of Chung Foo" is set in an abandoned mining town named Garrotte in the Sierras. The story is narrated by Polycarp, one-time warden and now the lone resident. When Garrotte was a boom-town, Chung Foo worked for Tai, a millionaire merchant and banker for a thousand Chinese immigrants. In a flashback, Tai is also the head of a tong called the See Yups, the largest of all the tongs in the Sierra foothills. Tai rules the See Yups with an iron hand, and none of them has ever been inside the Garrotte jail. Chung Foo is treated badly, however, because he disgraces the tong with his penchant for drink and his inability to learn business. He finally murders Tai, whose funeral is a major event in the region.

> For days the See Yups came pouring in: on foot, on horseback and by stage; came in from the river bars, the placer diggings, the deep mines of Mariposa, and in the white of mourning they filled Garrotte. Tai they sank deep with ritual in the graveyard, and ten joss-house men set on him trays laden with the blood and hair of bullocks, soup, wine and rice, all hidden under a mound of blue papers inscribed with prayers in vermilion.[65]

For no discernible reason, Chung Foo turns himself in and then hangs himself in his cell. This cheats the tong of their vengeance and they are angry. To avoid their wrath, the prosecuting attorney blames the warden, Polycarp, who fled town and only returns years later to tell this story.

The weakest element here is Chung Foo's giving himself up. One can understand suicide if he had been forcibly detained, but he apparently never considered trying to leave town. This flaw is similar to Pon Look's lack of sufficient motive for building a huge wall over a forty-year period. Though both characters are interesting and generally well drawn, their unexplained behavior still supports the notion that the Chinese immigrants on the frontier, and perhaps by extension Chinese Americans in general, are not expected to act in understandable ways.

In "Li Fang Serves Tea," Li Fang is the loyal domestic of the senile Capitano of a mercury mine. The mine was once famous, but has been closed many years. A new wartime demand for mercury has caused a steam-shovel crew to plan reopening it against the Capitano's will. Li Fang risks his life burning the timber supports of the mine, destroying it beyond any hope of recovery.

> Not since the hills were born had they beheld so unwonted a spectacle, that of a naked Chinaman, marching with dignity up the road, through the pines to the adobe. Li Fang bathed himself in the rain-tub at the door, dressed himself in the kitchen and made tea.[66]

When Li Fang takes the tea to his master, he finds the old man dead on the doorstep, where he had gone when he heard the distant cave-in, to die satisfied.

Li Fang is depicted as a loyal and self-willed individual whose motives are clear. This story is not set in frontier California, but slightly after, when sentiment for that past existed in people who had once lived it. Jones later expanded this story into a novel called *Vermilion* (1947).

Jones writes with obvious affection for his main characters and utilizes their viewpoints to some extent in his stories, though a white narrator, usually aged, often appears in a frame around them. Since Jones moved to California in 1911 and is writing in 1937, these elderly, garrulous white characters are quite possibly based on individuals with whom he had contact. He is obviously not writing about the frontier from personal experience, so the reader is exposed to the tales of frontier Chinese immigrants through two interpretations at least, of Jones and his source.

This point is important because these stories rely on certain familiar images of the Chinese immigrants. Despite Jones's sympathetic portrayal of Pon Look, he is satisfied to say that Pon Look's motive for his forty-year task is no more than a whim. He regards Chung Foo in the same way. In doing so, he has accepted the brand of inscrutability placed on them by white society, assuming that understanding their behavior is simply not a consideration. Quong Lee's motive for addicting to opium the man who framed him is clear enough, but of course Jones is utilizing here the image of the ruthless and vengeful opium dealer. Li Fang's being a loyal domestic servant is not a bad depiction, but it is another part of these traditional presentations. Jones's work indicates the strength with which these images had persisted from frontier times; even though he likes his characters and develops them fairly well, his underlying assumptions about their behavior are the same ones that were prevalent in American fiction in the 1800s. They have survived their first generation past the closing of the frontier.

The desire of certain white authors to sensationalize their depictions of Chinatown results in the creation of fantasy stories where American Chinatowns take the place of a Shangri-La. This is the most well-represented strain of the Yellow Peril and is the easiest to label as such. Frances Aymar Mathews, Hugh Wiley, and Lemuel de Bra purport to be writing about real Chinatowns, but their versions of Chinatown have combined some naturalists' beliefs about race and the muckrakers' enthusiasm for exposing the sordid without basing their fiction on reality in the manner that defined these schools. This development was possible because earlier fiction about Chinatown was already seriously lacking in accuracy. In order to describe a more fascinating setting than earlier authors had, for instance, Mathews takes the myth of underground tunnels in Chinatown and blithely expands it into three underground levels of city streets. Wiley and de Bra enlarge upon the alleged evils of Chinatown such as torture, murder, and disproportionate influence of the tongs with just as little attention to realism. Their reaching further into the realm of imagination for material, however, signals the end of fiction about crime-ridden, mysterious Chinatowns. Sensationalism quickly uses up subject matter, since each subsequent work must shock more than previous ones. Sensational fiction about the Chinatowns ceases to appear in mainstream fiction in the late 1920s.

Ernest Poole is a marginal entry in this category because he was not seeking to sensationalize Chinatown. However, his characters' impression of China is a fantasy, and their view of Chinatown is a stereotyped one with similar fantasy elements. This disreputable view of Chinatown has also been the most influential one. When feature films about Chinatown begin to appear, they show this side of the community. By presenting a consistent picture of Chinatown over the years, these authors developed a feeling of familiarity with Chinatown in their readers. Americans became familiar with terms such as tong, hatchet man, and opium den; the Six Companies, the Bachelor Society, and the restrictive laws confining Chinatown life remain largely unknown even now.

The first two Chinese American authors to write fiction offer an important contrast to the distorted presentations of Chinatown from white authors. The fiction of both Eaton and Tsiang is realistic and seeks to define the experience of Chinese America for the first time. In doing so, they expose the fiction of Mathews, Wiley, and de Bra as adventure fantasies and point out how the belief in the Yellow Peril affects the everyday lives of Chinese Americans. Eaton and Tsiang try neither to establish nor to deny the individual humanity of their characters, quite naturally writing with this quality as an assumption beneath mention.

The particular treatments of the Chinese Americans by Hergesheimer, Rideout, Shepherd, and Jones are not as important as the fact that all four presentations take place outside Chinatown and are intended as positive depictions. Their success is varied, with Rideout and Shepherd presenting sensitive portrayals of well-drawn, individual characters. Shepherd is especially effective, due to the experience he brings to his subject matter. Hergesheimer is as successful in creating a sympathetic character, but he fails to make Taou Yuen an individual distinct from her class of noble Manchu women. Jones exhibits the most influence from earlier Yellow Peril fiction. The pertinent works of these four authors appeared in the 1930s, and their diversification suggests that the Chinese Americans were the subject of increasingly realistic handling in American fiction. Two facts must be pointed out in this regard. One is that this is true in mainstream fiction only. Fu Manchu, Charlie Chan, and the Chinatowns of the pulp magazines develop their own use of stereotypes and warnings about the Yellow Peril in popular fiction. The second is that Japanese Americans become the victims of increasing hostility during this time. International politics are a factor here, and the American sympathy for China and hostility toward Japan in the 1930s are paralleled in white America's attitudes toward Chinese Americans and Japanese Americans. So the concept of the Yellow Peril does not die, but simply shifts for a time partly from mainstream fiction to the pulps and within mainstream fiction to the Japanese Americans, beyond the scope of this study.

VI
Fu Manchu and Charlie Chan

Fu Manchu and Charlie Chan are very different characters but they have an important relationship to each other in American popular culture. Fu Manchu is an evil genius who personifies the Asian threat, while Charlie Chan is a detective whose patience and intelligence solve murder mysteries in defense of civilized society. On the surface, they appear to be simple opposites. The Chinese ancestry of both characters tempts one to suggest that they represent the yin-yang symbol of Taoism that illustrates a dualist interpretation of the universe. Yet their origin is not, after all, Chinese. Fu Manchu and Charlie Chan were created by white authors Sax Rohmer and Earl Derr Biggers, respectively, for white readers. These two characters do not represent archetypal dualities such as good and evil, or even crime versus law. The duality they represent is racial, yellow versus white, with Fu Manchu embodying yellow power and Charlie Chan supporting white supremacy. The two characters will be examined separately with these roles in focus.

The Fu Manchu character is the first Asian role of prominence in modern literature to have a large American readership. Technically, the Fu Manchu series belongs to English literature, since author Sax Rohmer was English; however, the adoption of the Fu Manchu novels by the American public has established Fu Manchu as a major figure in American popular culture. Millions of copies of the Fu Manchu books have been sold in the United States, signaling a popularity that has led to adaptations in film, radio, television, and comics.[1] The tremendous popularity of Fu Manchu has also meant a great deal of literary influence, as the image of Fu Manchu has been absorbed into American consciousness as the archetypal Asian villain. For this reason the particular literary elements of the Fu Manchu novels will be examined for what they present to the American public, and for what subsequent American writers found desirable to emulate. This is done with the understanding that Fu Manchu may have a different significance in English culture.

All together, Rohmer wrote thirteen novels, three short stories, and one novelette about Fu Manchu and his arch-foe, British agent Sir Denis Nayland Smith. The first three novels constitute one unit, including *The Insidious Dr. Fu-Manchu* (1913), *The Return of Fu-Manchu* (1916), and *The Hand of Fu-Manchu* (1917), which stood for fourteen years as the complete series. (The character's name was hyphenated only in the first three novels.) All three works were serialized in British magazines prior to their appearance in the United States in book form. Throughout the 1920s, Rohmer wrote a variety of novels and short stories dealing with suspense, the occult, and with the Chinese in England. A few had at most a marginal relation to the Fu Manchu novels, in the form of minor characters and references. In the late 1920s, Rohmer went to New York to write a Fu Manchu serial for Collier's magazine, which eventually appeared in book form as *Daughter of Fu Manchu* (1931). This and the rest of the novels constitute a second group which appeared at intervals until 1959. However, the two main characters, the prevailing theme, and the type of plot devices used are all established in the first three novels, which will be considered first as a group.

Rohmer introduces Fu Manchu unequivocably as the representative of the Asian threat to the West.

> Imagine a person, tall, lean and feline, high-shouldered, with a brow like Shakespeare and a face like Satan, a close-shaven skull, and long, magnetic eyes of true cat-green. Invest him with all the cruel cunning of an entire Eastern race, accumulated in one giant intellect, with all the resources, if you will, of a wealthy government which, however, already has denied all knowledge of his existence. Imagine that awful being, and you have a mental picture of Dr. Fu-Manchu, the yellow peril incarnate in one man.[2]

Rohmer strengthens this image of the exotic, evil Asian by the use of three types of plot devices in these early novels. The most evocative device for the exotic aura around the character is an array of complex, original assassination techniques, which are usually successful. The development of the evil taint in Fu Manchu's personality is also achieved through his perpetration of nonfatal tortures and occasional assassination attempts that fail. The qualities of being exotic and evil are bound together by repeated statements to the effect that Fu Manchu represents a rising tide of Asian politics, and that his behavior is determined by his Asian culture and race.

In *The Insidious Doctor Fu-Manchu*, the plot consists of various efforts by Smith to prevent or solve certain murders and disappearances. First, Smith and his friend Dr. Petrie attempt to stop the latest in a rash of assassinations. Urgency heightens the suspense in this endeavor; however, in order to build the potency of the villain, Rohmer makes this attack on an undeveloped character successful. The killing is accomplished by the use of a scorpion, in an incident containing elements of both horror and mystery stories. First a letter is mailed to the victim, dipped in a certain perfume. The night after its arrival, one of Fu Manchu's servants introduces into the victim's study an unknown type of scorpion that locates the victim's hand through the perfume that has rubbed off the letter. The scorpion stings the hand fatally. The delicate planning required for this operation emphasizes the intricate lengths to which Fu Manchu will go and the scorpion itself, discovered in London, signifies the entry into England of the exotic, suggesting the jungle, Asia, and the foreign nature of Fu Manchu and his associates.

The murders committed by "The Call of Siva" offer the most challenge to the reader, as they present a locked-room mystery, where all the facts are presented long before the solution is disclosed. These deaths occur when victims, in upper-story rooms, are found lying on the ground beneath their windows, dead from the fall. In some incidents, they fell from rooms where the doors were locked and the windows completely inaccessible from the ground. One witness in the room actually has seen a victim yanked out the window, though no tangible means for causing this has been found. The only clue is a strange howling or cry outside the building, heard by some witnesses shortly before the victim's death. Smith is familiar with the mystery from his earlier days fighting the forces of Fu Manchu in Burma, where the cry was called "the Call of Siva" by a religious group.[3] An element of mysticism is added to the deaths by this use of the worshippers of Siva and the apparently disembodied voice. The Burmese origin of the phenomenon reinforces in the reader's mind Fu Manchu's status as a leader specifically of Asian people. The solution to the mystery clinches this reminder: in each murder, a member of the Indian religious cult *Thuggee* climbed to the roof of the building, and cried out to attract the victim to the window. When the victim's head was outside the window, looking around, the *Thug* would drop a fixed loop of silken cord over it, yank the victim out of the window, then pull up the cord as the victim fell out of the loop to the ground. The use of silk for the cord and a *Thug* for the crime itself maintain the Asian flavor of this crime, and by now, the reader begins to realize that crime by Asian people or objects means the presence of Fu Manchu behind the scenes.

In *The Return of Fu Manchu*, the assassination techniques are no longer specifically related to Asia, but are simply unusual and unpleasant. One character is known for carrying a cane with a knob in the shape of a snake's head. To eliminate him, a servant of Fu Manchu replaces it with a hollow tube holding a live adder, with its head in the place of the knob. Other killings are done by an Abyssinian half-man, half-baboon with the intelligence of a human and the strength and agility of the animal. Fu Manchu's use of the adder and the half-baboon represent a widening of his control from creatures of Asia to those of Australia and Africa. The breeding of the special scorpion and ape are gimmicks used here for the sake of mystery and suspense, but they are also the seeds of what blooms into clearly defined science fiction by the end of the third novel.

The last assassinations in the second novel are deaths by fright at the Gables mansion. Mysterious lights and ringing bells literally scare selected residents and guests to death. In this case, the servants of Fu Manchu have attached bells to mice and have released them within the walls of the building where they run in prescribed areas. The strange lights are accomplished with a flashlight, which at that time had not yet become a common item.

Only two assassination techniques appear in *The Hand of Fu Manchu*. The first is the "flower of silence," which produces poison. Since the poison affects the tongue very quickly, clear enunciation of complex words is early proof that one is not contaminated. Tradition states that saying "Sâkya Muni" is a charm against the poison, when of course it is actually just an indication that one has not been poisoned at all. By using one of the names of Buddha for this test and by giving India as the origin of the flower, Rohmer again focuses on Asia. A chest with a needle in the handle and a hidden syringe of poison inside has no connection with Asia, but—like the scorpion, the adder, the half-baboon, and the belled mice—it continues the association of sly, complex evil with the name of Fu Manchu.

The nonfatal crimes also heighten this sense of villainy. An attempt to kill Egyptologist Sir Lionel Barton involves filling a sarcophagus in his study with an invention of Fu Manchu's similar to chlorine gas. This extremely lethal cloud is described as seeming "to be alive. It moved over the floor, about a foot from the ground, going away from him and towards a curtain at the other end of the study."[4] Smith and Petrie later venture into London's Chinatown, disguised as Chinese, in search of Fu Manchu. When Fu Manchu discovers Petrie, he drops him through a trapdoor into the Thames. As he is carried by the current, he sees an apparent handhold; however, Smith, climbing down to his rescue, prevents him from grabbing it. The wooden beam actually hides the presence of two sharp, upturned sword blades, that sever the fingers of a victim against the pull of the current. The secondary level reasoning that places these blades creates a grudging respect in both the protagonists and the reader for the thoroughness of the villain, and also disgust for him as the perpetrator of such unnecessary and carefully considered cruelty.

The connection of being evil with being Asian does not rely only on symbolism and association. The theme, that Asian hordes are on the verge of sweeping through Europe and North America with only a few British heroes opposing them, runs explicitly throughout the first three novels. Suspects are chosen by racial background, and are always proven guilty. The assumption of Asian guilt and inferiority is open and unembarrassed. Smith finds that even Fu Manchu has lapses into childishness: "We owe our lives, Petrie, to the national childishness of the Chinese! A race of ancestor worshippers is capable of anything. . . ." Petrie, who is the narrator in the first three novels, often identifies suspects on the basis of race in the narrative: "Though highly educated, and possibly an American citizen, *Van Roon was a Chinaman.*"[6] Another killer's disguise was that of "a benevolent old gentleman whose ancestry was not wholly innocent of Oriental strains. . . ."[7] In regard to the struggle against these villains, Petrie gives the reader frequent reminders to the effect that "the swamping of the White world by Yellow hordes might well be the price of our failure."[8]

The other novels and short stories in the series continue Fu Manchu's efforts to conquer the white world through science-fiction methods, to be foiled by Smith and his secret-agent allies. After the third book, Petrie no longer narrates, though he occasionally still appears as a character. His replacements, like him, all act as viewpoint characters, sidekicks to Smith, and romantic leads; some also narrate. The next three novels in succession are *Daughter of Fu Manchu* (1931), *The Mask of Fu Manchu* (1932), and *The Bride of Fu Manchu* (1933). These three are narrated by Shan Greville, who is English; the first two continue to use England as a setting, while the third takes place on the French Riviera. The next two novels seem to indicate an awareness on Rohmer's part of an American audience; *The Trail of Fu Manchu* (1934), told in third person and set in London, features an American sidekick and romantic lead named Alan Sterling. Rohmer handles the fact that he is not British carefully, emphasizing his ancestry. He is introduced as

> a lean young man, marked by an intense virility. His
> features were too irregular for him to be termed handsome,
> but he had steadfast Scottish eyes, and one would have said
> that tenacity of purpose was his chief virtue . . . despite his
> Scottish name, a keen observer might have deduced from his
> intonation that Sterling was a citizen of the United States.[9]

In *President Fu Manchu* (1936), also written in third person, Smith
goes to the United States to prevent Fu Manchu's engineering the elec-
tion of one of his rare Caucasian servants to the presidency. His partner
here is Mark Hepburn, a captain in the U.S. Marine Corps on special
duty. He, too, has impeccable white ancestry, as a third-generation
Quaker with a half-Celtic mother.

The action returns to London in *The Drums of Fu Manchu* (1939),
which is narrated by Englishman Bart Kerrigan. However, this is the
last wholly British novel; in *The Island of Fu Manchu* (1941), Kerrigan
and Smith follow Fu Manchu to the Caribbean, where he is creating an
army of zombies, or walking dead, who will obey his commands and
staff a powerful, technologically advanced navy. The last three novels
all feature Americans as viewpoint characters written about in third
person. *The Shadow of Fu Manchu* (1948), set in New York, includes
an American named Dr. Morris Craig, whose credentials are not only a
British surname, but a manner of speech "particularly English,"[10] from
his training as "one of the most brilliant physicists Oxford University
had ever turned out."[11] Suspicion of the Asian race has not slackened
any in this later novel; another of Smith's American colleagues complains to a Harvard-educated secretary of his club about seeing an
"Asiatic" in the building and is assured, "Your complaint is before
me. . .I can only assure you that not only have we no Asiatic members,
honorary or otherwise, but no visitor such as you describe has been in
the club. . . ."[12] The Asian in the building, of course, is a spy in the
employ of Fu Manchu, and so justifies such complaints based on racial
grounds. In *Re-enter Fu Manchu* (1957), Smith is aided by Brian Mer-
rick, the son of a United States senator and a graduate of Oxford.
Finally, in *Emperor Fu Manchu* (1959), finished several weeks before
Rohmer died, Smith has another American colleague of Scottish
ancestry, U.S. government agent Tony McKay.

The increasing emphasis on American companions for Smith and
on settings in the western hemisphere may partly result from a desire of
Rohmer's to offer more variety of plot and setting. Also, *Collier's*
magazine in the U.S. had revived the series by commissioning

Daughter of Fu Manchu and *The Mask of Fu Manchu*. In fact, *Collier's* purchased not only several of the other Fu Manchu novels, but also the bulk of Rohmer's fiction from 1913 to 1946. The size of the potential reading market in the United States was probably at least a consideration; Nayland Smith's presence in every story maintains the British flavor and origin of the adventures, while occasional American companions may increase the attraction of the novels for American readers. Rohmer's friend and biographer Cay Van Ash writes that Rohmer decided in 1935 "to reward his American supporters by transferring the activities of Fu Manchu to the United States."[13] The first novel to follow this decision was *President Fu Manchu*.[14] Fu Manchu's success as a character was thus launched in a strictly British framework and was possibly boosted in the United States by certain conscious decisions by Rohmer along the way.

Prior to 1932, the people of China and their cousins throughout the world are not on record as objecting to the image of Fu Manchu as their representative in English-language fiction. Earlier complaints from China are understandably lacking; Fu Manchu first appeared between 1913 and 1917, when the nascent Republic of China, having overthrown the Manchu Dynasty in 1911, was degenerating into a titular government whose land was in reality governed piecemeal by various warlords. Incessant civil strife continued until early 1928, when the Kuomintang under Chiang Kai-shek defeated the other warlords and sent the Chinese Communists into the Long March, near extinction. While the Kuomintang never eliminated all their enemies nor regained all the foreign concessions, they did make the first substantial claim to being the national government of China that the world had seen for many years, so that the international situation had changed from 1917 to 1931, when *Daughter of Fu Manchu* resumed the series in *Colliers*.

In 1932, while *The Mask of Fu Manchu* was running in *Collier's*, Metro-Goldwyn-Mayer began production of a film by that title, starring Boris Karloff as Fu Manchu, Myrna Loy as his daughter, and Lewis Stone as Nayland Smith. The film was a hit, like its British predecessors, and MGM intended to produce sequels. However:

> They were curiously obstructed by urgent protests from the Chinese Embassy in Washington. The Chinese diplomats took a humorless view of Fu Manchu, whom they considered damaging to their "image." At this time, the West in general, and America in particular, was becoming alarmed by the rapid expansion of Japan in the Far East, and rather inclined to encourage China as a potential ally against this

threat. Consequently, the protest received closer attention than it might otherwise have done.

The Chinese were unable to influence the publication of the Fu Manchu stories (at that time; later, they were able, and did) but they were successful in holding up the production of further films. Sax's rather questionable financial advisers were furious, and actually suggested bringing an injunction against the Chinese government for "loss of revenue." But Sax, who considered the complaint understandable, even if absurd, refused to give his consent to any such proceeding.[15]

Nayland Smith apparently does come to admire Fu Manchu's abilities in the course of the series, though this change appears to be unrelated to any outside pressure. The change in attitude involves Smith's apparent growth of admiration for his foe's abilities during his endeavors to stop the encroachment of the Yellow Peril. At the same time, Fu Manchu develops a similar respect for the abilities of Smith and his associates who continually foil his designs for world domination. The mixture of all-out war between them and their recognition of each other's capabilities heightens the sense of spectacle when the two meet.

On several occasions in the early novels, Smith attempts, and urges his cohorts to attempt, killing Fu Manchu; in *The Insidious Doctor Fu Manchu*, from 1913, he screams at Petrie, *"It's Fu-Manchu! Cover him! Shoot him dead if—"* The sentence is cut off by the falling of a trapdoor beneath Petrie.[16] However, Smith's attitude is entirely different in 1948, when Fu Manchu makes his escape at the end of *The Shadow of Fu Manchu*. A colleague named Sam has fired three times after what he believes to be Fu Manchu's fleeing form, despite orders from Smith to cease fire. "'You fool!' Nayland Smith's words came as a groan. 'This was no end for the greatest brain in the world!'"[17] However, Sam has in fact only shot one of Fu Manchu's servants dressed like his master. Fu Manchu's escape has merely allowed Smith to voice his change in attitude toward his adversary. In *Re-enter Fu Manchu*, however, he expresses a doubt about this new consideration. At one point, Fu Manchu introduces a double for Smith into their intrigue; after the double is killed, the real Smith reports back to Fu Manchu, posing as his own double. He leaves without harming Fu Manchu, in order to convey his information about Fu Manchu's widespread plans to the authorities. He assumes that he will capture Fu Manchu when the plot as a whole is dismantled. At the end of the novel, when the plan has been foiled but Fu Manchu has escaped, Smith says, "I haven't settled down yet to the fact that that cunning fiend has escaped me again. In my crazy overconfidence I missed my chance. It was my duty to the world when I stood before him to shoot him. . . ."[18] These changes, superficial and waffling, do not ultimately alter the depiction of Fu Manchu's image or character.

The four short works about Fu Manchu are a novelette, "The Wrath of Fu Manchu" (1952), the most significant, which appeared in the *Star Weekly* of Toronto; and three short stories, "The Eyes of Fu Manchu" (1957), "The Word of Fu Manchu" (1958), and "The Mind of Fu Manchu" (1959), all of which appeared in *This Week* magazine. The last three are minor pieces relying on the reader's prior knowledge of Fu Manchu for their full impact. They were severely constrained by the length limitations of the magazine, and so utilize established parts of the Smith-Fu Manchu conflicts without expanding upon them.[19] "The Wrath of Fu Manchu" is a much more ambitious tale involving Smith's personal infiltration of Fu Manchu's advisory council. While it adds little new material to the saga, it does contain greater suspense and characterization, including the final appearance of Fu Manchu's daughter, Fah Lo Suee.

Sax Rohmer altogether wrote fiction consisting of forty-one novels, eleven collections of short fiction, and many other uncollected short stories.[20] Beyond those about Fu Manchu, few of these works involved the Chinese or the Yellow Peril. The novels *The Yellow Claw* (1915), set in London and Paris, and *Yüan Hee See Laughs*, set in London, involve mysteries surrounding Chinese mandarins in England. They never gained the popularity of the Fu Manchu stories, possibly because, appearing later, their crimes, techniques, and overall image seem to be mere spin-offs. While interesting, they seem weak compared to the image created in Fu Manchu.

The Golden Scorpion (1936) deals with Fu Manchu's secret organization, the Si-Fan, without including him or Nayland Smith. *Dope* (1919) and *Yellow Shadows* (1925) also involve crime in London's Chinatown, as do the short-story collections *Tales of Chinatown* (1922) and *Tales of East and West* (1932). In these stories, the emphasis is on the individual activities of Chinese criminals without the elements of science fiction or of maniacal mandarins in charge of worldwide organizations that help define the threat of Fu Manchu. Instead they are more mundane stories of crimes involving the Chinese in London. The contribution of these stories to the image of the Chinese is Rohmer's portrayal of all Chinatown inhabitants as morally depraved, dangerous, and degenerate. Similar figures appear in the Fu Manchu stories as the servants who actually commit the crimes he designs. None of these works approximate the popularity or impact of the Fu Manchu stories, but they can serve to illuminate further Sax Rohmer's vision of the Chinese. In this capacity, they confirm that his presentation of the moral nature of the Chinese in the West was consistent in his works throughout the many decades in which he wrote.

The greatest impact of Fu Manchu as a character derives from his function as a leader. Prior to his creation, the Chinese in the United States are pictured with variety in their scattered roles throughout the frontier, in their small hamlets, and in their Chinatowns. They are depicted as victims and rogues; they appear as servants, opium smokers, violent criminals, and passive laborers. Their evil characteristics are well established and dominate their image in American fiction during the last half of the nineteenth century. Yet, these characteristics are given to the Chinese as a group, without compelling characterization. Even Harte's memorable See Yup and Ah Fes are shown as representatives of the Chinese, not as outstanding personalities. The lack of powerful individual personalities amog the Chinese is clearest in the stories of invasion, where the activity of the infiltrating Chinese is presented as the result of an inhumanly strict obedience to shadowy figures in China. When leaders do appear, such as Woltor's Prince Tsa, their function is primarily symbolic.

By contrast, Rohmer places Fu Manchu atop the Chinatown in London, which represents the Chinese communities in the American West to American readers. Fu Manchu's tools are those same scum of the Chinatown opium dens, rough waterfronts, secret societies, and heathen religions whom earlier American fiction has already made familiar. His methods not only utilize, but actually rely on, the secrecy for which the Chinese had become known to white observers in the United States from the time of Bret Harte. He is not a remote leader, however. Like Robert W. Chambers's Yue-Laou and Dr. Doyle's Quong Lung, he supervises his programs personally, lending a profound and powerful, if slightly mad, character of genius to the adventures. As the leader and focal point of Chinese people in Western Europe and North America, Fu Manchu draws upon the old established images of the Chinese for the minor villains who obey his will. Simultaneously, he increases the impact of their images by using these servants and his own scientific genius for carefully organized, large-scale programs. Their individual crimes and depravity grow in stature by becoming parts of an international whole.

In a sense, Fu Manchu fills a power vacuum that had existed in the tales of Chinese immigration and infiltration; with his presence as "the yellow peril incarnate," the evils of Chinatown are seen as a clearly intelligent malevolence rather than as either a random one, or an inevitable one.[21] His character, like those of Sherlock Holmes, Tarzan, and Superman, becomes greater than any particular work of fiction in which he appears. By associating Fu Manchu with every evil aspect of the Chinese image that existed in the early twentieth century, Rohmer ensured that future Chinese villains would evoke memories of Fu Manchu for many years to come, in every wandering wisp of opium smoke, every fugitive trailing a queue, every dark, damp alley of Chinatown, and every sharp-taloned mandarin's silhouette.

Charlie Chan is only the second literary character of Asian descent whose name has become commonly recognized in the United States. As a protagonist, he is not a representative of the Yellow Peril, but, rather, an example of overcompensation in an author's attempt to break away from the Yellow Peril. Unlike Fu Manchu, Charlie Chan is known primarily through a total of forty-seven serial and feature films produced during the 1930s and 1940s, still seen on television.[22] Nevertheless, his origin lies in the novels by Earl Derr Biggers, who defined the character in six mysteries between 1925 and 1932. Biggers died in 1933, leaving subsequent film, stage, radio, and television productions to other writers. The character of Charlie Chan is developed in the first three novels, *The House Without a Key* (1925), *The Chinese Parrot* (1926), and *Behind That Curtain* (1928). The last three novels are *The Black Camel* (1929), *Charlie Chan Carries On* (1930), and *Keeper of the Keys* (1932). After developing the character to his satisfaction by the third novel, Biggers seems to have settled down to producing new mysteries without altering the mainstay of his work, much in the way Sax Rohmer produced ten Fu Manchu novels based on the characters he had established in the first set of three novels.

As a Chinese Hawaiian, Charlie Chan in Biggers's day represented a halfway point to Asia; Hawaii was a territory, not part of the United States proper, populated mainly by Hawaiians and Asian immigrants. At the same time, it was United States property, and white Americans controlled the economy and dominated the social structure of the wealthy. Asian immigration had been sufficiently established to make Charlie Chan's position as a detective there plausible, while antipathy in the country as a whole toward the Chinese made his having such a position on the mainland unlikely. Conceivably, if a novel had presented a Chinese detective on the West Coast at this time, it might not have been accepted by the public as Charlie Chan was. So Charlie Chan is located in Hawaii as a racially Asian man in a society controlled by white Americans, resulting in his definition here as an Asian American. Occasional cases on the mainland solidify this definition.

Charlie Chan's unique attribute as a literary character is his position as an Asian American protagonist. Appearing at a time when Fu Manchu, opium dens, and tong wars dominated American fiction about the Chinese in the United States, Charlie Chan was drawn in lines that no one could mistake as a threat.

> He was very fat indeed, yet he walked with the light dainty step of a woman. His cheeks were as chubby as a baby's, his skin ivory tinted, his black hair close-cropped, his amber eyes slanting. As he passed Miss Minerva he bowed with a courtesy encountered all too rarely in a work-a-day world, then moved on after Hallet.[23]

Much of the impact of Charlie Chan's character comes not just from his appearance and personality, but in the contrast of these with his career as a detective. Of all the many detectives in serious crime fiction, none is more out of shape, though some are equally so, and none is more meticulously polite. Not one is less hard-boiled or less imposing a figure than Charlie Chan. While Biggers does not claim that Charlie Chan represents all Chinese or Chinese Americans in the way that Fu Manchu is called "the yellow peril incarnate," Charlie Chan's solitary position as an Asian American protagonist renders him the representative of good Chinese American citizens simply by default. The resulting implication is that as a detective and protagonist, Charlie Chan is the best Chinese Americans have to offer.

In *The House Without a Key*, Biggers shows caution in regard to his racially innovative detective. The romantic interest and viewpoint character is young John Quincy Winterslip of Boston, descended from the Puritans. Charlie Chan himself enters the novel only on page seventy-six, though he then remains in the spotlight throughout the investigation of murder. He is absent from the final scene, when Winterslip concludes the romantic subplot.

Charlie Chan's investigatory technique mirrors his appearance, with totally submissive, apologetic speech and manners. When facing direct racism from a Bostonian cousin of the murdered man, he responds,

> "Humbly asking pardon to mention it, I detect in your eyes slight flame of hostility. Quench it, if you will be so kind. Friendly co-operation are essential between us." Despite his girth, he managed a deep bow. "Wishing you good morning," he added, and followed Hallet.[24]

Biggers carries this courtesy to absurdity when Charlie Chan questions a recalcitrant witness. At no time in this first novel does Biggers allow any hint of aggression, assertiveness, or temper to show in his detective. This investigator's methods are gentle chidings and a display of disappointment in order to elicit guilt feelings from the witness, who finally complains, "That slant-eyed Chinaman has been sitting here looking at me more in sorrow than in anger for the better part of an hour, and I've made up my mind to one thing. I shall have no more secrets from the police."[25]

Charlie Chan remains polite and unruffled regardless of the events in *The House Without a Key*. By presenting him as calm at all times, Biggers erases any emotion from Charlie Chan's personality except for an aura of apology, and maintains his low profile as an individual. This leaves primarily the image of cold cerebral abilities that he applies to his job. In tense moments, his calm is emphasized by the use of flowery speech, as in the apprehension of the murderer:

> A serene, ivory-colored face appeared suddenly at the broken window. An arm with a weapon was extended through the jagged opening.
>
> "Relinquish the firearms, Mr. Jennison," commanded Charlie Chan, "or I am forced to make fatal insertion in vital organ belonging to you."[26]

The successful conclusion of the murder investigation earns Charlie Chan praise from his former detractor, who says, "I congratulate you. You've got brains, and they count."[27] This development symbolizes a fundamental lesson in upward mobility: Charlie Chan is initially faced with direct racism, to which he responds politely. He does his job and is rewarded with acceptance—bestowed by a Bostonian woman of Puritan stock upon a Chinese American man, a fact that establishes in whose hands the power of acceptance lies.

Throughout the first novel, Charlie Chan remains essentially a racial novelty, as an assistant to his Captain Hallet, who participates in many of the proceedings, and as a confidante to the young Winterslip. The only mention of his personal background informs the reader that he has a cousin, Willie Chan, in Hawaii and that he himself has been there for twenty-five years. Biggers was conducting an experiment in presenting his Chinese American detective, and he illuminates his character as an individual much less than most mystery writers do with their detectives. After the success of the first novel, Biggers's confidence in his protagonist seems to increase.

In *The Chinese Parrot*, Biggers is ready to provide more information about Charlie Chan's background. In addition, he brings Charlie

Chan into the novel much sooner, though young white Bob Eden, heir to "the best-known jewelry store west of the Rockies," is again the viewpoint character and romantic lead. The reader finds that Charlie Chan's job as a detective represents upward mobility in a financial sense as well as a social one when a former employer recalls, "Long ago, in the big house on the beach, he was our number one boy."[28] His age is not mentioned. Later, Biggers even produces a flash of anger in Charlie Chan, though the scene is set up in such a way as to prevent any outburst from him. This story takes place on a ranch in California, where racism against the Chinese is expected. At this time, Charlie Chan is spying on a suspect while disguised as a servant named Ah Kim.

> "But fortunately no one was hurt. No white man, I mean. Just my old Chink, Louie Wong." Ah Kim had entered just in time to hear this speech, and his eyes blazed for a moment as they rested on the callous face of the millionaire.[29]

Biggers reveals his attitude toward Chinese domestic servants through Charlie Chan's rendition of Ah Kim during the murder investigation conducted by a local constable.

> "Ever see this Louie Wong before?" thundered the constable.
> "Me, boss? No, boss, I no see 'um."
> "New round here, ain't you?"
> "Come las' Fliday, boss."
> "Where did you work before this?"
> "All place, boss. Big town, litta town."
> "I mean where'd you work last?"
> "Lailload, I think, boss. Santa Fe lailload. Lay sticks on glound."[30]

Working-class backgrounds, heavy accents, and dull minds characterize the bulk of Asian characters in the series.

On other occasions, when Charlie Chan is free to protest racial insults if he chooses, he does not. One example of the racial comments he tolerates comes from Captain Flannery, who is in charge of the murder investigation in *Behind That Curtain*: "I'll have Manley of the Chinatown Squad bring the kid here to-night. They're all crazy about Manley, these Chink kids."[31] Charlie Chan is present during this conversation but the narrative does not turn to him at this point. No mention is made of his reaction or lack of one.

The fact that San Francisco's Captain Flannery, especially with

his Irish surname, exhibits racial antagonism toward Charlie Chan
while his regular superior in Hawaii, Captain Hallet, does not,
realistically contrasts the general attitudes in those two areas. When
Charlie Chan plays a hunch regarding the identity of a witness, Flannery grudgingly goes along with his line of investigation. When the
witness is not identified as expected by a second witness, Flannery ex-
plodes in anger and Charlie Chan responds typically.

> Profound contrition showed in Charlie's eyes. "I am so
> sorry. I have made stupid error. Captain—is it possible you
> will every forgive me?"
> Flannery snorted. "Will I ever forgive myself? Listening
> to a Chinaman—me, Tom Flannery. . . ."[32]

Later, Flannery says to the witness, "I apologize to you. You see, I got
foolish and listened to a Chinaman, and that's how I came to make a
mistake about your identity."[33]

Ultimately, Charlie Chan prevails. He establishes that the crucial
witness was not identified honestly by the second witness, and that his
hunch was correct all along. When the mysterious witness finally confesses her true identity, he indulges in a rare expression of triumph:
"Charlie looked grimly at Flannery. 'Now the truth arrives,' he said.
'That you once listened to a Chinaman is, after all, no lasting
disgrace.' "[34]

This victory represents a kind of revenge for any and all racial
harassment Charlie Chan has endured during his investigation, and is a
trademark in each of the first three novels. In the first, as mentioned,
his investigative success earns the acceptance of a Bostonian of Puritan
descent; in The Chinese Parrot, his triumph earns the respect of the
crusty old white California millionaire; next, he proves himself to Captain Flannery. After these first novels, the need for him to struggle for
acceptance apparently has faded. Only the fifth novel, Charlie Chan
Carries On (1930), contains even a trace of this phenomenon, and it
comes midway through the novel from Charlie Chan's English ally, Inspector Duff, who first met Charlie Chan in Behind That Curtain and
now has followed a murderer to Hawaii.

> Duff sat up. The easy manner with which Charlie rattled
> off names suggested that, after all, the matter was interest-
> ing him more than his sleepy eyes would indicate. Once
> again, Duff thought, he had been wronging the Honolulu
> policeman. Once again, as had frequently happened several
> years ago in San Francisco, he must hastily revise his opin-

ion of this Chinese.[35]

A new development replaces the old need to earn acceptance. Throughout the entire series, Charlie Chan quotes various supposed Chinese aphorisms. In the last three novels, Charlie Chan produces a greater number of these sayings and instead of ending each novel with a triumph proving his worth to a white racist, he ends his role in each novel with a saying. In *Charlie Chan Carries On*, he says to Mark Kennaway, the white romantic lead, "The Emperor Shi Hwang-ti, who built the Great Wall of China, once said: 'He who squanders to-day talking of yesterday's triumph, will have nothing to boast of tomorrow.'"[36] He ends the final novel, *Keeper of the Keys* (1932), saying, "Three things the wise man does not do. He does not plow the sky. He does not paint pictures on the water. And he does not argue with a woman."[37] At the end of *The Black Camel*(1929), he rhetorically questions an old Chinese domestic servant.

> Charlie gazed into the beady eyes, the withered yellow face of his compatriot.
> "Tell me something, Wu," he said. "How was it I came upon this road? Why should one of our race concern himself with the hatreds and the misdeeds of the *haoles*?"
> "Wha's mallah you?" Wu inquired.
> "I am weary," sighed Chan. "I want peace now. A very trying case, good Wu Kuo-ching. But"—he nodded, and a smile spread over his fat face—"as you know, my friend, a gem is not polished without rubbing nor a man perfected without trials."[38]

The Chinese American detective has on the surface progressed from the status of struggling minority to moral authority. The price is subtly expressed but significant: when struggling for acceptance, Charlie Chan clearly functioned as a member of an American minority relating with difficulty to whites. His moral authority is not derived from his experience or culture as an American, but from his heritage as an immigrant. The sayings emphasize the foreign origin of the character, not his trials and other experiences as a member of an American minority. Associating foreign status with increased respect eliminates the need to concede respect to the Asian American *as* an American. His struggles for acceptance are forgotten, as though he had immigrated as a member of the middle class, and had simply brought these gems of wisdom with him.

Charlie Chan's relationship to his home on Punchbowl Hill, his wife, and numerous children is developed only to a small degree. He is established as a devoted family man through brief comments and references to his home at various times. In *Behind That Curtain*, he expresses frequent anxiety about the case detaining him in San Francisco while his wife is about to give birth. Finally, when the case has been closed, he sneaks away from his colleagues in order to reach the ship for Hawaii before they present him with a new case. His eleventh child has been born already, and his anxiety to return underscores the importance of his family to him. At the same time, however, the manner of his departure adds to the humor of his character. First, he leaves through a window and fire escape in the same manner an important witness had earlier escaped him and the police. In addition, Biggers is striving for the same cuteness with which Charlie Chan had made his initial entrance in *The House Without a Key*. The image of a fat, famous detective climbing out of a window so he can go home unmolested by his admiring friends provides just enough of this cuteness.

Charlie Chan's devotion to his family supports his middle-class image, gained from the upward mobility of his moving from a houseboy's position on the beach to the middle-class existence of a police detective. Biggers does not, however, break entirely with older stereotypes. Chinese domestic servants appear in the series often, always speaking in broken English with heavy accents. Beginning in *The Black Camel*, Charlie Chan grudgingly accepts the aid of an admiring Japanese Hawaiian named Kashimo. Kashimo is a buffoon, always making idiotic mistakes that receive the patient criticism of his idol. Kashimo offers comic relief while enhancing the image of the Chinese Americans at the expense of the Japanese Americans. In *Charlie Chan Carries On*, Inspector Duff is introduced to Kashimo: "Kashimo studies to be great detective like you are," Chan explained to Duff. "So far fortune does not favor him. Only this morning he proved himself useful as a mirror to a blind man."[39]

Charlie Chan remains the only Asian American protagonist in American fiction before 1940 to have wide recognition and influence. As such, he is a role model of an Asian American male who is accepted by the likes of Puritan Bostonians and white Californians. He receives this acceptance because nearly every aspect of his character is a direct contravention of a trait of Fu Manchu. As a literary development, this is a logical technique, but using a reversal of Fu Manchu as a standard for creating a character produces a very particular result.

The villain is tall, bony, and yellow; the detective is shorter, chubby, and pink. The former is angry and threatening; the latter stays calm and apologetic. Fu Manchu speaks precise, accurate English;

Charlie Chan speaks in broken English with incorrect grammar. Fu Manchu represents his race; his counterpart stands away from the other Asian Hawaiians. Biggers's primary goal in characterizing a protagonist of Chinese descent was to assure his white readers that the character was not threatening to them in any way. Defining a character of toughness, daring, and romance, traits that are the mainstays of many fictional detectives, has nothing to do with the creation of Charlie Chan.

Charlie Chan's calm, apologetic, and passive tolerance of racial insults and harassment is an obvious sop to those who would be threatened by an Asian American detective with normal assertiveness and temper. His rotund figure is also important, symbolizing the opposite of the lean Fu Manchu. Charlie Chan is a middle-aged family man. The existence of his family and his devotion to it further reduce the chance of threat. In each novel, the romantic male lead is a young white man of Protestant British descent. Charlie Chan's activity as a protagonist is only that of intellect: he lacks the stern demeanor and physical impact of a Sherlock Holmes, the physical strength or toughness of a Philip Marlowe, or the hard-boiled and romantic drive of a Sam Spade. Charlie Chan's function in these novels is specifically to unravel the puzzle of a crime, and his bows and apologies to white characters are symbolic gestures to his white reading audience, constantly reminding them that he is a good fellow, harmless except for his singular concern of catching a murderer.

For Asian Americans, especially males, the role of Charlie Chan has a special significance. He is in a middle-class position of authority, is trusted by his white superior, and is accepted by the white characters around him. To the extent that literary protagonists can be role models, the depiction of Charlie Chan implies that his demeanor and personality are related to his social acceptance by white Americans. This implication is underscored by Biggers's failure to present other Asian American characters in positions of similar social acceptance and respect. In these novels, only Charlie Chan has succeeded. The rest of the Asian Americans who appear are taxi drivers, restaurant workers, domestic servants, or workers in other service occupations. They usually speak with heavier, lampooned accents and have less intelligence than Charlie Chan. He exemplifies the model-minority American, who is willing to be put through certain paces by white Americans in order to prove himself to them; who never exhibits direct anger, frustration, or displeasure at white people; and who has no desires involving white society other than the execution of his assigned job.

Fu Manchu and Charlie Chan represent the two extremes of

American fiction's presentation of Asian men in the West before 1940. To avoid any possible taint of the Yellow Peril, Biggers eliminates all assertiveness, sexuality, and variety of emotion from Charlie Chan, leaving him a continually self-effacing figure. Unlike Fu Manchu, Charlie Chan did not leave a legacy of numbers. Few Asian American protagonists have appeared in American fiction even to the present, and most of these have come from Asian American authors after 1940 or in popular culture dealing with the martial arts in the 1970s. The impact of Charlie Chan has been felt most impressively as an example of the acceptable Asian male in the United States, corresponding to, and reinforcing, certain expectations of some white and Asian Americans in real-life situations.

The duality represented by Fu Manchu and Charlie Chan in American popular culture is therefore created specifically by certain values and beliefs of white supremacy. These include a belief in the Yellow Peril. Fu Manchu is defined as a villain and the embodiment of the Yellow Peril because he is an Asian whose behavior is uncontrolled by Europeans and white Americans. Charlie Chan is not interpreted as part of the Yellow Peril because his subservient behavior to white Americans indicates that he has been, in a sense, domesticated and trained. That Charlie Chan has been tamed, however, implies that he conceivably could have been wild, or uncontrolled, and so he is a reflection of the Yellow Peril though not a part of it. The type of character that these values fail to create is that of an Asian American who is strong and independent and a contributing member of society, representing the many such people in American history. Belief in the Yellow Peril precludes the acceptance of such a character.

VII
The Pulps

The span of years between 1920 and 1940 represents the heyday of the pulp magazine. Pulps began with publisher Frank Munsey in 1882, and their descendants are still in existence today.[1] However, the period between the world wars saw the growth of the private investigator into a major American hero, the development of science fiction into a fully developed genre, an explosion of masked crime fighters and other adventurers, and the birth of legendary popular culture names such as The Shadow, Conan, and Doc Savage.[2] Hundreds of pulp titles appeared, some as often as every two weeks.[3] The height of the Yellow Peril in the pulps occurred in the 1930s, spurred by the success of Fu Manchu and the international events in Asia and the Pacific leading to World War II. A full selection of pulp magazines is not available, and many issues are too fragile and expensive actually to be handled and read. For this reason, the fiction examined in this chapter has been quoted extensively. It is a representative sampling of relevant work, not the complete run of Yellow Peril fiction that appeared in the pulps.

The 1930s were a period of encroachment by Japan on the Asian mainland. The internal strife in China had resulted, in 1928, in the recognition of the Kuomintang's government in Nanking under Chiang Kai-shek as the national government of China. Japan had become a world power after World War I and had continued its gradual expansion into the islands and mainland of Asia ever since that time. In the late 1920s, an increasingly militaristic and imperialistic policy began to take shape to confront the new Nanking government. For economic reasons, Japan entered Manchuria in 1931 from Korea, which was already controlled by Japan. This seizure of Chinese territory alarmed the major governments of the world and made the conflict and animosity between China and Japan common knowledge in the United States. China continued to consolidate and modernize its economy and society to some extent, but in 1937 Japan invaded China proper and opened what would become the Asian theater of World War II. In the stories of the Yellow Peril that appeared in the pulps, an awareness of a possible Asian military threat based on the power of Japan is mixed with plot devices and characters derived from the fiction of Sax Rohmer and with a resurgence of concepts that contributed to the American stories about Asian invasions in the late nineteenth century.

Original concepts about the Yellow Peril in the pulps are almost nonexistent. While Rohmer's Fu Manchu ran in the slick *Collier's* magazine, pulp writers copied Fu Manchu and his organization in precise detail and gave the Yellow Peril new life in the pulps. They also drew on older American concepts such as the vermin-ridden Chinatowns full of opium dens, vice, and secret passages, and on the prospect of military invasion by teeming yellow hordes. The pulps dealing with the Yellow Peril also began to solidify an image of Asian women in the United States for the first time, drawing primarily on Sax Rohmer's Fah Lo Suee, the daughter of Fu Manchu. First, however, Dashiell Hammett did offer original and unusual characters in a short story and in a novella, both of which appeared in *Black Mask*, the crime pulp that also published the first fiction by Raymond Chandler and Erle Stanley Gardner.[4]

Dashiell Hammett belongs to a sizeable group of authors whose work began in the pulps, to be recognized later as the fiction of major talents. Of the pulp authors considered here, he is the only one to have earned such a reputation, and his writing clearly outshines that of the others. With his background as a Pinkerton detective, he brought a realism to crime fiction upon which the "hard-boiled" school of such fiction was based; the realism of the two stories discussed here starkly contrast the adventure fantasies of the imitators of Sax Rohmer.

"The House on Turk Street" (1924) is narrated by the Continental Op, Hammett's anonymous private operative of the Continental Detective Agency. He is searching in a San Francisco neighborhood for a runaway boy when he stumbles across a gang of thieves about to leave the area with a fortune in stolen bonds. The gang includes an elderly white couple named Quarre, a tall, ugly, short-tempered white man named Hook, an attractive young white woman named Elvira, and a Chinese ringleader named Tai. Hook has seen the Op asking questions at every house in the neighborhood and when he knocks at their safe house, the gang ties him up, believing him to be in search of them.

The plot consists of arguments and treachery among the gang members as they prepare to make a permanent getaway, and the Op's use of their arguments and their violence in order to gain control of the situation. In the process, Hammett breaks ground with almost every aspect of Tai's character as a Chinese immigrant in the United States.

The Op first hears Tai's voice without seeing him, and notes that he speaks with a cultured British accent. Hammet does not develop Tai's background, but such an accent in a Chinese usually suggests a wealthy background in Hong Kong or Singapore. That would probably make his ancestry Cantonese, which is further suggested by his description as a "short fat Chinese, immaculately clothed in garments that were as British as his accent."[5]

Tai is cultured and probably wealthy, not a degenerate opium dealer or slumlord; he gives orders to white accomplices who are not bound to him by drugs or coercion, but merely in a selfish alliance like that of most fictional gangs. Hammett indicates an awareness of race, as Elvira once snaps, "Don't be altogether yellow." Tai responds, "it isn't a matter of color . . . it's simply a matter of ordinary wisdom."[6] This quiet response does not indicate, however, that Tai is cut in the mold of Charlie Chan. Hook learns this when he punches Tai.

> The force of the punch carried Tai all the way across the room, and threw him on his side in one corner.
>
> But he had twisted his body around to face the ugly man even as he went hurtling across the room—a gun was in his hand before he went down—and he was speaking before his legs had settled upon the floor—and his voice was a cultured British drawl.[7]

Later, the Quarres also learn how dangerous Tai can be.

> Tai had dropped the gun that had been in his hand, but he hadn't been searched. The Chinese are a thorough people; if one of them carries a gun at all, he usually carries two or three more. . . .
>
> Tai's hands moved. An automatic was in each.
>
> Once more Tai ran true to racial form. When a Chinese shoots he keeps on until his gun is empty.[8]

As the leader of a violent gang, Tai possesses intelligence, caution, and physical ability. He is decisive, though usually reserved in demeanor. Unlike Charlie Chan, his moral triumphs are accompanied by assertive actions that significantly change the plot. Most importantly, he represents a completely new kind of Yellow Peril.

Tai is a part of the Yellow Peril because he is Chinese by race and heritage, and threatens the security of the United States with major crimes. Unlike his predecessors, he is a capable sophisticate who, like many other criminals in fiction, is motivated by selfish, simple reasons, not racial mania or world politics. If yet another Asian villain in the United States has to appear in American fiction, at least this kind of role offers the realistic human traits so often lacking before 1940, and in many cases after.

Hammett turns to San Francisco's Chinatown in the novella "Dead Yellow Women" (1925). His opening paragraph, however, attempts to dispel or at least postpone any expectations the reader may be bringing to the story.

> She was sitting straight and stiff in one of the Old Man's chairs when he called me into his office—a tall girl of perhaps twenty-four, broad-shouldered, deep-bosomed, in mannish gray clothes. That she was Oriental showed only in the black shine of her bobbed hair, in the pale yellow of her unpowdered skin, and in the fold of her upper lids at the outer eye-corners, half hidden by the dark rims of her spectacles. But there was no slant to her eyes, her nose was almost aquiline, and she had more chin than Mongolians usually have. She was a modern Chinese American from the flat heels of her tan shoes to the crown of her untrimmed felt hat.[9]

Lillian Shan is the daughter of a wealthy immigrant from North China who has died, leaving her a mansion on the Pacific Coast away from San Francisco. Hammett demonstrates his knowledge of Chinese affairs and their relation to Chinese Americans in a brief description of her father's background and concerns. He includes Lillian Shan's Chinese name, Ai Ho, which sounds properly Mandarin, and ends with her father's decision not to move into Chinatown with the Cantonese for political and cultural reasons.

Lillian states that after a trip was unexpectedly cut short, she returned to find a strange Chinese man in her house, who tied her up with her maid, who was also of Chinese descent. The maid was accidently strangled while being bound and another dead Chinese woman was later found in the cellar by deputy sheriffs. Lillian's two remaining servants have disappeared. She hires the Continental Op to investigate, feeling that the regular authorities are doing too little.

The Op begins by hiring a young Pilipino American, Cipriano, who is eager to become a detective, assigning him to pick up any related hearsay in Chinatown.

> I found the lad I wanted in his cubbyhole room, getting his small body into a cerise silk shirt that was something to look

at. Cipriano was the bright-faced Filipino boy who looked after the building's front door in the daytime. At night, like all the Filipinos in San Francisco, he could be found down on Kearney Street, just below Chinatown, except when he was in a Chinese gambling-house passing his money over to the yellow brothers.[10]

Hammett again shows an awareness of subtle friction between Asian Americans with his Pilipino character. Since the Philippines were owned by the United States, the United States had passed a law in 1925 allowing Pilipinos to become citizens after three years of service in the Navy, where they served exclusively as stewards.[11] Cipriano, in answer to a question, observes, "Chinaboy don't talk much about things like that. Not like us Americans."[12] The story is further fleshed out with other minor characters such as a white stool pigeon named Dummy Uhl, who observes, "Things ain't been anyways quiet since the Japs began buyin' stores in the Chink streets, an' maybe that's got sumpin' to do with it."[13] Another character only mentioned is a Japanese American named Hasegawa who, with a white accomplice named Conyers, conned twenty thousand dollars out of the Japantown in Seattle. Hasegawa was caught; Conyers moved on to become the villain using Lillian Shan's mansion.

Eventually, the Op moves into the heart of Chinatown, which Hammett describes as earlier writers had: "If you leave the main thoroughfares and showplaces and start poking around in the alleys and dark corners, and nothing happens to you, the chances are you'll find some interesting things—though you won't like some of them."[14] The Op finds his way to the house of Chang Li Ching, whom Cipriano has learned is a key figure in Chinatown, likely to know about the affairs of Chinese Americans. Hammett presents the secrecy, the hidden doors and passageways, and broken English so familiar in fiction about Chinatown, but his characters continue to be distinctive. The Op is led to Chang Li Ching by a shuffling lackey who totes big guns and does not hesitate to use them; the door to the inner chamber is opened by another Chinese.

> But this was none of your Cantonese runts. He was a big, meateating wrestler—bull-throated, mountain-shouldered, gorilla-armed, leather-skinned. The god that made him had plenty of material and gave it time to harden.[15]

Chang Li Ching is an imposing figure of a different type.

The room was large and cubical, its doors and windows—if

any—hidden behind velvet hangings of green and blue and silver. In a big, black chair, elaborately carved, behind an inlaid black table, sat an old Chinese man. His face was round and plump and shrewd, with a straggle of thin white whiskers on his chin. A dark, close-fitting cap was on his head; a purple robe, tight around his neck, showed its sable linings at the bottom, where it had fallen back in a fold over his blue satin trousers.[16]

Chang Li Ching is a dignified, reserved individual. In order to avoid stereotyping him, Hammett lampoons the overly polite image of a self-effacing Charlie Chan-type character, giving both of his characters an awareness of the joke. Chang Li Ching begins.

"It was only the inability to believe that one of your excellency's heaven-born splendor would waste his costly time on so mean a clod that kept the least of your slaves from running down to prostrate himself at your noble feet as soon as he heard the Father of Detectives was at his unworthy door."

That came out smoothly in English that was a lot clearer than my own. I kept my face straight, waiting.

"If the terror of evil-doers will honor one of my deplorable chairs by resting his divine body on it, I can assure him the chair shall be burned afterward, so no lesser being may use it. Or will the Prince of Thiefcatchers permit me to send a servant to his palace for a chair worthy of him?"

I went slowly to a chair, trying to arrange words in my mind. This old joker was spoofing me with an exaggeration—a burlesque—of the well-known Chinese politeness. I'm not hard to get along with; I'll play anybody's game up to a certain point.

"It's only because I'm weak-kneed with awe of the mighty Chang Li Ching that I dare to sit down," I explained, letting myself down on the chair, and turning my head to notice that the giants who had stood beside the door were gone.[17]

The encounter drags on and the Op puts his questions about the deaths and disappearances connected with the Shan mansion. The Op does not learn anything from this visit, but gains an appreciation of Chang Li Ching: "I liked him. He had humor, brains, nerve, everything. To jam him in a cell would be a trick you'd want to write home about.

He was my idea of a man worth working against."[18]

Ultimately, the Op finds that Conyers, Chang Li Ching, and a young man named Garthorne are importing illegal Chinese immigrants, and probably opium, into the country through Lillian Shan's mansion. Garthorne's job is only to date her in order to keep her away from the mansion at certain specified times; he believes the smuggling involves liquor, as the story takes place during Prohibition. Lillian Shan eventually makes a separate agreement with Chang Li Ching, exchanging the use of her mansion in return for the safety of Garthorne, for whom she has developed an affection, from Conyers and her own safety from legal problems. The reason for her cooperation is that Chang Li Ching, who supports the anti-Japanese movement in China, is shipping guns illegally through her mansion to Chinese patriots in Asia. Lillian has been told that her murdered servants were spies for Japan's Chinese collaborators. This arrangement comes to light in a scene in Chinatown, where Lillian Shan no longer appears as a mannish Chinese American.

> The queen of something stood there! She was a tall woman, straight-bodied and proud. A butterfly-shaped headdress decked with the loot of a dozen jewelry stores exaggerated her height. Her gown was amethyst filigreed with gold above, a living rainbow below. The clothes were nothing!
>
> She was—maybe I can make it clear this way. Hsiu Hsiu was as perfect a bit of feminine beauty as could be imagined. She was perfect! Then comes this queen of something—and Hsiu Hsiu's beauty went away. She was a candle in the sun. She was still pretty—prettier than the woman in the doorway, if it came to that—but you didn't pay any attention to her. Hsiu Hsiu was a pretty girl: this woman in the doorway was—I don't know the words.[19]

Lillian Shan's explanation of her presence in Chinatown in traditional formal dress is that she has "come back to my people."[20] The Op dismisses this as he unravels the agreement she has made with Chang Li Ching. Her explanation, however, combines with her patriotic interest in China to remind the reader that she is, even as an American, concerned with her heritage. Balancing this new image of a Chinese American woman of strength, resolve, beauty, and physical presence is the figure of Hsiu Hsiu, a pretty slave girl who is four feet six inches tall, cannot speak English, giggles at the wrong moments, and betrays her master Chang Li Ching.

The Op solves the situation by tricking Chang Li Ching into kill-

ing Conyers in the belief that Conyers was actually running his guns to
the Japanese. Conyers's underlings are arrested; Garthorne is in the
clear, and Lillian Shan will be left alone. Hammett ends with a reitera-
tion of Chang Li Ching's character as a crime lord, in response to the
note Chang Li Ching sends the Op after he has discovered the
deception.

> "Greetings and Great Love to the Unveiler of Secrets:
> "One whose patriotic fervor and inherent stupidity com-
> bined to blind him, so that he broke a valuable tool, trusts
> that the fortunes of worldly traffic will not again ever place
> his feeble wits in opposition to the irresistible will and daz-
> zling intellect of the Emperor of Untanglers."
> You can take that any way you like. But I know the man
> who wrote it, and I don't mind admitting that I've stopped
> eating in Chinese restaurants, and that if I never have to
> visit Chinatown again it'll be soon enough.[21]

Hammett has combined the traditional images of Chinatown—secret passageways, giant bodyguards, slave girls, and illegal
aliens—with crucial developments of his own. Most importantly, he
presents Lillian Shan as an educated, sophisticated Chinese American
woman, still a rarity in American fiction. Her non-Cantonese
background is logical in this respect, since most of the Cantonese immigrants came from working-class backgrounds. In addition to Lillian
Shan, Hammett draws a precise character in Chang Li Ching, including, as he said, "humor, brains, nerve, everything." He still is a
ruthless, vicious, and impatient villain, with little redeeming value;
however, he is depicted with a realism and humanity that the other
Asian crime lords of the pulps lack. This is writing of high quality,
though largely done with the traditional view of the Chinese villain in
the United States.

Sax Rohmer's depiction of Fah Lo Suee, the daughter of Fu Manchu, presented American readers with the first clearly defined
characterization of an Asian woman they had seen. The novel did not
appear in a pulp, but first in *Collier's*; however, the character of Fah
Lo Suee left an important stamp on the characterization of Chinese
women who were depicted in the pulps and so she will be considered
here. As a book, *Daughter of Fu Manchu* (1931) depicts Fah Lo Suee
resuming the Fu Manchu series of novels by replacing her father as the
leader of the Asian threat against the white race. Her science-fictional
methods of assassinating, kidnapping, and drugging her victims are
taken directly from her father, as she draws together her father's

organization for the first time in many years. The plot is not distinct from the other novels in the series until the end, when she has captured Nayland Smith and the narrator Shan Greville. The significance of this novel for the image of the Chinese lies entirely in the characterization of Fah Lo Suee.

Fah Lo Suee's character contains three critical traits. These are exotic sensuality, sexual availability to a white man, and a treacherous nature. The first two are explicit exploitations of her female identity, while the third contains an element of this mixed with the image of treachery frequently attached to Asians.

Rohmer describes Fah Lo Suee slowly through the first half of the novel by giving Greville fleeting or distorted glimpses of her, often in disguise. His first look is at a small image in a photograph, over which he muses, "Brilliant, indeterminably oblique eyes. . .a strictly chiselled nose, somewhat too large for classic beauty. . .full lips, slightly parted . . . a long oval contour. . . ."[22] Shortly after this, Greville takes part in a stakeout, where he gains a brief look at a shapeless, robed figure carrying a torch in her hand, the only part of her visible.

> A delicately slender hand it was, nurtured in indolence—an unforgettable hand, delicious yet repellant, with pointed, varnished nails: a cultured hand possessing the long-square-jointed thumb of domination; a hand cruel for all its softness as the velvet paw of a tigress.[23]

As Fah Lo Suee gradually pushes her plans forward toward the reestablishment of her father's organization, her British opponents become more familiar with her. Greville first sees her face in person when he and Smith have infiltrated a meeting of her lieutenants.

> Her hair was entirely concealed beneath a jewelled headdress. She wore jewels on her slim, bare arms. A heavy girdle which glittered with precious stones supported a grotesquely elaborate robe, sewn thickly with emeralds. From proudly raised chin to slight, curving hips she resembled an ivory statue of some Indian goddess. Indeed, as I watched, I knew she was Kâli, wife of Siva and patronne of *Thugs* and *Dacoits*, from whom they derived their divine right to slay![24]

At this point, Fah Lo Suee's exotic beauty and inherent evil have become entwined. She captures Greville after discovering his identity, though Smith escapes, and she drugs her prisoner. He semiawakens to see

the green goddess with eyes of jade. I knew that her smooth
body was but a miraculous gesture of some eastern crafts-
man immortalized in ivory; that her cobra hair gleamed so
because of inlay and inlay of subtly chosen rare woods: her
emerald robe I knew for an effect of cunning light, her
movements for a mirage.

But when she knelt beside me, the jade-green eyes held
life—cold ivory was warm satin. And slender insidious
hands, scented lotus blossoms, touched me caress-
ingly. . . .[25]

Fah Lo Suee tells him of her political plans, her immense power, and of
her loneliness. He suddenly realizes,

This was a superwoman into whose hands I had fallen! And
what blindness had been upon me during our earlier if brief
association to close my eyes to the fact that she had con-
ceived a sudden, characteristically Oriental infatuation?[26]

Fah Lo Suee's treacherous nature is inherent in her activities. Her
attempts to reconvene her father's organization for her own use is a
clear betrayal of her father, and her personal interest in Greville poses
a threat to her own political interests as well as to the group she is
gathering behind her. Rohmer uses the unpredictability of her
behavior to heighten suspense. Because she is the first Asian woman of
prominence to come before American readers, the price of this device is
high: Asian women who follow in the American media exhibit the same
three traits of exotic sensuality, availability to white men, and
treachery, even through the 1970s. Only a few appear in the pulps and
unfortunately the most familiar names are in areas outside prose fiction. The next important figure with the traits of Fah Lo Suee is the
Dragon Lady of Milton Caniff's comic strip *Terry and the Pirates*, a
strong, glamorous, and willful Chinese villain. In the feature film "The
World of Suzi Wong," Nancy Kwan plays a worldly but hopeful prostitute who takes up with an American artist played by William
Holden, but fails to tell him the whole truth about herself as they
become involved. Characters of lesser significance have also exhibited
these qualities in film, television, and comics, in addition to fiction.
Some appeared immediately after Fah Lo Suee, however, in the pulps,
and a few of these will be surveyed in this chapter.

The Spider is a caped and masked vigilante hero modeled on the
Shadow. Each issue of *The Spider* magazine, which first appeared in
1933, carried a short novel about the main character and often a short

story or two. "Dragon Lord of the Underworld" (1933) appeared over the pseudonym Grant Stockbridge. Exact records are lacking, but this pseudonym was most often used by Norvell W. Page. Page often visited the magazine's editorial offices wearing a cape himself, and under his direction the Spider began to confront problems of a large and often grotesque nature.[27] In "Dragon Lord of the Underworld," a Chinese villain enters New York armed with a mass of black widow spiders.

The Spider is actually

> Richard Wentworth, scion of one of New York's oldest and wealthiest families, last lone member of an ancient line, dilettante of the arts, sportsman, amateur criminologist extraordinary.[28]

His duty as an Anglo-Saxon savior of the United States requires in this novel that he face the threat mounted by Ssu Hsi Tze, an imitation of Fu Manchu whose name is Mandarin for "Ruler of Vermin." He intends to unite all the criminals in the United States under his control and has taken this phony name as a title mocking his future subordinates. At the opening of the story, he already has in his employ most of New York's underworld and all of Chinatown. One assistant is a woman named Sanguh Liang-guh, Mandarin for "Three-piece Two-piece," symbolizing a full house in poker. Ssu Hsi Tze's following in Chinatown is unquestionably loyal. "All the Chinese worship this man as if he were a god," because he has spent much energy rallying China against Japanese encroachment.[29] In fact, resisting Japan is his purpose in taking money from the United States. However, the following description of the threat posed by Ssu Hsi Tze to the United States is also a description of the threat mounted by Fu Manchu to the white race.

> What the Chinese could accomplish here in America was fearful to contemplate. He would have the instant unquestioning obedience of every Chinese, to the death. He would bring into use the subtle intelligence of the Orient, the merciless, cold-blooded hate of the yellow races. Moreover, Ssu Hsi Tze, ruler of vermin, was privy to all sciences. . . . Especially those which engendered human pain and death. . . .[30]

Ssu Hsi Tze has two more attributes that echo the character of Fu Manchu. One is the hypnotic power he exercises through his eyes, which the Spider confronts the first time he looks at Ssu Hsi Tze. The Spider manages to resist this mental attack. When his mind clears, he sees the second quality that Ssu Hsi Tze shares with Fu Manchu, that of representing the mandarin class of traditional China with the rich cultural trappings and personal traits of this group.

> The throne was thick with a padding of imperial yellow satin and stood upon a low dais. The robe of the Chinese was yellow also, and a tiered and jeweled crown ringed his temples. He sat as impassively as an idol. . . .
> The hands rested unmoving upon the arms of the throne, fingers tapered and tipped with nail guards of transparent jade, of gold and silver. Upon his upper lip was a mustache snakelike black ends of which drooped at the corners.
> "You have asked to see Ssu Hsi Tze." The syllables hissed. . . .[31]

Ssu Hsi Tze's plan of operation in the United States is to bring all American criminals into a cohesive organization under his control by eliminating those who refuse. This is done by releasing black widow spiders to poison them, backed by gun-toting Chinese agents. When his human followers feel the need to use their guns, they shoot into their victims the Chinese character for death.[32] Shooting the pattern of a Chinese character into a victim first appeared in Hugh Wiley's "Tong."[33] The use of the spiders is patterned after Fu Manchu's use of scorpions, apes, and other animals and plants; as with those, the Asian origin of these spiders is sufficient proof of their owner: "'*Kara Khoum* spiders,' he told her sharply, 'from the Gobi. I guess there's no longer any doubt the black widows of Wilton come from Ssu Hsi Tze.'"[34]

In the same way, all appearances by Chinese and Chinese Americans signal evil actions to come at the direction of the villain. The final similarity to the fiction of Rohmer is in the gradual introduction of Sanguh Liang-guh, whose initial appearance is another fleeting one after the manner of Fah Lo Suee.

> And then the Spider's guns choked to silence. For he glimpsed a pale face peering back through a corner of that window, an oval lovely face the pale lips of which curved in a mocking smile, the eyes peeping out from beneath the pert brim of a cocked hat. A woman!
> . . .The girl, too, was Oriental, of that he was sure. Something in the cast of her features. . . .[35]

The second time she enters the story, she is leading the blindfolded Spider to an interview with Ssu Hsi Tze. She remains a mystery, however.[36] The Spider finally sees her late in his interview with Ssu Hsi

Tze. True to form as a character based on Fah Lo Suee, she then proves to be both beautiful and treacherous. Her sexual availability to the Spider also develops at this point. So far the author has been accurate in his presentation of traditional Chinese culture and the Mandarin dialect. However, he is under the mistaken impression here that Manchurians do not have the distinctive epicanthus of all East Asians: "But this woman was no Manchu, not pure blooded at any rate, for there was a distinct almond slant to her black dark eyes."[37]

> She was a little thing, not quite to his second vest button. A heady perfume enveloped them both, so close they stood. She remained motionless, staring up into his eyes. Her breath came more quickly, her eyelids dropped heavily. She swayed toward him and her lips parted.
> "If you would believe Ssu Hsi Tze," she breathed, "nothing, nothing would be denied you."
> . . ."Not even death," he said harshly. "Go and tell Ssu Hsi Tze you, too, have failed!"[38]

In addition to the traits of this novel that are derived from the fiction of Sax Rohmer, several more are familiar from earlier portrayals of the Chinatowns and Chinese immigrants. The first, which also resembles Rohmer's vision of London's Limehouse Chinatown, is the image of the Chinatown in New York as a nest of secret passageways, traps, tunnels, and fantastic hidden tortures.

> He knew the Orient, the death traps, its ingenious cruelty could contrive. Pits of fluffy ashes that were acid-poisoned and would burn through a man's lungs; showers of needles that would riddle a man with agonizing pain; a stairway that would fade away and plunge him into a spider pit.[39]

Another familiar concept is that the Chinese threat is especially overpowering through force of numbers. After five of Ssu Hsi Tze's followers have been killed, "Wentworth's eyes narrowed briefly. Five lives out of the the teeming millions of China! It was nothing, a spot of grease rubbed off the sleeve of time."[40] Tied with this concept are the assumptions that Chinatown is not an American community, but a transplanted part of Chinese society, and that Asians do not value life. "Human life was cheap in China—or in New York's Chinatown!"[41] Finally, the Spider also has as his ally an Irish American, police commissioner Patrick O. Flynn. Since Irish Americans are prominent in much American fiction during the 1930s, the importance of his presence should not be overestimated. Still, Irish Americans have appeared frequently in fiction dealing with Chinese Americans ever since frontier days, always in opposition to the Yellow Peril. This situation probably originates from the friction between the two groups that reached its height under Dennis Kearney. In any case, Flynn is another character in this tradition.

A man with an Irish surname takes the spotlight in the magazine titled *Wu Fang*. American FBI agent Val Kildare champions the United States against Wu Fang, a direct copy of Fu Manchu whose magazine ran for seven issues beginning in 1935. One novella about Wu Fang appeared in each issue with an unrelated short story or two, which sometimes dealt with Chinese threats. The *Wu Fang* novellas were written by Robert J. Hogan.[42]

In these stories, Val Kildare replaces Nayland Smith and the United States is the sole focus of intrigue. Otherwise, these are undisguised imitations of Rohmer's fiction that sometimes only slightly paraphrase Rohmer's words. Wu Fang's title, "Dragon Lord of Crime," is apparently taken from Ssu Hsi Tze. The first novella, "The Case of the Six Coffins" (1935), even begins in the Limehouse area of London.

> The keen ears of Wu Fang, Dragon Lord of Crime and Emperor of Death, had detected something—a sound of softly padding footsteps that came down the dark winding passage leading to his underground room at the bottom of London's Limehouse.
>
> . . . He was a tall yellow man with slim, drooping shoulders from which hung a mandarin robe of embroidered yellow silk. His long-fingernailed hands were clasped loosely behind him. His movements were profoundly dignified and deliberate like those of a kindly old doctor or college professor.
>
> His slanting eyes had widened now as they watched the open doorway and there was a strange light in the jade-green pupils that made them seem almost iridescent, like the eyes of a cat in the darkness.[43]

His brain is called "super-human."[44]

Wu Fang is evil and ruthless. In this novella, he has obtained a vial of an extremely lethal liquid and he plans a journey to the United States in search of its inventor and hence the formula. With enough of it, he intends to destroy the entire population of New York City, after which he can dictate terms of capitulation to all the governments of the world.

In the opening scene, he is arranging a test of the poison. He has white men and women in his employ as well as Asians and animals. A French follower arranges to have a pilot drop the liquid into the center of the chosen village one night. The next morning, Wu Fang rides in his chauffeured limousine to a cliff overlooking the town.

"The liquid is working well nicely," he breathed.

Then he spied two figures lying at the doorstep of another house. One—a woman—seemed to be crawling toward the other, who was a man. Perhaps even her husband. To anyone else, the sight would have been a pitiful one. A wife trying to help her husband—and both dying out there in the street. Dying from some cause they could not understand.

But Wu Fang smiled more broadly.[45]

Deciding from this test that larger amounts of the liquid could easily eliminate cities the size of London and New York, Wu Fang embarks for the United States. At this point, the focus of the story jumps to Val Kildare and Jerry Hazard, a reporter Kildare meets on board the *S.S. Bergenland* voyaging from London to New York. Both are normal pulp heroes in that they are courageous, intelligent, and honorable; in addition, they are young American men of Western European stock. Kildare has been hot on the trail of Wu Fang for some time and is taking a note back to his superiors that he obtained by killing an agent of Wu Fang. The note identifies the inventor of the poisonous liquid and Wu Fang must get it before he can proceed with his plan.

Unknown to Kildare, Wu Fang and a handful of his agents are on the *Bergenland*, smuggled aboard in six coffins. One of his agents is a beautiful Greek woman named Mohra who is being mysteriously forced into serving Wu Fang. Wu Fang's servants manage to steal the note Kildare has been carrying, but their attempts to kill him fail, of course. Kildare recognizes the power of his foe, whose organization rivals that of Fu Manchu, after which the author designed it. Equally significant are Wu Fang's weird experimental creatures. He owns a farm on which he raises every type of poisonous creature known and many that he has created himself through special breeding. In this story, he uses one creature in particular for several killings. When Kildare and Hazard open the six mysterious coffins in search of Wu Fang, they find not only him and his human agents, but also a disgusting horde of snakes and other small, venomous reptilian creatures, all of which obey the verbal commands of Wu Fang.

Kidnapping and torture are part of Wu Fang's treatment of Kildare and Hazard. Still following the pattern of Fu Manchu, he also kidnaps and tortures lesser figures, such as the inventor of the poisonous liquid and Mohra, after she rescues Kildare and Hazard for a reason the author neglects to explain. Finally, one of Wu Fang's agents attacks Kildare with a short, extremely heavy club. Like Nayland Smith and the Spider before him, Kildare identifies the mysterious tool's Asian origin, which is sufficient to link it to Wu Fang.

> "It must be filled with lead," Hazard guessed. Kildare shook his head. "No, it is made of a rare wood that grows only in the northern end of the Malay peninsula. White people call it iron wood because of its hardness and weight. The Malays make clubs out of it exactly like this."[46]

Hogan adds several more familiar items to the aura around Wu Fang that are present in the Fu Manchu stories but have an older history in American fiction as well. One is the vaunted inscrutability of the Chinese:

> "How the devil does anyone know we're here?" Hazard asked in a hoarse, tense whisper.
> "That," Kildare came back, "is the mystery of the East. Some things the Chinese do just don't make sense, but they do 'em."[47]

Another of these items is Hogan's version of New York's Chinatown, which for the first time is described as having an extensive underground, the way the Chinatown of San Francisco reputedly had in some earlier fiction.

> That was a terrible experience, passing down rotten, creaking stairs, through long twisted corridors as black as night. There wasn't a light anywhere. The foul smells of underground Chinatown were mingled with that indescribable, Oriental tang of the East.[48]

Kildare adds,

> "All of Chinatown is honeycombed with rooms and passages. I have known cases where families were found living underground, practising some sort of evil, whose kids grew to be ten or twelve years olds (sic) before they ever got out to see the light of day." [49]

Hogan does not have a woman of East Asian ancestry in this story. However, Mohra, the Greek, provides the same exotic mystery as Fah Lo Suee. Her eastern Mediterranean origin probably results from the original definition of the word "Oriental," which in some applications includes all of the Islamic world. Turkey ruled Greece until World War I and in the 1930s much of its cultural influence was still visible.

Wu Fang ended after seven issues, but the same publisher followed it with a similar magazine called *Dr. Yen Sin* in 1936, just a few months after the last issue of *Wu Fang* left the stands. Part of the reason for this last attempt at a magazine based on a Chinese villain similar to Fu Manchu may have been an unused *Wu Fang* cover painting, which appeared on the first issue of *Dr. Yen Sin*, as well as an apparently deep-seated belief in pulp publishing circles that the Yellow Peril was commercially viable.[50] Each issue of *Dr. Yen Sin* contained one novella about the villainous doctor and several short stories, all of which also dealt with a Chinese menace to the United States. The novellas were written by Donald E. Keyhoe under his own name. The only differences between Dr. Yen Sin and his predecessors Fu Manchu and Wu Fang are superficial; his eyes are tawny yellow instead of green, but are as hypnotic as those of Fu Manchu and Ssu Hsi Tze. In the first issue, he arrives in Washington, D.C., to begin his operations out of the Chinatown there rather than in New York or London.[51]

Keyhoe's effort to make the Yen Sin series sell better than the Wu Fang series mostly involved improving the hero. Yen Sin's foe is a white American named Michael Traile who is almost as weird as Yen Sin. Because of a surgical mistake on his brain as a child, Traile never sleeps. He studies constantly, is very edgy, rests in a sort of trance while conscious, and is very bitter about this trait that makes him different from everyone else. He is a free-lance secret agent working with the United States government because his physical youth is combined with the learning and experience of a much older individual due to his prolonged waking hours. The plot of this novella is diffuse, involving many cloak-and-dagger operations as Yen Sin tries to kill Traile and Traile searches for clues to Yen Sin's whereabouts in Washington's Chinatown. Yen Sin's purpose is to create war between Japan and the United States by robbing secret documents from the Japanese embassy, murdering Japanese diplomats, and framing American agents. His organization intends to rise to power afterward.

The differences between Dr. Yen Sin and Wu Fang are petty; despite their differences, Yen Sin remains a clear and extreme personification of the Yellow Peril. These differences are familiar baggage from other fiction about the Yellow Peril, simply neglected in characterizing Wu Fang and included in creating Yen Sin. The introductory blurb to the story suggests that readers who enjoyed the stories of Fu Manchu and Wu Fang will be at home here.

> Out of the teeming turbulent East had come Dr. Yen Sin—
> saffron-skinned wizard of crime—bringing to the capital of
> the West all the ancient Devil's-lore at his command—and
> a horde of Asian Hell-born to help him spawn it. But
> Michael Traile—The Man Who Never Slept—had crammed
> into his own keen brain the means to cope with the sinister
> doctor. For he knew even the secrets of the Dragon's
> Shadow and how to penetrate the yellow murder fog that
> had descended on the capital to mingle its blood-wisps with
> the mist from the Potomac.[52]

The Dragon's Shadow is a mysterious infection used to assassinate
enemies of Yen Sin and his Invisible Empire. It is also a delightfully explicit expression of fear of contamination from Asian people. When a
white victim is stricken, he takes on Asian racial characteristics as he
dies.

> His swollen lips were drawn back, and his eyes had a queer,
> pulled look. They narrowed, changed weirdly even as his
> face was changing, taking on a startling likeness to—
>   . . . Gone was the face of the Navy man. There before
> them was the yellow visage of a Chinese, his lips drawn
> back in a hideous smile. Traile's glance shot to the stricken
> man's hands. They, too, had yellowed. . . .[53]

Yen Sin's Invisible Empire, like Wu Fang's following, includes
men and women, Asians and whites. It is well established in major
cities all over the world. In Washington, its agents are placed for
political reasons. One attractive female agent is an unwilling Greek
forced into service like Mohra in the Wu Fang series. Another agent is
an attractive blonde in the British embassy to the United States; a man
is in the Japanese embassy; others are Burmese *dacoits*, who kill
enemies for Yen Sin the way their brethren kill for Fu Manchu. They
strangle with silken cords and shoot with blowguns. Traile calls them
"one of the deadliest species on earth."[54]

Traile is also the one white man who understands Yen Sin's large-
scale design.

> "I'm personally convinced that he dreams of heading a
> yellow rebellion against the white race. I've tried to make
> the officials here see it and they're at last waking up to the
> menace. Until Japan began slicing off China, he was well on
> the way to dominating Asia. Even the Soviet fears Yen Sin,
> and mentioning the Invisible Empire keeps the Japanese

War Office awake at nights."[55]

Keyhoe's choice of words to put in his hero's mouth is revealing. If Asians are planning to rebel against whites, then Traile and possibly Keyhoe apparently believe that Asians have subject status in some sense under whites, even if only economic. Traile's work at quelling this rebellion, of course, implies that this subordination should continue.

Keyhoe fits Yen Sin into the world politics of the 1930s reasonably well, as Yen Sin's plan relies on a situation that really existed in the Japanese government at that time. "The Japanese military clique waits only a good excuse to wage war on the United States. My work tonight is the first step in providing that excuse."[56]

The Greek woman, Sonya Damitri, takes the place of an Asian woman in this story. She, like Fah Lo Suee, is first glimpsed by the white hero in a passing car. Though Greek, she is considered "Oriental" and is just as exotic and treacherous as the daughter of Fu Manchu.

> Some delicate Oriental perfume added its haunting fragrance to her already exotic allure, and a different man than Michael Traile might readily have succumbed to the desperate appeal in her eyes. But he had known other agents of the Invisible Emperor, almost as lovely, and each as treacherous as a serpent.[57]

The last item in the story derived from Rohmer's plot devices is the now-predictable, mysterious Asian life form used to kill. Here, it is "*Shi-muh*—the Corpse-Flower of Tibet!"[58] This is a poisonous puffball similar to one used by Fu Manchu.

Other parts of the story are drawn from the American images of Chinatown and Chinese immigrants. The Chinatown of Washington, D.C., is assumed from the beginning of the story to be the base of Yen Sin's operations and Traile observes that it is "almost as bad as Limehouse—or the China Coast."[59] Contrasting the dark and threatening squalor of Chinatown is the Restaurant Occidental, an aptly named bastion of the white community on the edge of Chinatown where Traile is eating when the story opens. He knows his enemy is nearby and in control of the community: "Dr. Yen Sin has all the tongs completely cowed. . . . You could arrest every Chinese in Washington, and you wouldn't learn a thing."[60] Keyhoe is aware of Chinese dialects and uses them correctly; most Chinatown residents speak Cantonese, while Yen Sin speaks English, Hindu, Cantonese, Yunnanese, and apparently Mandarin, as befits the leader of a broadly based Asian organization. Keyhoe avoids the pitfall of some white American authors who mistakenly believed that the Chinese dialects were written differently in Chinese; when he wants to use a dialect in writing, he notes that it is the Yunnan dialect written phonetically.[61] Keyhoe also shows the reader dark, damp passages in Chinatown, secret rooms, and opium dens where the workers speak broken, clumsy English.[62] To complete their representation of the stereotype from the American frontier, they wear queues, even though this hairstyle actually went immediately out of use in 1911, with the fall of the Manchu dynasty in China.

Dr. Yen Sin lasted only three issues. The commercial failures of Wu Fang and this magazine are not indications, however, that the Yellow Peril or characters derived from Fu Manchu were losing their popularity. Basing a fictional magazine on a villain was a drawback because every reader knew that the ending of every story had to be the same; the hero thwarts the villain, but the villain escapes to return the following issue and is never completely defeated except by a lack of readers. Also, the reader saw little variety from one issue to the next, since the same hero battled the same villain in every issue. In contrast, the Fu Manchu series did not carry any particular magazine alone and theoretically the villain might die at the end of any given story; the reader had to finish each one in order to find out. Nayland Smith had a number of different sidekicks throughout the series, as well, who opened up new possibilities. Villains such as Ssu Hsi Tze who appeared in the magazines of heroes such as the Spider could appear with all the evil of Fu Manchu and in addition give the reader the satisfaction of a suitably violent, ignominious, and often colorful death before the hero moved on to conquer another villain in the next issue. This sense of progress is lacking in Wu Fang and Dr. Yen Sin, since Kildare and Traile are on virtual treadmills. In the late 1930s, villains representing the Yellow Peril continue to thrive in the magazines of heroes such as Operator 5, G-8 and his Battle Aces, the Shadow, and others. They are so consistently created in the mold of Fu Manchu that little else of significance can be said of them. One story, however, stands out in this latter half of the decade as an example of how the image of American Chinatowns, as discussed in chapter 5, could be effectively combined with a character derived from Fu Manchu to produce a sense of threat that seems less fantastic than the Invisible Empire and more frightening because of its somewhat greater plausibility.

Secret Agent X appeared for a time in Detective Mysteries, a pulp that featured different heroes during the 1920s and 1930s, as each began to lose sales and a successor was created.[63] Secret Agent X works closely with the FBI and is sponsored by an influential figure in Washington, but as a sort of vigilante he has also been marked a criminal by the police. He is known only as X and his real face is never described past his grey eyes, since he is constantly in one disguise or another. His stories appeared over the by-line of Brant House, a sardonic pseudonym of the publishing house. It was used by Henry Treet Sperry, Paul Ernst, and Paul Chadwick. However, which man wrote which stories is now as unknown as the identity of X himself.[64]

"Curse of the Mandarin's Fan" (1938) is a novelette set in the Chinatown of San Francisco. Secret Agent X is working with the FBI to stop heavy traffic in marijuana, hashish, and opium. His FBI contact is named John Worrel. Lon Hunter is a San Francisco reporter who says he is after a story about Chinatown crime, and Glenda Rice is a friend of his who is also a reporter after a good story. X gets involved in the investigation by drugging Hunter for several days and disguising himself as Hunter. He learns that a crime war is raging in Chinatown between a man named Chang, who trades in opium, and another group trying to push marijuana and hashish. Through the use of disguises, he infiltrates both groups and manages to destroy them.

Chang is the character based on Fu Manchu, but before he makes his entrance, John Worrel has ordered steak and mushrooms in a Chinese restaurant, where incense "masked the wholesome odor of American food."[65] When Hunter mentions his familiarity with a Chinatown back alley, Worrel scoffs,

> "I envy you newspaper men your imagination, your ability to see vicious villains in some of these parchment-faced old beggars of Chinatown. I'd like to be able to people these shadows with fearsome things. But I can't. Barbary Coast is gone. The yellow man's opium dens are gone. 'Frisco is clean."[66]

The point of the story seems to be disproving this idea. In fact, Worrel himself does not believe it and was just hoping to keep Hunter out of his way during the FBI investigation. When this is obviously impossible, Worrel tells Hunter about Chang to enlist his help. Chang came from the Limehouse of London, like Fu Manchu, according to a British police officer who is dying of "some insidious torment, the creation of an Oriental mind."[67]

Hunter seems to take a liberal stance on race when he asks the apparently Chinese waiter to translate the Chinese message on a fan he has received. He explains that he trusts the waiter because "I can read men. . . . Yellow or white. The Chinese are fundamentally honest."[68] Unknown to Hunter, but explained to the reader, X has disguised himself as Chinese and is posing as the waiter. Hunter has ironically declared a white man honest, not a Chinese immigrant as he believes, and despite what he says about the Chinese fundamentally, no decent or law-abiding Chinese adults appear in the story, though one trustworthy child has a small role. All the others are involved in the drug traffic and most are murderers.

The message on the fan is a curse sent to Hunter by Chang, presumably in response to the reporter's investigative efforts. After X has forcibly drugged Hunter and taken his place, he delves more deeply into the dark opium dens, filthy underground passages, trapdoors, and secret rooms that the author portrays in Chinatown. X finds the situation more complex than he had thought, and discovers at the end of the story that Chang's rival gang leader was Hunter himself. The dirty and damp mysteries of Chinatown and the drug trade are derived from the prevailing images of Chinatown in American fiction, but Chang and his organization are familiar takeoffs on Rohmer's fiction.

Chang himself makes a spectacular entrance:

> Standing in that square of pale light, which was evidently a doorway, was the figure of a Chinese. The man wore the traditional garb of a mandarin, a long coat of black silk. Worked into the black of the long coat were designs of coiling dragons which seemed painted there in cold flame.
> . . . The phosphorescence piped the edge of the Chinaman's cap and glowed in the mandarin bead at the top of the cap. Ends of his long mustache drooped from his slot of a mouth. His cheeks looked as though they had been carved from ivory—yellow-white and dead-looking. And deep in his burning eyes was a look of overwhelming sorrow and hatred, as though some hideous vice gripped his soul.[69]

Chang's character, by now predictable, is one of consummate evil. He delights in grotesque tortures and in assassination through obscure means. His following, however, is all Chinese, not multiracial or even multiethnic. In fact, one of X's early clues that Hunter is Chang's rival is the appearance of white killers in Chinatown, since Hunter has both white and Chinese criminals in his employ. Interestingly, although Hunter is a large-scale drug dealer and killer like Chang, he is described as handsome, urbane, and direct. He became involved with crime for a clear motive, needing to pay off large gambling debts. By contrast, the author does not seem to feel that Chang's evil actions require a motive. By this time, the idea was well established at least in the pulps that an old, intelligent Chinese mandarin could be inherently evil. No motive or cause is necessary beyond his ethnic and racial origin.

Chang's principal assistant is a young woman named Lim Toy. When X sees her, he realizes that she is

the most exquisite Chinese girl he had ever seen.

She wore a tantalizing garment of revealing silk and gold, long-skirted and unvarying in proportion from hips to ankles. This clinging skirt was slashed on either side to the knees so that every lithe step, as she crossed the dais, gave a glimpse of perfect limbs.[70]

Lim Toy has several tasks. One is to ornament Chang's opium establishments to attract customers and inspire their dreams with her image. X learns, however, that Lim Toy has fallen in love with Hunter. When she sees X disguised as Hunter in the company of Glenda Rice, she becomes bitterly jealous. She retaliates by planting drugs in Hunter's apartment to frame him. Her confusion disappears when the real Hunter surfaces to confront X, and she responds by betraying Chang's men, causing many deaths. In the process, she has become another literary descendent of Fah Lo Suee, combining her exotic allure with her betrayal of Chang in order to gain Hunter's good graces. That she turned against Hunter when she thought he was interested in the white woman emphasizes further her fickleness.

The shadow of Fu Manchu dominates the pulp versions of the Yellow Peril. Repeatedly, master Chinese villains clearly copied from him threaten to gain control of the United States, only to be stopped at the last moment by a white hero. Similarly, Asian women have been characterized in the mold of Fah Lo Suee in these stories, though none of them are featured villains the way the daughter of Fu Manchu is. The activities of these villains support two major subthemes of the Yellow Peril, that the United States is in danger of military invasion from East Asia and that American Chinatowns are both centers of sabotage in this endeavor and cesspools of dangerous and contagious crimes in their own right.

The nearly total lack of originality about the Yellow Peril in the pulps is due mainly to the nature of pulp magazines in general. They were a popular entertainment form whose appeal was aimed at the lowest common denominator in the reading audience. Editors and authors preferred to produce stories that contained characters and themes of proven commercial appeal, and fast-moving plots that allowed little time for character development or long expositions. Where the Yellow Peril was concerned, the fiction about Fu Manchu and Fah Lo Suee had been an unchallenged commercial success.

Stories of the alleged horrors in American Chinatowns also had a demonstrable popularity, and the growing military power of Japan in the 1930s created a natural renewal of interest in the idea of open war between Asia and the United States.

By combining blatant copies of Rohmer's two characters with these established subthemes of the Yellow Peril, the pulp authors served their purpose of presenting fiction that sold even in the highly competitive pulp market of this period. In light of this overall purpose, the harsh attitude taken by these authors toward the Chinese and Chinese Americans may not actually be evidence that they believed in the Yellow Peril. Certainly, however, they had no interest in realistic or balanced portrayals of these groups, either.

Conclusion: Wind from the Gobi

The Yellow Peril theme dominates American fiction about Chinese Americans between 1850 and 1940. It relies heavily on distortions of history and Chinese American society. The expression of this theme results less from empirical evidence supporting the fear of Chinese Americans than from social and philosophical beliefs held by white authors.

These distortions suggest that the impressions of Chinese Americans formed by white American readers during this ninety-year period were largely wrong. Further, these distortions created a faulty frame of reference by which depictions of Chinese Americans after 1940 would be interpreted. During and after World War II, new developments in Chinese America were evaluated according to a past that had never existed.

World War II bears a special relation to the Yellow Peril theme which will be briefly summarized here. In the late nineteenth century, the possibility of an armed invasion of the United States from Asia was so unlikely that the idea bordered at times on paranoia. Yet after decades of unfounded concern about the Yellow Peril, Americans suddenly discovered in 1941 that the imagined threat had become real. This is because the racist foundation of the Yellow Peril had permitted many attitudes and beliefs about the Chinese and Chinese Americans to be expanded to include the Japanese and Japanese Americans. To some, the attack on Pearl Harbor justified every word of Yellow Peril ideology ever uttered in the United States, and so the myth, instead of being discredited, remained embedded in American culture.

The American attitude toward China, and therefore Chinese Americans, improved temporarily in the 1940s, bringing about more sympathetic, though condescending, treatment of the Chinese and Chinese Americans in American fiction. However, the Communist Revolution in China combined the Yellow Peril with the red scare and returned the focus of the Yellow Peril theme to China. The Korean War then further brought these concepts into the literary treatment of Asian Americans. The Vietnam War, from its origins in the 1950s to its end in the 1970s, is yet another major development in this combined phenomenon. In short, the wars after 1941 between the United States and Asian nations kept the focus of discussions about the Yellow Peril centered on international events. The earlier perceptions of the Yellow Peril have tremendous influence, but the theme of the Yellow Peril acquires an essentially different character in this era. Perhaps most importantly, however, this theme continues to appear up to the present.

The historical and social distortions upon which the Yellow Peril theme relies need further study. My examination of fiction here offers a look at the depiction of Chinese Americans especially as it was presented in dramatic ways. Several of the other studies cited earlier include valuable considerations of the images of Chinese Americans presented in nonfiction.[1] However, these studies do not distinguish clearly between the Chinese and Chinese Americans. Though images of the two groups obviously overlap, this distinction is important to the analysis of these images, since the former are foreign people and the latter are Americans. All of the depictions of the Yellow Peril, however, were of course presented in the past. Their true worth lies in the implications they have for the present and future, not only in literature but in other areas of American culture as well.

The two most important areas affected by a belief in the Yellow Peril are international relations and Chinese America. No matter what events develop in the future between the United States and China, or any other East Asian country, all nations involved will be best served if governmental decisions are based on reliable information. While no responsible diplomats will consciously base their decisions on fiction they have read, the belief in the Yellow Peril expressed in American fiction is pervasive enough to be called a fundamental assumption of American culture. Such an assumption is especially dangerous when it is unrecognized, and can cause Americans to evaluate current events, for instance, in a particular way without a sound rationale. At the same time, Chinese Americans remain objects of fear due to the concept of the Yellow Peril. With Charlie Chan as a role model for them, some white Americans can expect, or require, that Chinese Americans conform to certain passive and subservient behavior patterns in order to improve their status in American society. Conversely, Chinese Americans who refuse this role model may find their self-assertion and ambition viewed as threats. The belief in the Yellow Peril is not a dry literary subject, but an active influence in some areas of American life.

Future research might usefully examine the intellectual relation between a belief in the Yellow Peril and the ideas of literary naturalism, Social Darwinism, and evolution. All of these provided a theoretical base for some white authors in the late nineteenth century from which to present racist ideas. Also, the attitudes of missionaries toward Chinese Americans in fiction are only a part of their attitudes toward Asians and non-Christians in general. Their condescension toward Chinese Americans implies a lack of respect for them that is not widely recognized and would bear more discussion.

The importance of international relations between the United States and Asian countries after 1940 lends significance to all the factors contributing to the American picture of the Yellow Peril. Two particularly important events that should be examined in light of the Yellow Peril theme are beyond the scope of this study: the imprisonment of Japanese Americans during World War II, while the German and Italian Americans remained free; and the passage of the Internal Securities Act during the Korean War, which authorized the similar incarceration in camps of American citizens deemed security risks. At this time, American soldiers were in combat against Chinese soldiers, causing particular concern over Chinese Americans as security risks. The extent to which Yellow Peril ideology affected wartime fear should be measured.

Probably the area most in need of further scholarly attention is fiction by the Chinese Americans themselves. Their achievements in this area reflect the artistic expression of a minority experience that is free of the racist strain of naturalism, of the sensationalized muckraking, and of the Christian condescension so prevalent in the fiction by white authors. Although Chinese American authors write from certain interests and viewpoints of their own, their work lacks the historical and social distortions of Yellow Peril fiction and also the Yellow Peril theme itself. This is the source material that can best counter the racist presentations of characters such as Fu Manchu and Charlie Chan.

Perhaps the central question is why so many authors indulged in deliberate distortion, presenting flights of fancy as realism. Lack of knowledge is part of the answer, but this does not explain why so many authors never bothered to research their subject. The various sociopolitical points the authors wished to make, and the pressure to write commercially for an equally uninformed public, are the answers.

The theme of a Yellow Peril from Chinese Americans includes many different social and political issues. The issues and arguments used to "prove" the existence of this Yellow Peril change over the ninety years considered here and contain many distortions of reality. Only the conclusion—that a threat from Chinese Americans did exist in some form—remains constant. This situation suggests that the fear of the Yellow Peril was more important than the reasons offered to argue its existence, and that at times the reasons may have been found or interpreted in order to fit the desired conclusion.

When the Chinese immigrants first arrived in the United States, they came into a society that already viewed them with hostility and condescension. Over the following ninety years, American fiction writers consistently portrayed Chinese Americans as threats to the security and welfare of the United States. Fear of an Asian threat throughout most of this period was poorly grounded in reality, and echoed to some degree the fears of a Mongol hurricane held by thirteenth-century Europeans. When Japanese planes appeared over Pearl Harbor a few years after the Japanese had occupied North China, the long wait for a wind from the Gobi was finally over.

Notes

Introduction

1 No special effort has been made to locate children's fiction on this theme, though some children's books have been included. For a discussion of children's fiction about the Yellow Peril, see J. Frederick MacDonald, "The 'Foreigner' in Juvenile Series Fiction, 1900–1945," *Journal of Popular Culture* 8 (May 1974): 534–48. For nonfiction about the Yellow Peril, see Richard A. Thompson, "The Yellow Peril, 1890–1924" (Ph.D. diss., University of Wisconsin, 1957), hereafter cited as Thompson, "Yellow Peril." For fiction and nonfiction about the Yellow Peril in a different time frame, see John Berdan Gardner, "The Image of the Chinese in the United States, 1885–1915" (Ph.D. diss., University of Pennsylvania, 1961), hereafter cited as Gardner, "Image."

2 Mary Coolidge, *Chinese Immigration* (New York: Henry Holt, 1909), p. 364.

3 Stuart Creighton Miller, *The Unwelcome Immigrant: The American Image of the Chinese, 1785–1882* (Berkeley and Los Angeles: University of California Press, 1969), p. 191. For a discussion of more recent American attitudes toward the Chinese and Chinese Americans, see Harold Isaacs, *Scratches on Our Minds: American Images of China and India* (New York: John Day, 1958).

4 Ibid., p. 192.

5 Ibid., p. 201.

6 Gunther Barth, *Bitter Strength: A History of the Chinese in the United States, 1850–1870* (Cambridge, Mass.: Harvard University Press, 1964), p. 212.

7 Attila and the Huns, also from Asia, are likewise recalled in history as savage barbarian conquerors in the declining years of the Roman Empire. This image has been diluted by their sharing it with

many other nomadic barbarians in those years, by their relatively brief period of significance in history, and by the break in the historical records and cultural continuity of European countries during the Dark Ages that the Huns helped bring down.

Chapter I

1 Mary Coolidge, *Chinese Immigration* (New York: Henry Holt, 1909), p. 80.

2 Paul Jacobs and Saul Landau with Eve Pell, *To Serve the Devil, Vol. 2, Colonials and Sojourners* (New York: Vintage Books, 1971), p. 129.

3 Ibid., p. 99.

4 Ibid., p. 100.

5 Bret Harte, "Wan Lee, the Pagan," in *Writings of Bret Harte*, Standard Library Edition (Boston: Houghton Mifflin, 1896), 2:262–79 (all subsequent references to work by Harte are to this edition of his writings); "The Queen of Pirate Isle," 14:269–88; "See Yup," 14:144–60; "Three Vagabonds of Trinidad," 17:186–201.

6 Bret Harte, "Wan Lee, the Pagan," 2:264.

7 Ibid., p. 270.

8 Ibid., p. 273.

9 Ibid., p. 279.

10 Ibid., p. 278.

11 Bret Harte, "The Queen of Pirate Isle," 14:278.

12 Bret Harte, "See Yup," 16:144.

13 Ibid., p. 146.

14 Ibid., p. 160.

15 Bret Harte, "Three Vagabonds of Trinidad," 17:188.

16 Ibid., p. 192.

17 Bret Harte, "A Belle of Canada City," 18:46.

18 Harte expressed views in various nonfiction works clearly indicating that he had a low regard for the tormentors of the Chinese. For example, in his 1863 essay "John Chinaman" (14:223), Harte writes:

> I don't know what was the exact philosophy that Confucius taught, but it is to be hoped that poor John in his persecution is still able to detect the conscious hate and fear with which inferiority always regards the possibility of even-handed justice, and which is the keynote to the vulgar clamor about servile and degraded races.

19 Bret Harte, "The Christmas Gift That Came to Rupert: A Story for Little Soldiers," 17:171.

20 Bret Harte, "N. N.: Being a Novel in the French Paragraphic Style," 1:155.

21 Bret Harte, "An Episode of Fiddletown," 2:139.

22 Bret Harte, "Gabriel Conroy," 13:326.

23 The Chinese appear as servants in the following:

1. "Devil's Ford" (1884), 5:158.
2. "Snow-bound at Eagle's" (1886), 5:158.
3. "A Millionaire of Rough-and-Ready" (1887), 5:266–67, 315, 320.
4. "A Phyllis of the Sierras" (1887), 6:267, 270, 310.
5. "The Bell-ringer of Angel's" (1894), 8:297.
6. "The Reformation of James Reddy" (1894), 10:254.
7. "Three Partners" (1897), 15:74.
8. "A Niece of Snapshot Harry's" (1900), 17:34
9. "The Youngest Miss Piper" (1901), 17:135.
10. "The Reincarnation of Smith" (1902), 17:295.
11. "Prosper's 'Old Mother'" (1903), 19:158, 161, 169.

A Chinese miner appears in "A Millionaire of Rough-and-Ready," 5:341. Chinese carriers are included in "Three Partners," 15:109. Chinese farm workers appear in "Snow-bound at Eagle's," 5:157, in "A Millionaire of Rough-and-Ready," 5:260, and in "A Buckeye Hollow Inheritance," 18:202.

24 "Plain Language from Truthful James," 12:129.

25 John Burt Foster, "China and the Chinese in American Literature" (Ph.D. diss., University of Illinois, 1952), p. 25 (Hereafter cited as Foster, "China").

26 Ambrose Bierce, "The Haunted Valley," in *The Collected Works of Ambrose Bierce* (New York: Neale, 1910), 3:150 (all subsequent references to work by Bierce are to this edition of his writings).

27 Ambrose Bierce, "Mortality in the Foothills," 12:316.

28 Ambrose Bierce, "The Night-Doings at 'Dead-man's,'" 3:207.

29 Ambrose Bierce, "Fantastic Fables," 6:165.

30 Ambrose Bierce, "A Radical Parallel," 6:212.

31 Foster, "China," p. 37.

32 Joaquin Miller, *First Fam'lies of the Sierras* (Chicago: Jansen, McClurg, and Cox, 1876), p. 42.

33 Ibid., p. 47.

34 Ibid., p. 48.

35 Ibid., p. 57.

36 Ibid., p. 252.

37 "Washee-Washee" is also the title of a poem about the Chinese in the United States which Miller wrote in 1884. By this time Miller's depiction is more positive, if still patronizing, suggesting that if the Chinese launderer will cleanse the corruption in Washington, he will be welcomed in the country by the general population. From Joaquin Miller, *Memorie and Rime* (New York: Funk and Wagnalls, 1884).

38 Margaret Hosmer, *You-Sing: The Chinaman in California: A True Story of the Sacramento Flood* (Philadelphia: Presbyterian Publication Committee, 1868), p. 15.

39 Ibid., p. 17.

40 Ibid., p. 119.

41 Ibid., p. 136.

42 Ibid., p. 148.

43 Ibid., preface.

Chapter II

1 Betty Lee Sung, *Mountain of Gold* (New York: MacMillan, 1967), p. 54.

2 Atwell Whitney, *Almond-Eyed: The Great Agitator: A Story of the Day* (San Francisco: A. L. Bancroft, 1878), p. 10.

3 Ibid., p. 15.

4 Ibid., p. 31.

5 Ibid., p. 72.

6 Ibid., p. 29.

7 Ibid., p. 168.

8 Robert Woltor, *A Short and Truthful History of the Taking of California and Oregon by the Chinese in the Year A.D. 1899* (San Francisco: A. L. Bancroft, 1882), p. 58.

9 Ibid., p. 77.

10 Ibid., p. 79.

11 Ibid., p. 81.

12 Pierton W. Dooner, *Last Days of the Republic* (San Francisco: Alta, California, Publishing House, 1880), p. 102.

13 Ibid., p. 130.

14 Ibid., p. 149.

15 Oto E. Mundo, *The Recovered Continent: A Tale of the Chinese Invasion* (Columbus, Ohio: Harper-Osgood, 1898), p. 289.

16 Ibid., p. 194.

17 For other discussions of these novels, see Thompson, "Yellow Peril"; Gardner, "Image"; and Foster, "China." I was not able to locate any contemporary secondary sources.

Chapter III

1 Limin Chu, *The Images of China and the Chinese in the "Overland Monthly," 1868–1875, 1883–1935*, (San Francisco: R. and E. Research Associates, 1974), p. 305. Hereafter cited as Chu, *Images of China*.

2 Lorelle, "The Battle of Wabash," *Californian* 2 (Oct. 1880): 364–76.

3 *Californian* 5 (April 1882): 385.

4 Chu, *Images of China*, p. 308.

5 Adah F. Batelle, "The Sacking of Grubbville," *Overland Monthly* 2d ser. 20 (Dec. 1892): 573.

6 William W. Crane, "The Year 1899," *Overland Monthly* 2d ser. 21 (June 1893): 579–89.

7 R. P. Pearsall, "The Revelation," *Overland Monthly* 2d ser. 58 (Dec. 1911): 485–94.

8 Chu, *Images of China*, p. 322.

9 Emma F. Dawson, "The Dramatic in My Destiny," *Californian* 1 (Jan. 1880): 5.

10 Limin Chu points out that Tong's name is a slight variation of Tseng-ko-lin-sing, the name of a Manchurian general in the mid-nineteenth century. Chu, *Images of China*, p. 324.

11 Ibid.

12 Phil More, "Chung's Baby," *Overland Monthly*, 2d ser. 31 (March 1898): 233.
Other stories in this category are:

S. S. Boynton, "Tales of a Smuggler," *Overland Monthly*, 2d ser. 21 (Nov. 1893): 511.

J. C. Nattress, "An Encounter with Chinese Smugglers," *Overland Monthly*, 2d ser. 23 (Feb. 1894): 206.

John H. Walsh, "Mr. Poudicherry and the Opium Smugglers," *Overland Monthly*, 2d ser. 56 (Sept. 1910): 273.

Amos George, "Playing the Game," *Overland Monthly*, 2d ser. 57 (Jan. 1911): 35.

13 Charles R. Harker, "The Revenge of a Heathen," *Overland Monthly*, 2d ser. 15 (April 1890): 386.

14 L. Warren Wigmore, "The Revenge of Ching Chow," *Overland Monthly*, 2d ser. 82 (Feb. 1924): 60. Other stories in this category are:

Francis J. Dickie, "The Creed of Ah Sing," *Overland Monthly*, 2d ser. 66 (Dec. 1915): 497.

James F. Kronenberg, "The Avenging Joss," *Overland Monthly*, 2d ser. 82 (Sept. 1924): 393.

E. E. Underwood, "When an Oriental Meets an Oriental," *Overland Monthly*, 2d ser. 84 (April 1926): 107.

15 Frank Norris, "Thoroughbred," *Overland Monthly*, 2d ser. 25 (Feb. 1895): 196. For a detailed discussion of the Chinese immigrant in novels by Frank Norris, see p. 223.

16 Norris, "Thoroughbred," p. 199.

17 Ibid., p. 200–201.

18 For a detailed consideration of this novel, see p. 98.

19 G. Emmerson Sears, "Baxter's Beat," *Overland Monthly*, 2d ser. 55 (March 1910): 293.

20 Marian Allen, "Ah Foo, the Fortune Teller," *Overland Monthly*, 2d ser. 65 (March 1915): 249.

21 Gordon Grant, "The Provocation of Ah Sing," *Overland Monthly*, 2d ser. 79 (Jan. 1922): 25.

22 Ibid., p. 68. Other stories in this category are:

Sarah Comstock, "Ways That Are Dark," *Overland Monthly*, 2d ser. 32 (Dec. 1898): 500.

Robert B. Grant, "Finders, Keepers," *Overland Monthly*, 2d ser. 38 (Dec. 1901): 430.

Olive Dilbert, "The Chinese Lily," *Overland Monthly*, 2d ser. 42 (Sept. 1903): 184.

George C. Evans, "The Long Black Box," *Overland Monthly*, 2d ser. 45 (April 1905): 317.

John A. Murray, "The Mandarin's Birthday Gift," *Overland Monthly*, 2d ser. 56 (July 1910): 75.

J. E. Hasty, "The City of Romance: the Episode of the Green Dragon," *Overland Monthly*, 2d ser. 76 (Aug. 1920): 39.

Frederick C. Rothermel, "Foo Soon, the Heathen," *Overland Monthly*, 2d ser. 72 (Jan.-Feb. 1921): 23.

23 E. Lincoln Kellogg, "A Partly Celestial Tale," *Overland Monthly*, 2d ser. 26 (Sept. 1895): 315.

24 Ibid., p. 318.

25 Ibid., p. 319.

26 M. Austin, "The Conversion of Ah Lew Sing," *Overland Monthly*, 2d ser. 30 (Oct. 1897): 307; reprinted, 2d ser. 78 (Sept.

1921): 33.

27 Sui Sin Far, "A Chinese Ishmael," *Overland Monthly*, 2d ser. 34 (July 1899): 43. Sui Sin Far is the pseudonym of Edith Eaton. Most of her stories are much less violent and sensational. (See p. 130)

28 Marguerite Stabler, "The Sale of Sooy Yet," *Overland Monthly* 35 (May 1900): 414.

29 Andriana Spadoni, "Devils, White and Yellow: A Story of San Francisco's Chinatown," *Overland Monthly*, 2d ser. 44 (July 1904): 80.

30 James Hanson, "The Winning of Josephine Chang," *Overland Monthly*, 2d ser. 75 (June 1920): 493.

31 James Hanson, "Behind the Devil Screen," *Overland Monthly*, 2d ser. 78 (Nov. 1921): 19. The other story in this category is: Robert Hewes, "A Little Prayer to Joss, Ah Foon Metes Out Oriental Justice," *Overland Monthly*, 2d ser. 81 (Aug. 1923): 10.

32 Ambrose Bierce, "The Haunted Valley," *Overland Monthly* 8 (July 1871): 88. For a detailed consideration of "The Haunted Valley," see p. 22.

33 Frank Norris, "After Strange Gods," *Overland Monthly*, 2d ser. 24 (Oct. 1894): 375.

34 Hazel Havermale, "The Canton Shawl," *Overland Monthly*, 2d ser. 64 (Sept. 1914): 269.

35 Esther B. Bock, "Ah Choo," *Overland Monthly*, 2d ser. 76 (Sept. 1920): 49.

36 Jeanette Daily, "Sweet Burning Incense," *Overland Monthly*, 2d ser. 77 (Jan.-Feb. 1921): 9.

37 Steve Fisher, "Shanghai Butterfly: A Short, Short Story," *Overland Monthly*, 2d ser. 91 (Nov. 1933): 158. The other story in the category is: Sarah Comstock, "A Great Gulf Fixed," *Overland Monthly*, 2d ser. 32 (Dec. 1898): 499.

38 Mrs. James Neall, "Spilled Milk," *Overland Monthly* 5 (Nov. 1870): 431.

39 Prentice Mulford, "Pete," *Overland Monthly* 6 (April 1871): 370.

40 Flora De Wolfe, "Ti Lung," *Overland Monthly*, 2d ser. 3 (May 1884): 553.

41 C. E. B., "An Episode of the Turnpike," *Overland Monthly*, 2d ser. 4 (July 1884): 46.

42 Mary T. Mott, "Poor Ah Toy," *Californian* 5 (April 1882): 371.

43 Chu, *Images of China*, p. 394.

44 Ibid., p. 395.

45 Horace Annesley Vachell, "The Conscience of Quong Wo," *Overland Monthly*, 2d ser. 24 (Nov. 1894): 504.

46 Mary Bell, "Sing Kee's Chinese Lily," *Overland Monthly*, 2d ser. 30 (Dec. 1897): 531.

47 Chu, *Images of China*, p. 400.

48 Eunice Ward, "Ah Gin," *Overland Monthly*, 2d ser. 49 (May 1907): 393.

49 Lucy Foreman Lindsay, "Sang," *Overland Monthly*, 2d ser. 69 (Jan. 1917): 57.

50 Chu, *Images of China*, p. 401. Other stories in this category are:

T. Duncan Ferguson, "The Joss That Answered Prayer," *Overland Monthly*, 2d ser. 30 (Dec. 1897): 531.

Marion E. Hamilton, "Wong," *Overland Monthly*, 2d ser. 63 (June 1914): 569.

Edith Hecht, "His First Client," *Overland Monthly*, 2d ser. 68 (July 1916): 21.

Daisy De Forest Skaggs, "Hawaiian Yesterday," *Overland Monthly*, 2d ser. 77 (March 1921): 30.

51 The Stevensons, "Chinatown: My Land of Dreams," *Overland Monthly*, 2d ser. 73 (Jan. 1919): 42. Other stories in this category are:

Howard Lathrup, "A Pioneer of 1920," *Overland Monthly* 4 (April 1870): 303.

Sara Comstock, "Kwai-Tzse," *Overland Monthly*, 2d ser. 32 (Dec. 1898): 501.

Amy M. Parish, "The Ghost of Fan-Tai," *Overland Monthly*, 2d ser. 43 (March 1904): 194.

Minnie D. Kellogg, "The Big Butter Buddha," *Overland Monthly*, 2d ser. 43 (March 1904): 184.

Lizzie G. Wilcoxson, "The Tangent of a Tiff: A Tale Wherein Mrs. Hill, Yip Hung, and a Beauty Doctor Are Concerned," *Overland Monthly*, 2d ser. 50 (July 1907): 77.

Gurdon Edwards, "The History of Chop-Suey and Fan-Tan," *Overland Monthly*, 2d ser. 51 (April 1908): 345.

James Hanson, "The Divorce of Ah Lum," *Overland Monthly*, 2d ser. 77 (March 1921): 35.

James Hanson, "According to the Sages," *Overland Monthly*, 2d ser. 83 (Oct. 1925): 487.

52 Owen C. Treleaven, "Poison Jim Chinaman," *Overland Monthly*, 2d ser. 74 (July 1919): 40. Other stories in this category are:

Jesslyn H. Hull, "A Yellow Angel," *Overland Monthly*, 2d ser. 67 (March 1916): 189.

Charles W. McCable, "Only a Squaw Man—Kind Feelings Lodge in Many Unlikely Places," *Overland Monthly*, 2d ser. 76 (Dec. 1920): 51.

Chapter IV

1 *U.S. Census of Population, 1950 and 1960, Non-White Population by Race,* cited in Betty Lee Sung, *Mountain of Gold* (New York: MacMillan, 1967), p. 320.

2 Maud Howe, *The San Rosario Ranch* (Boston: Roberts Brothers, 1844), p. 10.

3 Ibid., p. 62.

4 Ibid., p. 128.

5 Ibid., p. 158.

6 Ibid., p. 236.

7 Ibid., p. 303.

8 William Henry Bishop, *Choy Susan and Other Stories* (Boston: Houghton Mifflin, 1885), p. 10.

9 Ibid., p. 6.

10 Ibid., p. 9.

11 *Little Ah Yee of the Opium Dens* (1886) by Emma Cable is classified as fiction but actually is not. The author was a Presbyterian missionary in the Chinatown of San Franscisco, in charge of home visitations. The book contains excerpts from her annual reports to the mission board from 1880 to 1885 concerning a Chinese American girl who is eight years old when the reports begin. The reports end with the girl's death from cholera. See Foster, "China," p. 157.

12 William Norr, *Stories of Chinatown: Sketches in the Chinese Colony of Mott, Pell and Doyers Street* (New York: William Norr, 1892), p. 4.

13 Ibid., p. 27.

14 Ibid., p. 72.

15 Ibid., p. 75.

16 Ibid., p. 79.

17 Ibid., p. 83. Other stories in the collection are: "The Romance of Chuck Connors," "Mrs. Morrissey's Present," and "'Round the Opium Lamp."

18 Harry M. Johnson, *Edith: A Story of Chinatown* (Boston: Arena, 1895), p. 5.

19 Ibid., p. 21.

20 Ibid., p. 34.

21 Robert W. Chambers, "The Maker of Moons," in *Hauntings and Horrors: Ten Grisly Tales,* ed. Alden H. Norton (New York: Berkeley, 1969), p. 4.

22 Ibid., p. 6.

23 Ibid., p. 7.

24 Ibid., p. 22.

25 Ibid., p. 26.

26 Ibid., p. 35.

27 Ibid.

28 Ibid., p. 47.

29 Ibid., p. 49.

30 Ibid., p. 52.

31 Edward Townsend, *A Daughter of the Tenements* (1895; reprint ed., Upper Saddle River, N.J.: Literature House, 1970), p. 78.

32 Ibid., p. 223.

33 Ibid., p. 228.

34 Edward Townsend, *Near a Whole City Full* (New York: Dillingham, 1897).

35 Chester Bailey Fernald, *The Cat and the Cherub and Other Stories* (New York: Century, 1896), p. 42.

36 Chester Bailey Fernald, *Chinatown Stories* (London: William Heineman, 1900), p. 80. The other stories in *Chinatown Stories* are: "The Law of the Barbarians," "The Monkey That Never Was," "The Gentleman in the Barrel," "The Man Who Lost His Head," "The Pot of Frightful Doom," and "Chan Tow, the Highrob."

37 Arthur Hobson Quinn, *American Fiction: An Historical and Critical Survey* (New York: D. Appleton Century, 1936), p. 519.

38 May Lamberton Becker, *Golden Tales of the Far West* (New York: Dodd, Mead, 1935), p. 277.

39 Gertrude Atherton, *The Californians* (New York: B. W. Dodge, 1898), p. 51.

40 Ibid., p. 116.

41 Ibid., p. 345.

42 Ibid., p. 190.

43 Ibid., p. 294.

44 Ibid., p. 331.

45 Frank Norris, *Moran of the Lady Letty: A Story of Adventure off the California Coast* (Garden City, N.Y.: Doubleday, Doran, 1928), p. 197.

46 Ibid., p. 188.

47 Ibid., p. 212.

48 Ibid., p. 237.

49 Ibid., p. 248. The author of this study is a "See Yup."

50 Ibid., p. 251.

51 Ibid., p. 252.

52 Ibid., p. 268.

53 Ibid., p. 279.

54 Ibid., p. 300.

55 Ibid., p. 294.

56 Ibid., p. 322.

57 Frank Norris, *Blix* (Garden City, N.Y.: Doubleday, Doran, 1928), p. 33.

58 Frank Norris, *McTeague: A Story of San Francisco* (Garden City, N.Y.: Doubleday, Doran, 1928), p. 105.

59 Mary E. Bamford, *Ti: A Story of San Francisco's Chinatown* (Chicago: David C. Cook, 1899), p. 7.

60 Ibid., p. 9.

61 Ibid., p. 22.

62 Ibid., p. 38.

63 Ibid., p. 93.

64 Foster, "China," p. 178.

65 Dr. C. W. Doyle, *The Shadow of Quong Lung* (Philadelphia: Lippincott, 1900), p. 7.

66 Ibid., p. 39.

67 Hezekiah Butterworth, *Little Sky-High or the Surprising Doings of Washee-Washee Wang* (New York: T. Y. Crowell, 1901), p. 7.

68 Ibid., p. 14.

69 Ibid., p. 46.

70 Ibid., p. 42.

71 William E. S. Fales, *Bits of Broken China* (New York: Street and Smith, 1902), p. 9.

72 Ibid., p. 14.

73 Ibid., p. 75.

74 Ibid., p. 86.

75 Ibid., p. 164.

76 Ibid., p. 171. Other stories in this collection are: "Poor Doc High," "The Red Mogul," and "A Mott Street Incident."

77 Foster, "China," p. 186.

78 Nellie Blessing Eyster, *A Chinese Quaker: An Unfictitious Novel* (New York: Fleming H. Revell, 1902), p. 20.

79 Ibid., p. 28.

80 Ibid., p. 37.

81 Ibid., p. 173.

82 Ibid., p. 294.

83 Jack London, *Tales of the Fish Patrol* (Cleveland: International Fiction Library, 1905), p. 225.

84 Jack London, "The Unparalleled Invasion," in *Curious Fragments: Jack London's Tales of Fantasy Fiction*, ed. Dale L. Walker (Port Washington, N.Y.: Kennikat, 1975), p. 112.

85 Ibid., p. 116.

86 Jack London, *The House of Pride and Other Tales of Hawaii* (New York: Regent, 1912).

87 Jack London, *On the Makaloa Mat* (New York: MacMillan, 1919).

88 Andrew Sinclair, *Jack: A Biography of Jack London* (New York: Harper and Row, 1977), pp. 229–30.

89 Earle Labor, *Jack London* (New York: Twayne, 1974), p. 20.

90 E. Spence de Pue, *Dr. Nicholas Stone* (New York: G. W. Dillingham, 1905), p. 95.

91 Ibid., p. 181.

92 Helen Green, *At the Actors' Boarding House and Other Stories* (New York: Nevada, 1906), p. 129.

96 Ibid., p. 130.

94 Lu Wheat, *Ah Moy: The Story of a Chinese Girl* (1906, as *The Third Chinese Daughter: A Story of Chinese Home Life;* reprint ed. New York: Grafton, 1980), p. 32.

95 Ibid., p. 78.

96 Ibid., p. 122.

97 Ibid., p. 135.

Chapter V

1 For a detailed consideration of magazine fiction about the depiction of Chinese Americans and Chinese, see Sue Fawn Chung, "From Fu Manchu, Evil Genius, to James Lee Wong, Popular Hero: A Study of the Chinese American in Popular Periodical Fiction From 1920 to 1940," *Journal of Popular Culture* 10, no. 3 (March 1977): 534–47.

2 Frances Aymar Mathews, *The Flame Dancer* (New York: G. W. Dillingham, 1908), p. 273.

3 Ibid., p. 275.

4 Ibid., p. 370. Though Manchuria was originally a country separate from China, Manchurians in China had been absorbed into Chinese culture by this time.

5 Edith Eaton ("Sui Sin Far"), *Mrs. Spring Fragrance* (Chicago: A. C. McClurg, 1912). Hereafter cited as Eaton, *Mrs. Spring Fragrance.* For biographical information, see Sui Sin Far, "Leaves from the Mental Portfolio of an Eurasian," *Independent* 66 (21 Jan. 1909): 125–32.

6 See p. 53.

7 Eaton, *Mrs. Spring Fragrance*, p. 1.

8 Joseph Hergesheimer, *Java Head* (New York: Alfred A. Knopf, 1918), p. 56.

9 Ibid., p. 76.

10 Ibid., p. 77.

11 Ibid., p. 110.

12 Ibid., p. 117.

13 Ibid., p. 134.

14 Ibid., p. 218.

15 Ibid., p. 243.

16 Ernest Poole, *Beggar's Gold* (New York: MacMillan, 1921), p. 7.

17 Ibid., p. 79.

18 Ibid., p. 195.

19 Ibid., p. 228.

20 Foster, "China," p. 215.

21 Hugh Wiley, *Jade: And Other Stories* (New York: Alfred A. Knopf, 1922), p. 105.

22 Hugh Wiley, *Manchu Blood* (1927; reprint ed., New York: Books for Libraries, 1971), p. 13.

23 Ibid.

24 Ibid., p. 37.

25 Ibid., p. 41.

26 Ibid., p. 43.

27 Ibid., p. 45.

28 Ibid., p. 47.

29 Ibid., p. 51.

30 Ibid., p. 91.

31 Ibid., p. 102.

32 Ibid., p. 221.

33 Ibid., p. 57.

34 Ibid., p. 146.

35 Ibid., p. 102.

36 Hugh Wiley, "In Chinatown," *Collier's* 93, no. 26. (30 June 1934): 12–13.

37 Hugh Wiley, "The Thirty Thousand Dollar Bomb," *Collier's* 94, no. 4 (28 July 1934): 17.

38 Hugh Wiley, "No Witnesses," *Collier's* 97, no. 7 (15 Feb. 1936): 10–11.

39 Wiley's inability to characterize Wong as a realistic Chinese American may result from an inability to avoid Chinese American stereotypes unless he neglected Wong's personal life completely.

40 Lemuel de Bra, *Ways That Are Wary* (New York: A. L. Burt,

1925), p. 165.

41 Ibid., p. 308.

42 *Sunset* 54 (June 1925): 86.

43 Ibid., p. 87.

44 Henry Milner Rideout, *Tao Tales* (New York: Duffield, 1927), p. 3.

45 Ibid., p. 4.

46 Foster, "China," p. 225.

47 H. T. Tsiang, *China Red* (New York: the author, 1931), p. 25.

48 Ibid.

49 H. T. Tsiang, *And China Has Hands* (New York: Robert Speller, 1937), p. 10.

50 Ibid., p. 21.

51 Ibid., p. 23.

52 Ibid., p. 27.

53 Ibid., p. 28.

54 Ibid., p. 34.

55 Ibid., p. 61.

56 Ibid., p. 62.

57 Ibid., p. 66.

58 Ibid., p. 164.

59 Charles R. Shepherd, *Lim Yik Choy* (New York: Fleming H. Revell, 1932), p. 164.

60 Ibid., p. 168.

61 Ibid., p. 231.

62 Idwal Jones, *China Boy* (Los Angeles: Primavera, 1936), p. 16.

63 Ibid., p. 17.

64 Ibid., p. 22.

65 Ibid., p.67.

66 Ibid., p. 90.

Chapter VI

1 Fu Manchu's world readership includes millions more.

2 Sax Rohmer, *The Insidious Doctor Fu-Manchu* (1913; reprint ed., New York: Pyramid, 1961), p. 17 (hereafter cited as Rohmer, *Insidious*).

3 Ibid., p. 95.

4 Ibid., p. 69.

5 Sax Rohmer, *The Return of Dr. Fu-Manchu* (1916; reprint ed., New York: Pyramid, 1961), p. 76.

6 Ibid., p. 136.

7 Ibid., p. 182.

8 Sax Rohmer, *The Hand of Fu-Manchu* (1917; reprint ed., New York: Pyramid, 1962), p. 111.

9 Sax Rohmer, *The Trail of Fu-Manchu* (1934; reprint ed., New York: Pyramid, 1964), p. 15.

10 Sax Rohmer, *The Shadow of Fu-Manchu* (1948; reprint ed., New York: Pyramid, 1963), p. 10 (hereafter cited as Rohmer, *Shadow*).

11 Ibid., p. 9.

12 Ibid.

13 Cay Van Ash and Elizabeth Sax Rohmer, *Master of Villainy: A Biography of Sax Rohmer*, ed. Robert E. Briney (Bowling Green, Ohio: Bowling Green University Press, 1972), p. 235 (hereafter cited as Van Ash, *Villainy*).

14 Ibid., p. 297.

15 Ibid., p. 214. The "absurdity" of such complaints is debatable. They have become more common in regard to the mass media in the 1970s by many American minorities and other definable groups; currently, a group called Asian Americans for a Fair Media makes such watchdogging one of its prime functions.

16 Rohmer, *Insidious*, p. 40.

17 Rohmer, *Shadow*, p. 157.

18 Sax Rohmer, *Re-Enter Fu-Manchu* (1957; reprint ed., New York: Pyramid, 1960), p. 158.

19 Van Ash, *Villainy*, p. 286.

20 Ibid., p. 291.

21 Rohmer, *Insidious*, p. 17.

22 Frank Chin, "Interview: Roland Winters," *Amerasia Journal* 2 (fall 1973): 1.

23 Earl Derr Biggers, *The House Without a Key* (New York: P. F. Collier & Son, 1925), p. 76.

24 Ibid., p. 84.

25 Ibid., p. 145.

26 Ibid., p. 311.

27 Ibid.

28 Earl Derr Biggers, *The Chinese Parrot* (1929; reprint ed., New York: Bantam, 1975), p. 1.

29 Ibid., p. 11.

30 Ibid., p. 117.

31 Earl Derr Biggers, *Behind That Curtain* (1928; reprint ed., New York: Bantam, 1974), p. 119.

32 Ibid., p. 203.
33 Ibid., p. 216.
34 Ibid., p. 217.
35 Earl Derr Biggers, *Charlie Chan Carries On* (1930; reprint ed., New York: Bantam, 1975), p. 233.
36 Ibid., p. 126.
37 Earl Derr Biggers, *Keeper of the Keys* (1932; reprint ed., New York: Bantam, 1975), p. 216.
38 Earl Derr Biggers, *The Black Camel* (1929; reprint ed., New York: Bantam, 1975), p. 218.
39 Biggers, *Charlie Chan Carries On*, p. 127.

Chapter VII

1 Ron Goulart, *An Informal History of the Pulp Magazine* (New York: Ace 1972), p. 10 (hereafter cited as Goulart, *Pulp*).
2 Ibid., p. 7.
3 Ibid., p. 28.
4 Ibid., p. 114.
5 Dashiell Hammett, "The House on Turk Street," *The Continental Op* (New York: Random House, 1966), p. 103.
6 Ibid.
7 Ibid., p. 105.
8 Ibid., p. 116.
9 Dashiell Hammett, "Dead Yellow Women," *The Big Knockover* (New York: Random House, 1966), p. 191.
10 Ibid., p. 196.
11 Violet Rabaya, "Filipino Immigration: the Creation of a New Social Problem," in *Roots: An Asian American Reader*, ed. Amy Tachiki et al. (Los Angeles: UCLA Asian American Studies Center, 1971), p. 190.
12 Hammett, "Dead Yellow Women," p. 197.
13 Ibid., p. 203.
14 Ibid., p. 207.
15 Ibid., p. 211.
16 Ibid., p. 212.
17 Ibid.
18 Ibid., p. 214.
19 Ibid., p. 240.
20 Ibid., p. 241.
21 Ibid., p. 249.

22 Sax Rohmer, *Daughter of Fu-Manchu* (1931; reprint ed., New York: Pyramid, 1964), p. 37.

23 Ibid., p. 42.

24 Ibid., p. 98.

25 Ibid., p. 99.

26 Ibid., p. 105.

27 Goulart, *Pulp*, p. 63.

28 Grant Stockbridge, "Dragon Lord of the Underworld," *The Spider* 6 (July 1935): 13.

29 Ibid., p. 28.

30 Ibid., p. 25.

31 Ibid., p. 26.

32 Ibid., p. 9.

33 See p. 138.

34 Stockbridge, "Dragon Lord," p. 18.

35 Ibid., p. 10.

36 Ibid., p. 30.

37 Ibid., p. 31.

38 Ibid., p. 56.

39 Ibid., p. 32.

40 Ibid., p. 39.

41 Ibid., p. 18.

42 Goulart, *Pulp*, p. 195.

43 Robert J. Hogan, "The Case of the Six Coffins," *Wu Fang* 1 (Sept. 1935): 7–8.

44 Ibid., p. 12.

45 Ibid., p. 13.

46 Ibid., p. 17.

47 Ibid., p. 70.

48 Ibid., p. 71.

49 Ibid., p. 73.

50 Ibid., p. 74.

51 Goulart, *Pulp*, pp. 95–96.

52 Donald E. Keyhoe, "The Mystery of the Dragon's Shadow," *Dr. Yen Sin* 1 (July-Aug. 1936): 6.

53 Ibid.

54 Ibid., p. 30.

55 Ibid., p. 10.

56 Ibid., p. 15.

57 Ibid., p. 61.

58 Ibid., p. 17.

59 Ibid., p. 34.

60 Ibid., p. 9.
61 Ibid., p. 28.
62 Ibid., p. 29.
63 Goulart, *Pulp*, p. 89.
64 Robert Kenneth Jones, *The Shudder Pulps* (West Linn, Oreg.: FAX Collector's Editions, 1975), pp. 81, 90.
65 Brant House, "Curse of the Mandarin's Fan," *Detective Mysteries* 13 (Feb. 1938): 10.
66 Ibid., p. 12.
67 Ibid., p. 13.
68 Ibid.
69 Ibid., p. 19.
70 Ibid., p. 16.

Conclusion

1 For a study of nonfiction on the Yellow Peril theme in a limited time span, see Richard Austin Thompson, "The Yellow Peril, 1890–1924" (Ph.D. diss. University of Wisconsin, 1957); John Berdan Gardner, "The Images of the Chinese in the U.S., 1885–1915" (Ph.D. diss. University of Pennsylvania, 1961); Harold R. Isaacs, *Scratches on Our Minds: American Images of China and India* (New York: John Day, 1958).

Bibliography

Primary Sources
Books

Atherton, Gertrude. *The Californians.* New York: B. W. Dodge, 1898.
Bamford, Mary E. *Ti: A Story of San Francisco's Chinatown.* Chicago: David C. Cook, 1899.
Becker, May Lamberton. *Golden Tales of the Far West.* New York: Dodd, Mead, 1935.
Bierce, Ambrose. *The Collected Works of Ambrose Bierce.* 12 vols. New York: Neale, 1910.
Biggers, Earl Derr. *Behind That Curtain.* 1928. Reprint. New York: Bantam, 1974.
———. *The Black Camel.* 1929. Reprint. New York: Bantam, 1975.
———. *Charlie Chan Carries On.* 1930. Reprint. New York: Bantam, 1975.
———. *The Chinese Parrot.* 1924. Reprint. New York: Bantam, 1974.
———. *The House Without a Key.* New York: P. F. Collier, 1925.
———. *Keeper of the Keys.* 1932. Reprint. New York: Bantam, 1975.
Bishop, William Henry. *Choy Susan and Other Stories.* Boston: Houghton, Mifflin, 1885.
Butterworth, Hezekiah. *Little Sky-High or the Surprising Doings of Washee-Washee Wang.* New York: T. Y. Crowell, 1901.
De Bra, Lemuel. *Ways that Are Wary.* New York: A. L. Burt, 1925.
De Pue, E. Spence. *Dr. Nicholas Stone.* New York: G. W. Dillingham, 1905.
Dooner, Pierton W. *Last Days of the Republic.* San Francisco: Alta, California Publishing House, 1880.
Doyle, C. W., M.D. *The Shadow of Quong Lung.* Philidelphia: Lippincott, 1900.
Eaton, Edith [Sui Sin Far]. *Mrs. Spring Fragrance.* Chicago: A. C.

McClurg, 1912.

Eyster, Nellie Blessing. *A Chinese Quaker: An Unfictitious Novel*. New York: Fleming H. Revell, 1902.

Fales, William E. S. *Bits of Broken China*. New York: Street and Smith, 1902.

Fernald, Chester Bailey. *The Cat and the Cherub and Other Stories*. New York: Century, 1896.

———. *Chinatown Stories*. London: William Heineman, 1900.

Green, Helen. *At the Actors' Boarding House and Other Stories*. New York: Nevada, 1906.

Hammett, Dashiell. *The Big Knockover*. 1966. Reprint. New York: Vintage, 1972.

———. *The Continental Op*. 1974. Reprint. New York: Vintage, 1975.

Harte, Bret. *Writings of Bret Harte*. 20 vols. Standard library edition. Boston: Houghton Mifflin, 1896.

Hergesheimer, Joseph. *Java Head*. New York: Alfred A. Knopf. 1918.

Hosmer, Margaret. *You-Sing: The Chinaman in California: A True Story of the Sacramento Flood*. Philadelphia: Presbyterian Publication Committee, 1868.

Howe, Maud. *San Rosario Ranch*. Boston: Roberts Brothers, 1884.

Johnson, Harry M. *Edith: A Story of Chinatown*. Boston: Arena, 1895.

Jone, Idwal. *China Boy*. Los Angeles: Primavera, 1936.

London, Jack. *Curious Fragments: Jack London's Tales of Fantasy Fiction*. Edited by Dale L. Walker. Port Washington, N.Y.: Kennikat, 1975.

———. *The House of Pride and Other Tales of Hawaii*. New York: Regent, 1912.

———. *On the Makaloa Mat*. New York: MacMillan, 1919.

———. *Tales of the Fish Patrol*. Cleveland: International Fiction Library, 1905.

Mathews, Frances Aymar. *The Flame Dancer*. New York: G. W. Dillingham, 1908.

Miller, Joaquin. *First Fam'lies of the Sierras*. Chicago: Jansen, McClurg, and Cox, 1876.

———. *Memorie and Rime*. New York: Funk & Wagnall's, 1884.

Mundo, Oto E. *The Recovered Continent: A Tale of the Chinese Invasion*. Columbus, Ohio: Harper-Osgood, 1898.

Norr, William. *Stories of Chinatown: Sketches from Life in the Chinese Colony of Mott, Pell and Doyers Street*. New York: the author, 1892.

Norris, Frank. *Blix*. Garden City, N.Y.: Doubleday, Doran, 1899.

———. *McTeague: A Story of San Francisco*. Garden City, N.Y.:

Doubleday, Doran, 1899.

―――. *Moran of the Lady Letty: A Story of Adventure off the California Coast.* Garden City, N.Y.: Doubleday, Doran, 1898.

Poole, Ernest. *Beggar's Gold.* New York: MacMillan, 1921.

Rideout, Henry Milner. *Tao Tales.* New York: Duffield, 1927.

Rohmer, Sax. *Daughter of Fu-Manchu.* 1931. Reprint. New York: Pyramid, 1964.

―――. *The Hand of Fu-Manchu.* 1917. Reprint. New York: Pyramid, 1961.

―――. *The Insidious Doctor Fu-Manchu.* 1913. Reprint. New York: Pyramid, 1961.

―――. *Re-Enter Fu Manchu.* 1957. Reprint. New York: Pyramid, 1968.

―――. *The Return of Dr. Fu-Manchu.* 1916. Reprint. New York: Pyramid, 1961.

―――. *The Shadow of Fu Manchu.* 1948. Reprint. New York: Pyramid, 1963.

―――. *The Trail of Fu-Manchu.* 1934. Reprint. New York: Pyramid, 1964.

Shepherd, Charles R. *Lim Yik Choy.* New York: Fleming H. Revell, 1932.

Townsend, Edward. *A Daughter of the Tenements.* 1895. Reprint. Upper Saddle River, N.J.: Literature House, 1970.

Tsiang, H. T. *And China Has Hands.* New York: Robert Speller, 1937.

―――. *China Red.* New York: the author, 1931.

Wheat, Lu. *Ah Moy: The Story of a Chinese Girl.* New York: Grafton, 1908. 1906 (as *Third Chinese Daughter: A Story of Chinese Home Life*). Reprint.

Whitney, Atwell. *Almond-Eyed: The Great Agitator: A Story of the Day.* San Francisco: A. L. Bancroft, 1878.

Wiley, Hugh. *Jade: And Other Stories.* New York: Alfred A. Knopf, 1922.

―――. *Manchu Blood.* 1927. Reprint. New York: Books for Libraries, 1971.

Woltor, Robert. *A Short and Truthful History of the Taking of California and Oregon by the Chinese in the Year A.D. 1899.* San Francisco: A. L. Bancroft, 1882.

Stories

Allen, Marian. "Ah Foo, the Fortune Teller." *Overland Monthly*, 2d ser.65(March 1915): 249–53.

Atkinson, Edwin V. "A Study in Ochre." *Overland Monthly*, 24 (July 1894): 45–50.

Austin, M. "The Conversion of Ah Lew Sing." *Overland Monthly*, 2d ser. 30 (Oct. 1897): 307–12; reprinted in 2d ser. 78 (Sept. 1921): 33–35, 65–66.

B., C. E. "An Episode of the Turnpike." *Overland Monthly*, 2d ser. 4 (July 1884): 46–48.

Batelle, Adah F. "The Sacking of Grubbville." *Overland Monthly*, 2d ser. 20 (Dec. 1892): 573–77.

Bell, Mary. "Sing Kee's China-Lily." *Overland Monthly*, 2d ser. 30 (Dec. 1897): 531–38.

Bierce, Ambrose. "The Haunted Valley." *Overland Monthly* 7 (July 1871): 88–95.

Bock, Esther B. "Ah Choo." *Overland Monthly*, 2d ser. 76 (Sept. 1920): 49–56, 87–91.

Boynton, S. S. "Tales of a Smuggler." *Overland Monthly*, 2d ser. 22 (Nov. 1893): 511–16.

Chamber, Robert W. "The Maker of Moons." In *Hauntings and Horrors: Ten Grisly Tales*, edited by Alden H. Norton. New York: Berkeley, 1969.

Comstock, Sarah. "A Great Gulf Fixed." *Overland Monthly*, 2d ser. 32 (Dec. 1898): 499–500.

———. "Kwai-Tzse." *Overland Monthly*, 2d ser. 32 (Dec. 1898): 501–2.

———. "Ways That Are Dark." *Overland Monthly*, 2d ser. 32 (Dec. 1898): 500–501.

Crane, William W. "The Year 1899." *Overland Monthly*, 2d ser. 21 (June 1893): 579–89.

Dailey, Jeanette. "Sweet Burning Incense." *Overland Monthly*, 2d ser.77 (Jan.-Feb. 1921): 9–14.

Dawson, Emma F. "The Dramatic in My Destiny." *Californian* 5 (April 1882): 5–14.

De Wolfe, Flora. "Ti Lung." *Overland Monthly*, 2d ser. 3 (May 1884): 553–54.

Dickie, Francis J. "The Creed of Ah Sing." *Overland Monthly*, 2d ser. 66 (Dec. 1915): 497–500.

Dilbert. Olive. "The Chinese Lily." *Overland Monthly*, 2d ser. 42 (Sept. 1903): 184–88.

Edwards, Gurden. "The History of Chop-Suey and Fan-Tan." *Overland Monthly*, 2d ser. 51 (April 1908): 345–50.

Evans, George C. "The Long Black Box." *Overland Monthly*, 2d ser. 45 (April 1905): 317–21.

Ferguson, T. Duncan. "The Joss That Answered Prayer." *Overland Monthly*, 2d ser. 44 (Nov. 1904): 501–3.

Fisher, Steve. "Shanghai Butterfly: A Short, Short Story." *Overland Monthly*, 2d ser. 91 (Nov. 1933): 158.

George, Amos. "Playing the Game." *Overland Monthly*, 2d ser. 57 (Jan. 1911): 35–38.

Grant, Gordon. "The Provocation of Ah Sing." *Overland Monthly*, 2d ser. 79 (Jan. 1922): 25–26, 68.

Grant, Robert B. "Finders, Keepers." *Overland Monthly*, 2d ser. 38 (Dec. 1901): 430–31.

Hamilton, Marion E. "Wong." *Overland Monthly*, 2d ser. 63 (June 1914): 569–70.

Hanson, James. "Behind the Devil Screen." *Overland Monthly*, 2d ser. 77 (Nov. 1921): 19–24, 65–66.

———. "The Divorce of Ah Lum." *Overland Monthly*, 2d ser. 77 (March 1921): 35–38.

———. "The Winning of Josephine Chang." *Overland Monthly*, 2d ser. 75 (June 1920): 493–98.

Harker, Charles R. "The Revenge of a Heathen." *Overland Monthly*, 2d ser. 15 (April 1890): 386–90.

Hasty, J. E. "The City of Romance: the Episode of the Green Dragon." *Overland Monthly*, 2d ser. 76 (Aug. 1920): 29–42, 93.

Havermale, Hazel H. "The Canton Shawl." *Overland Monthly*, 2d ser. 64 (Sept. 1914): 269–72.

Hecht, Edith. "His First Client." *Overland Monthly*, 2d ser. 68 (July 1916): 21–23.

Hewes, Robert. "A Little Prayer to Joss, Ah Foon Metes Out Oriental Justice." *Overland Monthly*, 2d ser. 81 (Aug. 1923): 10, 46, 48.

Hogan, Robert J. "The Case of the Six Coffins." *Wu Fang* 1 (Sept. 1935): 6–95.

House, Brant. "Curse of the Mandarin's Fan." *Detective Mysteries* 13 (Feb. 1938): 10–52.

Hull, Jesslyn H. "A Yellow Angel." *Overland Monthly*, 2d ser. 67 (March 1916): 189–90.

Kellogg, E. Lincoln. "A Partly Celestial Tale." *Overland Monthly*, 2d ser. 26 (Sept. 1895): 315–19.

Keyhoe, Donald E. "The Mystery of the Dragon's Shadow." *Dr. Yen Sin* 1(July-Aug. 1936): 6–108.

Kronenberg, James F. "The Avenging Joss." *Overland Monthly*, 2d ser. 82 (Sept. 1924): 393–94, 414–15.

Lathrup, Howard. "A Pioneer of 1920." *Overland Monthly* 4 (April

1870): 303–12.

Lindsay, Lucy Forman. "Sang." *Overland Monthly*, 2d ser. 69 (Jan. 1917): 57–61.

Lorelle. "The Battle of Wabash." *Californian* 2 (Oct. 1880): 364–76.

McCable, Charles W. "Only a Squaw Man—Kind Feelings Lodge in Many Unlikely Places." *Overland Monthly*, 2d ser. 76 (Dec. 1920): 51–54.

More, Phil. "Chung's Baby." *Overland Monthly*, 2d ser. 31 (March 1898): 233–35.

Mott, Mary T. "Poor Ah Toy." *Californian* 5 (April 1882): 371–81.

Mulford, Prentice. "Pete." *Overland Monthly* 6 (April 1871): 370–71.

Murray, John A. "The Mandarin's Birthday Gift." *Overland Monthly*, 2d ser. 42 (Sept. 1903): 184–88.

Nattrass, J. C. "An Encounter with Chinese Smugglers." *Overland Monthly*, 2d ser. 23 (Feb. 1894): 206–15.

Neall, Mrs. James. "Spilled Milk." *Overland Monthly* 5 (Nov. 1870): 431–34, 437–38.

Norris, Frank. "After Strange Gods." *Overland Monthly*, 2d ser. 24 (Oct. 1894): 375–79.

———. "Thoroughbred." *Overland Monthly*, 2d ser. 25 (Feb. 1895): 196–201.

Pearsall, R. P. "The Revelation." *Overland Monthly*, 2d ser. 58 (Dec. 1911): 485–94.

Rothermel, Frederick C. "Foo Soon, the Heathen." *Overland Monthly*, 2d ser. 72 (Jan.-Feb. 1921): 23–26.

Sargent, Ellen C. "Wee Wi Ping." *Californian* 5 (Jan. 1882): 60–70.

Scofield, Charles. "Fan Show's Thanksgiving." *Overland Monthly*, 2d ser. 24 (Nov. 1894): 551–52.

Sears, G. Emmerson. "Baxter's Beat." *Overland Monthly*, 2d ser. 55 (March 1910): 293–98.

Skaggs, Daisy De Forest. "Hawaiian Yesterdays." *Overland Monthly*, 2d ser. 77 (March, 1921): 30.

Spadoni, Andriana. "Devils, White and Yellow: A Story of San Francisco's Chinatown." *Overland Monthly*, 2d ser. 44 (July 1904): 80–84.

Stabler, Marguerite. "The Sale of Sooy Yet." *Overland Monthly*, 2d ser. 35 (May 1900): 414–16.

Stevensons, the. "Chinatown: My Land of Dreams." *Overland Monthly*, 2d ser. 73 (Jan. 1919): 42–45.

Stockbridge, Grant. "Dragon Lord of the Underworld." *The Spider* 6 (July 1935): 4–102.

Sui Sin Far (Edith Eaton). "A Chinese Ishmael." *Overland Monthly*,

2d ser. 34 (July 1899): 43–49.

Treleaven, Owen C. "Poison Jim Chinaman." *Overland Monthly*, 2d ser. 74 (July 1919): 40–45.

Underwood, E. E. W. "When an Oriental Meets an Oriental." *Overland Monthly*, 2d ser. 84 (April 1926): 107–9, 115, 127.

Vachell, Horace Annesley. "The Conscience of Quong Wo." *Overland Monthly*, 2d ser. 24 (Nov. 1894): 504–8.

Walsh, John H. "Mr. Poudicherry and the Opium Smugglers." *Overland Monthly*, 2d ser. 56 (Sept. 1910): 273–77.

Ward, Eunice. "Ah Gin." *Overland Monthly*, 2d ser. 63 (June 1914): 569–70.

Wigmore, L. Warren. "The Revenge of Ching Chow." *Overland Monthly*, 2d ser. 82 (Feb. 1924): 60, 81, 87.

Wilcoxson, Lizzie G. "The Tangent of a Tiff: A Tale wherein Mrs. Hill, Yip Hung and a Beauty Doctor are Concerned." *Overland Monthly*, 2d ser. 50 (July 1907): 77–80.

Wiley, Hugh. "In Chinatown." *Collier's* 93, no. 26 (30 June 1934): 12–13.

———. "No Witnesses." *Collier's* 97, no. 7 (15 Feb. 1936): 10–11.

———. "The Thirty Thousand Dollar Bomb." *Collier's* 94, no. 4 (28 July 1934): 17.

Secondary Sources

Barth, Gunther. *Bitter Strength: A History of the Chinese in the United States 1850–1870*. Cambridge, Mass.: Harvard University Press, 1964.

Chin, Frank. "Interview: Roland Winters." *Amerasia Journal* 2 (fall 1973): 1–19.

Chu, Limin. *The Images of China and the Chinese in the "Overland Monthly," 1868–1875, 1883–1935*, San Francisco, R. and E. Research Associates, 1974.

Chung, Sue Fawn. "From Fu-Manchu, Evil Genius, to James Lee Wong, Popular Hero: A Study of the Chinese American in Popular Periodical Fiction from 1920 to 1940." *Journal of Popular Culture* 10, no. 3 (March 1977): 534–47.

Coolidge, Mary. *Chinese Immigration*. New York: Henry Holt, 1909.

Eaton, Edith (Sui Sin Far). "Leaves from a Mental Portfolio of an Eurasian." *Independent* 66 (21 Jan. 1909): 125–32.

Foster, John Burt. "China and the Chinese in American Literature, 1850–1950." Ph.D. dissertation, University of Illinois, 1952.

Gardner, John Berdan. "The Image of the Chinese in the U.S., 1885–1915." Ph.D. dissertation, University of Pennsylvania, 1961.

Goulart, Ron. *An Informal History of the Pulp Magazine.* New York: Ace, 1972.

Higham, John. *Send These To Me.* New York: Atheneum, 1975.

Isaacs, Harold R. *Scratches on Our Minds: American Images of China and India.* New York: John Day, 1958.

Jacobs, Paul, and Landau, Saul, and Pell, Eve. *To Serve the Devil.* Vol. 2. *Colonials and Sojourners.* New York: Vintage, 1971.

Jones, Robert Kenneth. *The Shudder Pulps.* West Linn, Oreg. FAX Collector's Editions, 1975

Kellogg, Minnie P. "The Big Butter Buddha." *Overland Monthly,* 2d ser. 43 (March 1904): 184.

Labor, Earle. *Jack London.* New York: Twayne, 1974.

Miller, Stuart Creighton. *The Unwelcome Immigrant: The American Image of the Chinese, 1785–1882.* Berkeley and Los Angeles: University of California Press, 1969.

Quinn, Arthur Hobson. *American Fiction: An Historical and Critical Survey.* New York: D. Appleton Century, 1936.

Rabaya, Violet. "Filipino Immigration: The Creation of a New Special Problem." In *Roots: An Asian American Reader,* edited by Amy Tachiki et al. Los Angeles: UCLA Asian American Studies Center, 1971.

Rohmer, Elizabeth Sax, and Van Ash, Cay. *Master of Villany: A Biography of Sax Rohmer.* Edited and with a foreword by Robert E. Briney. Bowling Green, Ohio: Bowling Green University Press, 1972.

Sinclair, Andrew. *Jack: A Biography of Jack London.* New York: Harper & Row, 1977.

Spoehr, Luthor W. "Sambo and the Heathen Chinese: California's Racial Stereotypes in the Late 1870's." *Pacific Historical Review* 2d ser. 42 (1973): 185–204.

Steiner, Stan. *Fusang.* New York: Harper & Row, 1979.

Sung, Betty Lee. *Mountain of Gold.* New York: MacMillan, 1967.

Thompson, Richard Austin. "The Yellow Peril, 1890–1924." Ph.D. dissertation, University of Wisconsin, 19578.

Index